Diaspora, Politics, and Globalization

Diaspora, Politics, and Globalization

Michel S. Laguerre

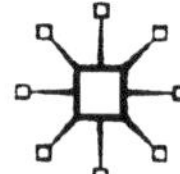

DIASPORA, POLITICS, AND GLOBALIZATION

First published in 2006 by
PALGRAVE MACMILLAN™
175 Fifth Avenue, New York, N.Y. 10010 and
Houndmills, Basingstoke, Hampshire, England RG21 6XS
Companies and representatives throughout the world.

PALGRAVE MACMILLAN is the global academic imprint of the Palgrave Macmillan division of St. Martin's Press, LLC and of Palgrave Macmillan Ltd. Macmillan® is a registered trademark in the United States, United Kingdom and other countries. Palgrave is a registered trademark in the European Union and other countries.

ISBN-13: 978–1–4039–7452–5
ISBN-10: 1–4039–7452–7

Library of Congress Cataloging-in-Publication Data

Laguerre, Michel S.
Diaspora, politics, and globalization / Michel S. Laguerre
p. cm.
Includes bibliographical references and index.
ISBN 1–4039–7452–7 (alk. paper)
1. Transnationalism—Political aspects—Case studies.
2. Globalization—Political aspects—Case studies. 3. Haitian Americans—Politics and government. I. Title.

JZ1320.L34 2006
320.973089′9697294—dc22 2005057928

A catalogue record for this book is available from the British Library.

Design by Newgen Imaging Systems (P) Ltd., Chennai, India.

First edition: July 2006

10 9 8 7 6 5 4 3 2 1

Printed in the United States of America.

For Sibby and Norm Whitten, Jr.

Contents

List of Tables

Preface and Acknowledgments

The study of diasporic politics has much to tell us about the democratic process in the host country, the homeland, and the strengths or weaknesses of the political organizations of the diaspora. Diasporic politics has been studied so far in terms of the relations of the diaspora with hostland and homeland politics. In essence, this book provides an alternative approach to the conventional wisdom in this field of inquiry by focusing on the diaspora as forming a political system of its own, sustained by the political and organizational infrastructures of the sending and receiving countries. In so doing, it establishes the parameters of such a transnational political system and explains its mode of operation. It shows how place and time shape the practice of diasporic politics in its transnational deployment. For example, these variables help to explain why the diaspora may shift its political engagement from homeland to hostland or from hostland to homeland to achieve specific goals and thus helps explain the flexible shape the transnational political system may take at any given time.

With regard to the role of place or location in diasporic politics, we will see how different relations with different segments of the diaspora depend on the nature of the political process in either site and the projected goal contemplated. A specific diasporic site may be called upon for help by the homeland government to achieve a specific outcome, while another site may be contacted for a different reason. Similarly, a specific hostland government may at times use the services of the local diaspora in its diplomatic and trade relations with the homeland, while at other times it may simply ignore such cosmopolitan political actors.

Homeland governments, in this sense, are influential in redesigning the hierarchy of importance of different diasporic groups in different locations, seen as political constituencies. Some diasporic groups form the core of projected overseas constituencies because they consist of government loyalists, while other diasporans sometimes stand at a lower echelon or on the periphery because they need to be neutralized as a result of their critical stance vis-à-vis the homeland government.

Such a hierarchy of diasporic sites developed by the homeland government to tap the resources of the diaspora may not correspond to the perception that the diaspora has of itself, however, and tends to disaggregate depending on the ebbs and flows of the homeland's political and ideological orientation. For example, the Miami Haitian American community was more important for the survival of the Aristide government than was the Boston or New York community. That was so because this proletarian community was more in tune with the grassroots orientation of the Aristide government than the other middle-class communities were.

From time to time, cosmopolitan leaders in the diaspora are asked to play broker roles vis-à-vis the homeland government on behalf of the government of a particular hostland. Just as the homeland government inadvertently or consciously creates a hierarchical division within the diaspora, these legitimate political practices also fragment the social architecture of the diaspora.

Diasporic politics is not only played out abroad, but also at home, by returnees whose dediasporization constitutes a new form of incorporation in the transnational circuit of cross-border political engagement. Returnees develop their own informal groups, meet occasionally to celebrate former hostland holidays such as the Fourth of July or to enjoy a televised American sporting event, serve at times as ambassadors of goodwill, for example explaining U.S. traditions and democratic practices, and sometimes create their own political parties, as in the case of Israel Ba'aliya or Israel Beiteiny, each with a handful of elected parliamentarians in the Knesset.

Although the hierarchy of diasporic places depends on the intensity of their linkages to the homeland, the strengths of these relationships may shift or oscillate over time. For example, a hostile attitude toward the homeland government may metamorphose into a friendly relationship or vice versa, as happened with the Haitian American community in Miami vis-à-vis Haiti after the collapse of the Duvalier dynastic regime in 1985. A relationship of the homeland government with a specific site may change in intensity once the issue that brought them together is resolved, as happened in the case of the relations of the Israeli government with French Jewry in the summer of 1982 as a result of the bombing of the Goldenberg Restaurant on the Rue des Rosiers in the Jewish Quarter in Paris. Likewise interest in homeland political affairs may be generated in the diaspora because of political turmoil and may subside once the situation returns to normal.

Time is also an important variable in the processes of diasporic politics. Temporal shifts help us to understand generational changes in diasporic politics from a primary focus on homeland politics and a secondary focus on hostland politics to a primary focus on hostland politics and a secondary focus on homeland politics.

Time is also of the essence in the way in which the homeland government, on occasion, concentrates its attention on helping a segment of the diaspora that is struggling to gain legal status in the host country. This usually occurs within a strictly delimited temporal moment and is not an ongoing process. For example, newly arrived refugees usually become a matter of immediate concern for the hostland government and therefore it may seek the collaboration of the homeland government for the resolution of the crisis. The intervention of the homeland government in diasporic affairs then resolves the impending problem caused by the refugee crisis. When the crisis is over, the homeland government shifts its attention to other matters. Refugees then are either able to return home or provided with a legal immigrant status. This intervention thus characterizes a specific moment in homeland-diaspora relations. It simply shows how time structures this aspect of diaspora-homeland political relations.

Special events in the diaspora or the homeland are also occasions when diaspora-homeland relations become intense. Temporal intervals thus cadence or provide a rhythm to diaspora-homeland relations. One may speak, for example, of the electoral campaign year, when both sides are engaged in intense relations to help a candidate in the homeland win the contest or for a candidate in the homeland to seek financial donations among diasporic communities to help finance his campaign. Problems that a diaspora community may confront in a host country may also intensify the interest of the homeland and other diasporic sites. These specific circumstances are moments during which diasporic interventions in homeland affairs or homeland interventions in diasporic affairs are deployed. While on the one hand place indicates the direction and geographic distribution of these transnational political interventions, temporal changes characterize the moments when such transactions occur and how they fracture the temporal political landscape.

The content of this book was presented and discussed in various academic forums, and I am thankful to members of those audiences who raised questions or provided comments that helped me to sharpen the thrust of the argument. A portion of chapter 1 was presented at a symposium on transnational citizenship organized by the University of Quebec in Montreal, October 14, 1998. Chapter 2 was delivered at the "States and Diasporas" conference organized by the Italian Academy and the Institute of Latin American and Iberian Studies at Columbia University, May 8, 1998. Chapter 3 was presented at a colloquium at Georgetown University on October 14, 1999. Chapter 4 was prepared for an international conference at the University of Kent, Canterbury, and read at a conference organized by Trinity College in Washington, DC, in January 2003. Chapter 5 was delivered as a keynote address at a joint symposium organized by Tulane University and Loyola University in New Orleans and held on April 14, 2004.

I am most grateful to the following scholars, who contributed in many different ways to the completion of this project: Robert Smith, Robert Maguire, Nicola Short, Jason Ackleson, Bonnie Hurd, Micheline Labelle, Frantz Voltaire, Georges Anglade, Jean Robert Elie, Jean Claude Icart, Marc Prou, Gurton Auguste, Serge Auguste, Harry Fouche, Franck Henry, Bob Joseph, Alice Blanchet, Jocelyn McCalla, Jean-Glovert Laguerre, Ramona Hernandez, and Wesner Emmanuel. I am also thankful to anonymous reviewers for their insightful suggestions and comments and to the following publishers: University of California Press, London School of Economics, and Ediciones Libreria LaTrinitaria for allowing me to republish here revised versions of my articles, "Homeland Political Crisis, the Virtual Diasporic Public Sphere, and Diasporic Politics." *Journal of Latin American Anthropology*, vol. 10, no 1, pp. 206–225, 2005; "State, Diaspora and Transnational Politics." *Millennium: Journal of International Studies*, vol. 28, no 3, pp. 633–651, 1999; and "Diasporic Lobbying in American Politics," *in Desde La Orilla: Hacia Una Nacionalidad Sin Desalojos*, edited by Silvio Torres-Saillant, Ramona Hernandez, and Blas R. Jimenez. Santo Domingo: Ediciones Libreria La Trinitaria, 2004, pp. 421–440.

In the course of the preparation of this book, both graduate and undergraduate students at the University of California at Berkeley helped me in transcribing interviews, performing bibliographic searches in several databases, surfing the Web in search of information on Haitian American elected officials, and compiling data for the tables in the book. Among them, I want to thank more particularly Debbie Yeh, Shridhar Seralathan, Sara Pickett, Bethany Burns, Jodie Atkinson, Jennifer Lee, Raymond Pascual, Lauren Kaplan, Sara Zeiger, Alina Shlyapochnik, Robert Klein and Laura Tolkoff.

The reference librarians at the Doe Library and the Institute of Governmental Studies at the University of California at Berkeley promptly located materials for me in the various databases available in these research facilities. Bruce Cain, a leading specialist on ethnic politics and the director of the Institute of Governmental Studies; Nelson Polsby, a leading specialist on the U.S. Congress; and Jack Citrin, an expert on immigration and political incorporation have provided me with the inspiration for this book, and Marc Levin, Debbie Yeh, Mark Tokaro, Hanbinna Park, Liz Wiener, and Louise Salazar have provided the necessary administrative backup for the completion of the project.

A special thanks is due to the staff of the Berkeley Center for Globalization and Information Technology, the research site where most of the drafts of this book were prepared and to Gabriella Pearce, Julia Cohen, and Erin Ivy at Palgrave Macmillan Press. Last but not least, I very much appreciate Bud Bynack's commentaries, suggestions, and editorial skills in transforming the manuscript into a much more readable and enjoyable piece of scholarship. I am, however, solely responsible for any shortcomings that may still remain with the text.

Introduction: Mapping the Global Arena of Diasporic Politics

Human migration is seldom a uniform process. It does not affect all the communities in either the homeland or the hostland in the same fashion.[1] In any country, some areas are more prone to migration in large numbers than others. Border zones, in particular, have been the sites of international migration well before some hinterland communities have joined the process because this has always been a mechanism of survival for their residents. They have also served as destination points for would-be immigrants on the other side of the frontier. Border towns such as Belladere in Haiti and Elias Piña in the Dominican Republic or Tijuana in Mexico and San Diego in the United States are examples of this cross-border access and incorporation.

Likewise, different communities in the homeland and hostland also have different experiences of migration. In the hostland, for example, some are more often used as communities of refuge than others, and differences in state policies differently affect diasporic communities. While individuals may be incorporated as citizens (ability to vote, to seek political office, etc.), their ethnic institutions (e.g., the voodoo church) may not get official state approval, are not considered as legitimate institutions, and therefore must function below the radar of the state. Such individuals are both inside and at the gates of the hostland nation-state. They have one foot in as incorporated individuals through citizenship and the other foot out because their ethnic institutions may lag behind, either because these can be ignored without injuring the group (thereby maintaining the privatization of such institutions) or simply because their institutions may not be seen by the mainstream to be compatible with existing institutional structures.

What engages us here, therefore, is the segmentation or fragmentation of the historicized process of migration and diasporization. Approaching this process in terms of immigration from country to country flattens migration into a homogeneous practice. Focusing instead on the zones in which it principally occurs discloses the heterogeneity and stratification of the process in terms of both the forms of diasporization it generates and its effect on specific areas of the homeland and the hostland. Likewise, it reveals the heterogeneity of the process of incorporation in the receiving state. Such an approach shows that heterogeneity of inscription in the social system, instead of homogeneity, is the norm. This heterogeneity is also seen in the political arena, and this study will unveil some of these practices in order to draw the spatial parameters—national, local, regional, transnational, and even global—of diasporic politics.

Studies of ethnic politics often hide this aspect of diasporic reality because of their focus on the local state, that is, the new place of residence of the immigrants and not on transnational relations. The emphasis in such an approach is placed on whether the immigrants vote in electoral contests at the local or national level or whether they are engaged in civic actions through any of the institutions of civil society.[2] This vision is based on the notion that assimilation is a way of judging the adaptability of immigrants or of gauging their contribution to society. That approach is not meant to explain the transnational political practices of the immigrants, since the homeland is not added to the equation or seen as relevant to their political participation.[3]

Traditionally, one speaks of the state or the relations between states as two distinct arenas of political practices, since they provide the ground for national or domestic politics and international relations, respectively.[4] In this approach, the state is conceived of as the organizing principle necessary to understand the logic of political action. This understanding is arrived at because of the assumption that the nation is enclosed in the state and therefore state politics coincides with national politics. However, with large numbers of diasporans engaging in transnational politics, transforming the homeland into a transnation-state, this assumption can no longer be sustained. In international relations, the homeland inscribes the diaspora in its economic planning because of the remittance factor, a source of extra national income to be sustained. In domestic politics, the receiving state, while maintaining the diasporans in a condition of marginalization, is mainly interested in their socioeconomic integration, their co-optation in the political process, and their participation in civic organizations.[5]

This book therefore takes a different approach. It identifies the diaspora as the locus of a new form of political practices, maps the distinguishable features (structure, geography, and agency) of diasporic politics, and explains its forms of operation. One gets a different vision of politics, depending on whether the focus is on the state (national politics), the relations between states (international relations), or the diaspora (diasporic politics) as an identifiable component of the nation, both hostland and homeland. Each positions its political actors inside specific parameters (national, international, or transnational) that differently partition the political field of action.

The diaspora approach to politics allows us to establish the linkages between the diaspora and hostland politics, between the diaspora and homeland politics, and between diasporic communities in various sites. It documents how this transnational engagement affects all of these elements while contributing to the integration of the diaspora into the receiving country. This field of politics—"ethnic politics" constitutes just one of its components—needs to be identified as a separate arena so that its contribution can be evaluated at their just measure and not be simply subsumed incorrectly under the rubric of domestic politics and international relations. I am not suggesting that the field of diasporic politics has been forgotten or altogether neglected, but rather that locating it within domestic politics or international relations does not do it justice. Therefore I am proposing to relocate it in the transnational or global field, where its border-crossing political practices can better be examined.[6]

In contrast to the arenas of domestic and international politics, diasporic politics is a transborder protopolitical system, because its existence depends on its successful encroachment on both the hostland and homeland political systems. Domestic politics and international relations are based on the duly recognized legal institutions of the state and gain their legitimacy from their relations to these institutions and legal instruments. Diasporic politics, by contrast, is based on transnational practice and the transnational stretch of state institutions. It grafts itself onto these institutions while also developing its own nonprofit organizations to accomplish particular goals. Diasporic politicians operate inside diasporic organizations, inside the formal organizations of the sending and receiving states, and within the transnational tentacles of the political institutions of the homeland and the hostland. At times, they use one institution (e.g., the Democratic Party in the United States) to consolidate another (the electoral process in the homeland). Diasporic politics connects various political organizations and actors to each other, changes or influences the dynamics of local politics by reinscribing local politics inside a transnational circuit, and in the process establishes a political arena distinct from the national political system, but nevertheless shaped by it. It develops an alternative political sphere geographically delimited by its participation in both hostland and homeland politics.

Although diasporic politics is supposed to help the integration of the community into society, it nevertheless serves as a dividing factor that fractures the diasporic community in terms of national orientation. Diasporic political engagement amplifies the ethnic and the transnational orientation of the community. While "ethnic politicians" and neighborhood activists who are engaged in ethnic politics stress the need for the political integration of the community into the hostland, "diasporic politicians" stress both the welfare of the community and their attachment to homeland affairs as an important incentive of their political participation in the hostland political process. This, according to Salojee and Semiatycki,[7] suggests "differences of priorities, goals and ideology between representatives of the same community in the formal and non-formal political spheres." This fracture, which epitomizes opposite polar political orientations among segments of the community, may also be singled out as an intrinsic component of diasporic politics.

Focusing on the amorphous, transborder, heterogeneous character of diasporic politics is important because it allows us to map the global contours of diasporic political engagement. This has several consequences. For example, it can provide an alternative way of framing the question of national security because of the transnational virtual communities in which diasporans participate and their ever-growing use of the Internet for communication with the homeland and other diasporic sites.[8] In this book, however, the ultimate focus will be on a larger issue. Examining the transnationality of diasporic politics allows us a way to begin to reframe the whole issue of the relations between the global and the local in the processes of globalization.

The peculiarities of diasporic politics are many. Its political agents are cosmopolitan politicians who straddle and participate in two political systems or more. They operate within a transnational or global circuit. To put it another way, such a diasporic political system is located or deploys its variable shape within a transnational or global universe and can influence negatively or positively all the sites in the network, including the hostland and the homeland. Unlike the other political systems, it does not have a fixed territorial space and has an evolving form of governance without a government. It does not operate in and over a legally recognized state of its own because its domain of action expands with the birth of new diasporic sites and crosses the boundaries of two or more states. It is a transborder political arena that cannot be understood simply by locating it inside the hostland and its politics, as various studies of integration, political participation, and voting behaviors so far have done, or inside the homeland and its politics, where it has been ignored or seen as a marginal para-political practice. Diasporic politics has its own logic, different from the logic of hostland or homeland politics, and it provides a new angle from which we can study both, along with the broader logic of globalization itself.

Diasporic Globalization

The transborder, transnational nature of diasporic politics requires that any approach to diasporic politics must be framed within the context of globalization theory instead of state or international relations theories. It is therefore crucial to explain the modalities of diasporic globalization. Globalization is itself inherently heterogeneous because it is manifested locally with different shapes as a result of local constraints of history, society, and culture. The phenomenon is expressed differently in various niches because of the different macro- and microcircuits in which it is deployed or that serve as its infrastructure. Diasporic globalization is one such macrocircuit. Its tentacles are rooted in more than one country and reterritorialize the boundaries of the transnational arena of diasporic politics. It is thus important to define the meaning and scope of diasporic globalization: Diasporic globalization implies human migration, voluntary or involuntary, the dispersion of the emigrants to more than one site, the connection of the various sites to each other through various forms of social interaction, and the maintenance of transnational relations between the homeland and the resettled émigrés. These border-crossing practices are symbolic of the expansion of the nation beyond its jurisdictional boundaries. Diasporic globalization is the matrix of relations between and among homeland and diverse diasporic sites constituting a multinational arena that operates through mechanisms that influence each site, including the governments of both hostland and homeland. While it is important to achieve an understanding of the multilateral networks in order to understand bilateral networks, an understanding of the latter can be achieved fully only inside this larger context of relationships. Diasporic globalization is a modus operandi that contextualizes and expresses local-global relations.

Although the relations of a diasporic site to the homeland constitute a nexus of analysis and have been the principal locus of studies of transnational communities, this approach has produced biased results because it privileges one side of the equation (diaspora-homeland relations) and tends to ignore the other (diaspora-diaspora relations). What the global approach adds is the plurality of expressions of these transnational relationships, reframing this field of study.

The relations of a site to the homeland cannot be understood fully outside the context of the relations to other sites by both parties (diaspora-diaspora relations and the homeland's relations with other sites). These site-to-site relations are diverse, hierarchized, and have distinct contents. For example, Haitians in France, in the United States, and in Canada relate differently to Haiti because of the size of the different diasporic communities, the greater or lesser influence that they may have over politics in each state, and the different policies of each state, which allow the diasporans to intervene successfully in one setting, but not in another. Likewise, the Jewish immigrant population is in a better position to influence U.S. foreign policies than the policies of the European Union or any of its constituent countries. It is so not simply because of the political strength of the population, but also because of different government structures that make possible these different levels of political participation, which may lead to different levels of success.

On the one hand, the relations of the diasporic site with the homeland are influenced by interdiasporic relations. In a time of political crisis, a diaspora may do (or not do) things for the homeland by taking into consideration the actions of other diasporic sites in order to (or not to) duplicate these efforts. To plead in 1991 for the return of President Aristide to Haiti, Haitian Americans left, for example, the operation of lobbying the Ottawa government to Haitian Canadians. On the other hand, interdiasporic relations can also be influenced by relations with the homeland. Haitian Americans and Haitian Canadians have in the past collaborated in a number of projects in an effort to help the establishment of democracy in Haiti and sometimes at the request of politicians in Haiti.

The global diasporic arena constitutes the expanded national niche that provides the context within which actions taken by the homeland and diasporas can be framed and understood. What needs to be understood is how that larger arena operates, the modalities of the relationships that develop there, and the interface between the global and the local.

Focusing on diasporic globalization is the newest attempt at framing the diasporic question, including the transnational arena of diasporic politics. Three operational approaches have been used so far in the study of diasporas. First, the *assimilation, integration, and incorporation scheme* concerns itself with the nation-state and the ability of immigrants to adapt to the hostland society.[9] In contrast, the *transnational approach* downplays assimilation to highlight the relations with the homeland as the proper arena to understand bipolar or multiple identities.[10] In this scheme, border-crossing practices linking the diaspora to the homeland become the mechanisms by which such relations are maintained. The *diasporic globalization approach* developed here reframes the study of the diaspora by stressing the importance of the multinational context brought about by the multilateral relations of diasporic sites in various countries among themselves and with the homeland. It reproblematizes the concepts of the homeland, the hostland, and the diasporas within a much larger universe in which units influence each other and in the process turn this multitude of sites into a connected arena of social practice. In this frame of reference, the logic of one's action or of a social/institutional practice may depend not only on one's residence in a hostland but also on the social context of the multinational universe in which one is embedded. And it is this frame of reference, therefore, that affords us a clearer understanding of the relations between the local and the global.

The Diasporic Political Field

The continuing migration of Haitians to the United States, the establishment of strong Haitian American communities in several states, and the transnational relations that are maintained between the country of origin and the country of residence have led to the practices of diasporic politics, a transnational political field with unique features different from earlier forms of national and international politics.[11] Because the issues they are concerned with are different, the political actors are sometimes different, the space of their political action is different, their agendas are different, and the expectations of the homeland from them are different. They occupy a third political space out of which they are expected to choreograph their political maneuvers. This transnational political process has affected homeland politics, the diaspora in its ethnic political practices, and hostland politics.

Mainstream politics as it has been studied so far in the context of the nation-state and in the international context includes relations between states and the role of multinational corporations and transnational civil organizations in state politics. In both theoretical orientations, diasporic politics is not theorized as an autonomous domain, despite its transnational nature and its positioning inside homeland and hostland politics while differentiating itself from both and maintaining its independent status. This is probably due to the fact that ethnic politics within the assimilation frame of reference is seen as a component of hostland politics whereby ethnics are encouraged to engage in political participation so as to bring about the smooth incorporation of their communities into the larger context of democratic politics. Even when their influence on American foreign policy is studied, it is seen as either a contribution or a hindrance to the national democratic process.[12] In both visions, diasporic politics is not seen or identified as an independent sphere of action that escapes, in a certain fashion, the grip of both hostland and homeland politics, but at the same time incorporates them and influences the shape of both. Hence the need to map the parameters of this political field, to identify its modes of action, and to examine the ways in which it influences national politics in the homeland and hostland and the new context it creates for the exercise of ethnic politics, that is, its modus operandi for the integration of the diasporic community in the hostland.

Transnational Informants

The data for this book was collected through informal and formal interviewing, participant observation in Boston and New York, and library research. For more than twenty years, I have been observing and participating in Haitian American diasporic social and political events, in both Canada and the United States. In the course of these years, I have entertained many conversations with diasporic leaders who were involved in political struggles to overthrow the Duvalier regime or to help Aristide regain the national office of the presidency when he was in exile in Washington, DC, from 1992 to 1994. I have read, on and off, the diaspora media, both print and Internet-based, that comments on diasporic political engagement on behalf of specific causes. When I am on the East Coast of the United States, I also listen to Haitian American radio and watch Haitian American television programs, as was the case from summer 2001 to June 2002, when I was a visiting scholar in the Program in Science, Technology, and Society at MIT.

The data for the book was first garnered through informal conversations and interviews with community leaders and activists in Boston, Chicago, Silicon Valley, Montreal, Miami, New York, and Paris. Two activists on the West Coast were particularly very generous with their comments and shared with me their pains, successes, and worries in times when the Haitian political situation looked bleak. I also spoke to several people who comprised the rank and file of these diasporic civic and benevolent associations.

The data on dediasporization was collected from formal interviews with a handful of government officials who had been living in the United States or Canada, who returned to Haiti to occupy, in some cases, high-level government positions and who later reemigrated overseas to resume life in the diaspora. Some of them served either as chief of staff for a prime minister or as cabinet ministers, businessmen under contract with the government to provide specialized services, or legislators in Haiti between 1994 and 2004, the period during which the Lavalas Party controlled the apparatus of government.

More systematic interviews were undertaken in the summer of 2004 with 12 diasporans who live in New York, Miami, Washington, DC, Boston, Chicago, and Montreal. Interviews were tape-recorded, with their permission, for further analysis. Among them were a professional woman who served as staff for Prime Minister Malval and Michel, the chief of staff for Prime Minister Malval, a former cabinet minister in the first Aristide administration, a former senator, a former diplomat from the Haitian embassy in Paris, three consuls who had previously served in the Haitian consulates of Boston or New York, a medical doctor in Miami who is very active in diasporic politics, two heads of Haitian community centers in New York, a community leader in Chicago who regularly travels to Haiti, and a diasporic businessman in the San Francisco Bay Area who has a computer enterprise in Port-au-Prince and commutes back and forth.

While I was interested in learning the facts about specific events, I was keen on eliciting the interpretations, analyses, and meanings that these cosmopolitan political actors attributed to these occurrences. The data that I am presenting in this book covers a specific period in the history of the diaspora, that is, between 1986, when the dynastic Duvalier regime collapsed, and 2004, the bicentennial anniversary year of the independence of Haiti, when President Aristide was forced to resign his position and leave the country.

While the Haitian diaspora data is based on actual field research with members of the community, the rest of the material concerning similar experiences of other ethnic groups comes from library research or published sources. I felt that it was necessary to bring these additional data in for comparative purpose and to show the global applicability of the global approach to diasporic politics developed in this book.

Outline of the Chapters

In order to explain the specific nature of diasporic politics and to develop a theoretical framework to guide our analysis, this introduction has identified the transnational parameters that distinguish diasporic engagements from domestic politics and international relations. We have established that diasporic politics partakes in both hostland and homeland politics, which provides it with a spatial basis of operation and mechanisms of political intervention. The model of diasporic globalization provides the frame of reference within which the meanings, operation, and dynamic interaction of diasporic politics can be interpreted, inferences about its systematic deployment can be made, and the itinerary of its trajectory can be understood.

Chapter 1 presents an array of diasporic political practices, from the formal to the informal and the virtual. It analyzes the elections of six Haitian Americans to the state legislatures of Massachusetts, New Hampshire, Illinois, and Florida, the conditions that led to their victories at the polls, and their styles of diasporic politics. It presents examples of types of cosmopolitan diasporic politicians and explains how they intervene in hostland and homeland politics. It furthermore explains how transnationality has affected the practices of some but not of others. The aim of the chapter is to familiarize the reader with these political practices so that their extraterritorial tentacles can be understood.

Chapter 2 explains how diasporic political intervention in homeland affairs has reshaped the structure of governance there. The example of Haiti shows that Haitian American transnational political practices have led to the recognition of the diaspora as a department of the Haitian state ("the tenth department") and to the creation of a ministry for diasporic affairs. It shows the dependence of local politicians on diasporic money and technical knowledge to enhance the possibility for the success of their political careers. Perhaps more importantly, it discusses how these forms of diasporic interventions have resulted in a redefinition of the state. The chapter also presents five models of state-diaspora relations and explains how each has differently affected diasporic integration into American society. Furthermore, it elaborates on diaspora-grassroots relations to show both their positive and negative effects on homeland politics and explains how local conflicts have been transnationalized because of these cross-border interactions. It argues that the locus of international relations has shifted from relations between nation-states to relations between transnation-states.

Chapter 3 examines the diasporic lobbying process by focusing on the participation of Haitian American lobbyists in American politics. It defines various forms that diasporic lobbying took during the Duvalier dynasty and the administrations of President Jean Bertrand Aristide, delineates the tactics used by lobbyists, and examines the effect of lobbyists on U.S. foreign policy and on the conduct of democratic politics in Haiti. It compares the Haitian American lobby with that of more established groups, such as the Jewish, Irish, and Greek lobbies in Washington DC. It shows how through lobbying, transnational rival blocs have emerged, thereby complicating the possibility for resolution of internal conflicts. It explains that lobbying has its own life cycle, with initial, peak, and decline phases related to the failures or accomplishments of the group and the turns of events in the homeland. It shows the difficult positions in which lobbyists place themselves when they lobby on behalf of the country and not on behalf of government policies of which they do not approve. It also explains how information technology is the newest tool used by lobbyists to conduct their business vis-à-vis politicians in both the U.S. federal system and the homeland government. What this chapter shows unequivocally is that now, more than ever, diasporic lobbyists trade their votes and those of the communities they represent for the welfare of their homeland, and in so doing they have become very noisy.

Chapter 4 focuses on the forced resignation in 2004 of President Jean Bertrand Aristide and provides an analysis of Haitian American transnational political practices based on the diasporic globalization approach developed above. It shows the circular movement in which a diasporic political actor became prime minister in the homeland and the president formally became once more a member of the diaspora. It discusses the modalities of the deployment of the diasporic public sphere and explains how the Internet has been used as a primary means of communication between various segments of the diaspora to access news about Haiti and to analyze the ebbs and flows of the Haitian political crisis. It shows that the collapse of a regime is a privileged moment in which to understand the multiple ramifications of diasporic politics because of the repositioning or replacement of the old guards by different diasporic leaders as a result of regime change in the homeland.

Chapter 5 argues that the process of diasporization implies the possibility for dediasporization and rediasporization, just as the process of globalization implies the possibility for deglobalization and reglobalization. It explains how various nation-states have developed elaborate procedures for dediasporization, how any outcome depends on the roles played by the individual, state, and society and on what is entailed to regain a lost prediasporic status. It establishes a typology of dediasporization practices to show the diversity of forms depending on the parameters of homeland constitutional arrangements and special laws or ordinances. It briefly discusses the legal implications of the Dual Nationality Law of Mexico, which is not a dual citizenship law. This analysis is undertaken to show the multiple facets of the dediasporization process. The chapter argues that the globalization process is made of forward and backward movements and that dediasporization is one such disentanglement in the transnational network of local nodes.

The concluding chapter explains the implications of diasporic politics in the everyday life of the community, discusses the evolution of the political consciousness of Haitian Americans, and analyzes the reasons behind the shift from nonelected to elected officials as representatives of the aspirations of the community. It explains how Haitian Americans engage in ethnic politics for the welfare of the community and as a mark of their patriotism and loyalty to the United States, but at the same time it shows how they maintain a transnational orientation by attempting to influence American foreign policy vis-à-vis Haiti when the homeland is going through a crisis. It finally argues that because of this double stance of the community, approaching diasporic politics via globalization theory, rather than approaching ethnic politics via assimilation theory, does a better job of dealing with both sides of the political orientation of Haitian Americans.

1

The Practice of Diasporic Politics

On September 27, 2005, Michaëlle Jean, was sworn in as the 27th Governor General of Canada. Born in Port-au-Prince, Haiti in 1957, and fleeing François "Papa Doc" Duvalier's dictatorial regime, she immigrated with her parents to Québec in September 1968, and later completed her undergraduate and graduate training in comparative literature at the University of Montreal. She is an award winning journalist, broadcaster and filmmaker who had been working for many years at Radio-Canada. Selected by the Prime Minister of Canada, Paul Martin, and appointed by Queen Elizabeth II, she became the third woman (after Jeanne Sauvé and Adrienne Clarkson) to serve as Canada's Head of State, Vice-Regal Representative, and Commander-in-Chief of the Canadian Armed Forces.

The field of "ethnic politics" in the United States has dealt with a number of issues pertaining to the participation of "ethnic minorities" in American political affairs. These issues are framed with the assumption that the active political participation of minorities will further their incorporation and assimilation in American society. This vibrant literature focuses on a variety of phenomena: on the role of race and ethnicity;[1] on voting behavior and political participation;[2] on ethnic leadership and empowerment;[3] on ethnic coalitions, conflicts, and ideology;[4] on mobilization for collective action;[5] and, of course, on foreign policy, involvement with the homeland, and dual nationality.[6] These works have shed enormous light on the political integration of immigrant communities.

However, less effort has been expanded to redefine the field so as to take stock of the globalization process, the transnational activities of diasporas, and the multicultural practices of states. Some analysts have proceeded in that direction by adding a transnational outlook to the assimilationist approach to ethnic politics, by stressing the transnational aspect at the expense of the ethnic dimension, or simply by reenvisioning the field altogether so as to reproblematize the categories.[7] This chapter proposes a reconceptualization of the field of diasporic politics by focusing on the recent political experiences of the Haitian American diaspora. Thus describing and explaining how transnational political practices operate in these instances is the focus of this chapter.

The chapter describes a representative sample of forms that Haitian American diasporic political practices take so as to show how they anchor the political process of the home- and hostland. The aim of diasporic politics is to influence both homeland and hostland policies or political practices on behalf of the homeland and the residential diasporic community. The services of these cosmopolitan activists are sought by politicians in the homeland and the hostland either to strengthen or to undermine the governmental regime, and this consolidates their recognized status as transnational brokers. Their actions are aided by cheap air transportation, periodic visits to the homeland, and the use of e-mail, telephone, or facsimile to keep alive the communication within the transnational circuit.

Diasporic politics has both informal and formal aspects, both with virtual components. This type of politics is undertaken both by activists who operate on their own or through nonprofit organizations and by individuals who seek elective office. After examples of the practices used by diasporic lobbyists and activists to help the homeland as brokers or go-betweens, informal government strategists, influence peddlers, and transnational activists, the chapter focuses on recent legislative elections in which six Haitian American candidates won the contest, analyzing the trajectory of the political involvement of the diasporic community from street protest to institution building and formal participation in American politics. It examines the transnational parameters of diasporic politics and the political implications of its deployment. It does so to realign the theory of diasporic politics with the reality of the globalization process.

The Diasporic Politician as Go-Between or Broker

The informal component of diasporic politics takes many forms. One is as a go-between or broker between politicians of the homeland and the political establishment of the hostland. What follows is a salient example as reported to me by a Haitian American computer engineer who lives in the San Francisco Bay Area and served as a broker from 1992 to 1994 between Congresswoman Maxine Waters and the exiled President Jean Bertrand Aristide.

> One Saturday evening in 1993, President Jean Bertrand Aristide, while in exile in Washington, D.C., received a call around eleven P.M. from a friend and advisor, Romelus, Bishop of Jérémie, in Southern Haiti. The call was urgent due to an emergency that required immediate attention for the protection of Romelus' life. An anti-Aristide group protected by the military, but in alliance with the pro-status-quo establishment, had been shooting in the air with their weapons near the residence of the bishop in an effort to silence him, to scare his flock, and to demobilize the pro-Aristide citizenry. Unable to get protection from the de facto authorities, he sought help from the diasporic president.
>
> Being new to the Washington area and overseeing a government-in-exile with an ad hoc operational structure and transitory seat of government, President Aristide relied on his ambassador and local acquaintances for help, but to no avail. The ambassador was unable to do much, because it was a weekend, and his contacts in the State Department and the White House were safely at home enjoying the delights of their time off. However, President Aristide called me in California to make me aware of the impending situation and to seek my help. I was able to inform Congresswoman Maxine Waters (D-Los Angeles) of the issue, and she immediately touched base with Secretary of State Warren Christopher. The secretary spoke to Aristide that evening and provided needed assurances concerning the security of the Catholic bishop.

By means of the informal activities of a go-between, a local political problem created in the homeland thus shifted from homeland politics to hostland politics and was reinscribed inside the transnational field of diasporic politics. This is an instance where the local becomes globalized and the global becomes central in the production of a local solution.

The next example shows the involvement of political activists in Montreal in attempting to influence Canadian foreign policy vis-à-vis Haiti during the Haitian crisis that led to the forced resignation of President Aristide in 2004. One of the leaders of the group who met on several occasions with members of the party in office in Ottawa and whom I interviewed has the following to say:

> Lobbying is an American practice, which is done in a much more discreet fashion in Canada. It is not a legal activity. It is evident that Haitian

> Canadians have had access to federal parliamentarians in order to obtain the support of Canada when we were pushing for the return of Aristide to Haiti to resume his presidency in the early 1990s. Let me give you an example. In the months prior to the resignation of Aristide, we were able to meet as a group with the Prime Minister of Canada to define our position. At the request of the Prime Minister, we (19 Haitians) were invited to meet with him. Since the Prime Minister did not know much about Haiti, he had asked to meet with us before he met with the secretary general of the UN.
>
> We met for about three hours with the Prime Minister in his Montreal office. There were people of diverse political affiliations who attended the meeting: Georges Anglade and Claude Jean François (two former cabinet ministers in Haiti), Frantz Voltaire (head of a documentation center), Jean Claude Icart (head of a Haitian service center), Daniel Holly (a university professor), the president of a Haitian women group, etc. We were mostly from Montreal since 95 percent of the community lives in Montreal. In fact, it constitutes 10 percent of the population of Montreal. So it has a political weight different from that of the rest of the Haitian population dispersed throughout Canada, and we had access to the cabinet ministers.
>
> For example, during the months of the crisis, I met with the cabinet minister who was in charge of the Haiti dossier. I met with him at least three times. He came to dine with us, and we sent him reports. During the same period, when the Canadian ambassador traveled from Haiti to Canada, he always stopped in Montreal to give a briefing to Haitian organizations on Canadian policy practices in Haiti.
>
> Most of us have ministerial contacts. In my case, I have working relations with five cabinet ministers. For example, during the crisis, I had the cell phone number of the cabinet minister who was in charge of the Haiti dossier because he told us not to hesitate to call if we wanted to talk to him. Evidently this was about the Haitian dossier. He is not a personal friend, but an associate in the context of governmental relations.

This example shows how hostland politicians construct pro-homeland diasporic activists as partners in the search for a solution to homeland problems and as an additional source of information on the homeland. They are then seen by the hostland government as potential allies that may support its foreign policy vis-à-vis the homeland.

The Diasporic Politician as Government Strategist

Another form in which the informal component of diasporic politics appears is in the role played by diasporans as informal government advisors. In 1994, two Haitian American lobbyists in California organized a brainstorming session for which they invited me and other participants from Quebec, Montreal, Port-au-Prince, New York, Miami, Chicago, and Washington, DC. The idea was to discuss and prepare a plan of action for Aristide before his return to the National Palace in Haiti. This group of professionals (academicians, business people, and employees of international organizations) gathered for a weekend in Los Angeles at a hotel managed by a Haitian American. One lobbyist paid for the plane tickets and the other for the lodging. American political actors in key positions in the Democratic Party were invited to address the group, and Aristide called on the second day of this miniconvention for a progress report.

During the course of the weekend, several issues were raised pertaining to the staffing of ministries, the handling of the military problem, the relations of the government with the business elite, and larger issues of public administration. A set of recommendations was discussed and proposed to Aristide for possible implementation.

Such informal relations have the potential to become formal. One member of the group later became prime minister, another served as director of international affairs in the Ministry of Foreign Affairs, and three others were offered cabinet posts (Ministry of Foreign Affairs, Ministry of Education, Ministry of Public Health) but declined the invitation.

This was an ad hoc diasporic organization that was created to deal with a specific problem, and it was dismantled shortly thereafter. In this case, the diaspora served as a policy formation site for the homeland and provided strategists on behalf of the government that they supported. Once again we see a circuit from the local to the global and back again completed by means of the transnational status of diasporic politics.

The Diasporic Politician as Influence Peddler

Although President Aristide had been living in Washington for a while during the last year of the first George Bush administration and during the presidential campaigns, he was not officially invited to attend the festivities of the Clinton presidential inauguration. A Haitian American lobbyist in California who was invited through the office of Congresswoman Waters thought that an invitation could give Aristide a good opportunity to rub shoulders with other important political leaders. Since the invitation was, as usual, for two, he brought Aristide along with him for the festivities at the White House. Upon returning from Washington, DC, this lobbyist had called to inform me of what had happened.

This represented an unheard-of breach of diplomatic protocol. On the one hand, the lobbyist felt that Aristide had to be there to keep the attention of American policy makers on the political crisis in Haiti, but on the other, the uninvited president would be accompanied not by his Washington ambassador or his exiled minister of foreign affairs, but by a diasporan who was not an official member of his government. The two officials in charge of the portfolio of the diplomatic relations between Haiti and the United States were left out of potential transactions that clearly fell under their aegis.

This case shows how a diasporan was able to transform himself into an unpaid lobbyist and provide a homeland government official access to the Washington political establishment. What could not be done through the official channels was recuperated and accomplished through informal means. These informal politicians provide a backup for the smooth operation of the formal machinery of government, a backup that is transnational, not simply local.

The Diasporic Politician as Transnational Activist

The most routine way in which transnational diasporic politics is undertaken is through transnational interaction between individuals who live in the hostland with individuals who reside in the homeland. This takes various forms, including satellite political bureaus that maintain contacts with the office headquarters, activists in grassroots organizations who contact their peers, individuals who speak via telephone to family and friends about the political situation, and those who use the Internet for discursive political practices through the medium of virtual communities, cybersalons, and chat rooms.

Most Haitian political parties have affiliates in the United States—individuals who support the cause, who provide advice on strategies, who recruit sympathizers, and who engage at times in fund-raising on behalf of the headquarters. According to a Haitian American leader in New York City,

> There are several people who claim allegiance to one or another political party. I think people like Jean Vernet, who was running for a seat on the City Council have been more closely associated with KONACOM in Haiti. The Parti Ouvri Barìè, the official representative after Renaud

> Bernardin, who became the general secretary of the Party in Haiti, was François Pierre Louis. At the same time, François Pierre Louis was in New York, heading a community action program.

These are informal organizations, created on an ad hoc basis to help a friend, without necessarily creating any formal office and without incorporation in the machinery of the U.S. government as a foreign political bureau. Such leaders may travel to Port-au-Prince from time to time as part of the leadership of the political party to attend meetings, to discuss strategies, or to participate in political caucus prior to general elections. The Lavalas Party has affiliate bureaus in New York, Chicago, Washington, DC, Miami, Oakland, and Boston. Members of these informal organizations are sometimes selected to serve in the Haitian diplomatic corps in the United States (so far at the consular office level as has happened in Boston, Chicago, and New York).

Networks of activists have routinely been in contacts with non-governmental organizations (NGOs) in Haiti on issues pertaining to human rights, democracy, and political empowerment. They have coordinated their activities with their counterparts in Haiti, traveled to Haiti to meet with them, and provided the locals some guarantees that their actions will be supported even if they get in trouble with the law. This offers an extra level of protection for individuals who otherwise would not have taken such risks to protest against government actions. In their activities, these individuals see themselves as watchdogs of the government and of the bourgeoisie on behalf of civil society. As cosmopolitan politicians, they seamlessly operate inside the political sphere of the homeland while residing outside its jurisdictional boundaries. With them, the local becomes globalized.

Conversations that are held over the phone constitute a major arena of diasporic politics. Here information on what is known abroad about the government is communicated to friends and family in the homeland, advice is provided on whom to vote for during the elections, money is wired to help finance the campaigns of candidates, counsel is provided to incite political action, and intelligence is provided to undermine the activities of opponents. Every evening, the international telephone lines between the United States and Haiti are more often than not busy as the politics of the country is analyzed, spiced up, and deconstructed by transnational correspondents. And of course in the homeland, the content of this vast expanse of conversations will be later shared with one's neighbors and professional acquaintances. Here is how a former government official characterizes these transnational telephone conversations and the problem of accessing at times of crisis any of the phone lines that connect North America to Haiti.

> The telephone lines were busy. Empirically speaking, I can tell you about my own experience. I tried, on several occasions in periods of crisis, to call people in Port-au-Prince, and I could not get connected. Since my family no longer lives in Haiti, all of my calls were political. During the crisis, I was called upon to intervene on both radio and television programs, and I called colleagues in Port-au-Prince to give me their analysis of the situation. I did so to verify information before I appeared on television. For example, I would call Mr. X and say: "Tell me, you are on the ground with a lucid and objective mind. How do you assess the evolution of things in Haiti?" I speak as an analyst, and not as a reporter or the head of a political party. I always call Port-au-Prince to get a sense of things. I had four to five interlocutors in Haiti whom I could call to inform me about things, and it was always difficult to contact them because one could not connect to Port-au-Prince easily because the lines were busy.

A new virtual public sphere in which people discuss their views of the political situation in Haiti has been created with the use of the Internet.[8] Every night, Haitian chat rooms become sites for spirited conversations about Haitian politics. Opinions vary from well informed and moderate to nonsensical and pompous. Of course, between the conversants sits a large group of anonymous onlookers whose identity is not known because they do not venture to share their opinions on the issues on the Net.

This virtual sphere, which is open only to those who have access to a computer, tends to be dominated mostly by North American conversations, because the correspondents in Haiti may not have free access and must pay for the time they are online. This limits their participation and at the same time amplifies the participation of the diaspora. The extent to which online conversations during electoral campaigns feed off-line conversations among prospective voters in Haiti is yet to be carefully documented, but the potential for such transnational effects in the political arena cannot be ignored.

Diasporans as Homeland Government Officials in the Hostland

Diasporans who are selected by the homeland government to serve as ambassadors or consuls in the hostland are called upon to provide a service to both their country of birth and their local community. They are not required to go through the dediasporization process because individuals who are occupying these functions are not mandated by the constitution to do so. The following two case studies reported by two diasporans who served as consuls in New York or Boston explain well the kind of issues they had to resolve pertaining to their relations with the Haitian government and the local diasporic community of which they are a member. These case studies shed light on their appointment, the administration of the office during their tenure, and the exit or return to their routine diasporic life.

The Haitian Consulate of New York City

A Haitian American who once formerly served as the consul general in New York provided an assessment of his term in office in an interview:

> What often happens is that the person that they select is the one that the President or Cabinet Minister likes. That's the heart of the problem. It's not simply a matter of competence, it's a certain affinity for a person. In my case, I was selected both by the government and, in an indirect manner, by the diasporic population, because I did not know anybody in the government. They selected me because they wanted to project a new façade. They were looking for someone who is serious, has a good reputation, and is respected by the community.
>
> When the Minister of Foreign Affairs called me and informed me that I was named Consul General in New York, I must tell you that I did not expect anything from the Haitian government, because I was too busy doing my not-for-profit work in Manhattan. Minister Clermont who, I believe, was transferred from a position at the United Nations to head the Ministry of Foreign Affairs, requested that I give him an answer in two days. I did not take the offer seriously because I am a little bit of an independent mind.
>
> They wanted to project a different image of the government. That's why they called on people in the diaspora. During the Avril administration, I received a call informing me that I was selected to serve as the mayor of Port-au-Prince. I turned down the offer. When Clermont called to offer me the job, I was confused because I was not involved in Haitian politics. Ertha Trouillot was president then. Thus, some friends encouraged me to take the job because, as they said, I was going to make history, since this was the first time a woman served as president of Haiti. Frankly, I did not want to get mixed up with Haitian politics, which is a very dirty game, but they said since you have always spoken

about the need for major change in Haiti, you should take this opportunity to serve the country.

I spent two weeks without responding to the Foreign Minister, he had to call a second time to find out about my response. I begged him to wait for two more days, and then I accepted the offer.

I am telling you all of this to say that they really needed me. When I took the post, I selected my own manager to prevent the ministry from employing someone whose role would be to spy on me. The minister objected, because I selected the brother of the consul that I was replacing. He was already an employee at the consulate. I selected him because of his experience, and finally the Foreign Minister agreed with my choice.

I was under the impression that I was in control of things. The president had much respect for me. There were two cabinet ministers, Guy Dalemand and Dr. St. Louis, who worked very closely with me. Whenever there was something in Haiti, they called me to inform me about it and asked for my advice on several occasions. The president also called me from time to time. This created a little bit of tension in the Ministry of Foreign Affairs, as they were aware that the president was asking me for advice instead of going to the minister who is in charge of this portfolio.

In New York, there were some activists who wanted to get rid of me as Consul General. One man with whom I grew up in the same neighborhood and with whom I used to play soccer when I was in high school, Wilson Désir, wanted the post and attacked me often on the air through a community radio program. From time to time, he attempted to undermine my authority by criticizing the functioning of the consulate. He sent his cronies to harass me.

He succeeded to a certain extent, because he was named Consul General after I left the office. I participated in community protests and was up front at the AIDS march that blocked the Brooklyn Bridge. I did not have a problem with the community per se, except with Wilson Désir. There was another one who asked to be given a check every month, and I refused to do so. This one also went to the radio station to say that the consulate is a mess.

The population was happy with my administration because of some of the new practices that I introduced. For example, the Vice Consul regularly went to the airport to speak to incoming immigrants who had passport or visa problems. Luckily, my wife, who used to work at the UN and in some consulates in Europe, trained the staff of the consulate on my behalf.

The New York consulate is somewhat different from the others, and soon I was having problems with the president. My wife and I usually spent the month of August in Aruba, where we have a timeshare, and the Haitian ambassador in Caracas always invited us when we were nearby. He was a childhood friend. Once upon a time, while we were on our way to the airport for one such trip to Aruba and Caracas and the taxi driver was waiting for us, I received a phone call from the president who said, "I heard that you are on your way to Caracas. Well at six P.M., I will have a cabinet meeting, and I want you to be there. I want to introduce you to the rest of the cabinet as the new Minister of Foreign Affairs." I thanked her for the confidence she had in me, but I told her that I was not ready for Port-au-Prince. She was not happy with my response, and the two ministers cited above tried to no avail to convince me to change my mind.

The president had a friend who lived in Queens, the wife of a medical doctor. She had left her husband here and went to live in the National Palace with the president. She used to pay me compliments as a polite young man. In the consulate, there was a good deal of corruption. When I took the job, there were people who came to tell me, "Consul, I am supposed to receive a check from the office every month because of the spying work I do on behalf of the consulate." I dismissed them one after the other, although I was ready to help them with money from my own pocket if they were in dire need.

[This woman] who used to pay me compliments came one day to ask me for $1000 from the general account of the consulate, and I turned her down with the proviso that I had no authority to do so and I referred her to the Ministry of Foreign Affairs.

That's precisely the reason why I did not want to get involved in Haitian politics, because of that pervasive level of corruption. Since I rejected the offer to serve as Foreign Minister, the president became a little bit cold toward me when she received me in Port-au-Prince.

[This woman] came a third time to the consulate to ask for more money, implying that she was going to buy something for the president. During my last trip, the president did not invite me to her residence, as had been the case in the past. I concluded that she was not happy with me.

The two cabinet ministers mentioned above did not want me to leave the government. (One was working as a radiologist in Chicago and was the brother-in-law of the president. He had left his position to serve in the government.) They told me that they were going to send me to the UN and Yves Auguste would go to the OAS. I simply turned down the offer.

The place where I work is a consortium of Haitian centers. I was the director of the Haitian Center in Manhattan, one of the members of the federation. I was in charge of the education program. When I accepted the job of Consul General, I spoke to the director of the consortium, who himself was going to be named ambassador by Aristide. I left the consulate in 1990, and he became ambassador in 1991. Since I had taken a leave of absence, I later returned to my previous job.

The Haitian Consulate of Boston

A group of activists who have been active supporters of Aristide sought to get one of their leaders selected for the post of consul in Boston, spent several weeks discussing in their radio and television programs their project for the office in an attempt to drum up some support from the community, sent one of their leaders to Port-au-Prince to meet with the president and his staff, then later found out that someone who was not a member of the group, someone who was living quietly in the city and served on and off as an economic consultant to the Haitian government, was named to the position. In this interview, the former consul in Boston, who has reintegrated the diasporic community, reflects on the issues that he has confronted during the period of his tenure in office.

> There were people above me, the ambassador in Washington, D.C., and also, of course, the Minister of Foreign Affairs in Port-au-Prince. Since I was appointed by the president, I had direct contact with him whenever I needed to report my observations to him. The Lavalas activists in Boston were hoping to get the post for one of their leaders, and they did not get it. They began early on to criticize me and did so publicly through the radio and television programs they controlled. For example, they claimed that I was illiterate and that I had not attended any secondary school, therefore I did not have even a high-school diploma. In fact, they did not know where I studied, since I was abroad in Moscow completing an M.S. in economics.
>
> Senator Kennedy had invited me to attend one of his stump meetings for his reelection, and the activists spent weeks criticizing me for representing the country poorly, implying that I should have left the job of lobbying the Massachusetts senator to them, who better understood the nuances of American politics. Several pro-Lavalas activists did their best to destabilize whatever I was trying to do on behalf of the government.
>
> When I took control over the consulate, there was a debt of $20,000 and an active account of $2,000. Eventually I paid the debt. When I came in, there was literally no office furniture there. So I bought new furniture, and I totally decorated the office with new desks, chairs, file cabinets, a safe box, and a television set.
>
> I also installed a network of computers. Since I was living in the United States, where every public office has them, I had to do the same for the Consular Office. For this, I was reprimanded by the Minister of Foreign Affairs, who told me that his own office in Haiti did not have a computer, and therefore I should not purchase computers for the Boston bureau. I must say that it was the only Haitian consulate in the world

that had them. You see, my own boss told me that I did not have the right to do this. I did so for efficiency, but also to keep track of the people who were financial abusers in the office.

I was not able to collaborate with the Lavalas activists in Boston and was therefore isolated, to some extent, from the base. I was cleaning up the system. For example, state employees in Haiti are supposed to receive their salaries every other month but they seldom do. In contrast in Boston, I created a different system, and the consulate employees received their salaries every month. I invested my own money in the consulate in order to pay the employees on time.

The activists took a hostile stance because they were hoping to get my job, and I was the one selected. That division did not make much sense, since we were all working for the president. Aristide called them once from Haiti to ask them to put some water in their wine. But they continued to make false statements on the air about me.

My dismissal in the form of forced resignation was due to the Boston activists, who had been undermining my role at the consular office, and I concurred with views expressed within the government that it was necessary for me to leave. There were "chek zonbi" [checks made out to individuals who appeared on the payroll list, but were not consulate employees] that I revoked. This created some tension among some members of the diasporic community, and I dismissed some people who were taking office supplies to send to friends or families in Haiti. Even the foreign minister, who sent me the form to fire an employee, called later to say that the people at the National Palace wanted him to rescind the order. It was the time when Aristide himself came up with the "zero-tolerance" policy. I told the minister that I was inspired by this and had just applied the zero-tolerance policy in the case of this employee. I gave him my word that if the employee could not be dismissed, then I would submit my resignation.

There were two employees who never showed up to the consular office and who used to receive their checks each month. There was one who worked as a security guard in the National Palace and had been receiving a check for $2,000 every month from the consulate. There was also a lawyer who received $3,000 per month, and I had never seen her in the office. To bring more transparency to the office, I established a new system whereby employees had to punch their attendance cards when they came to work, and if you did not punch your card, you did not get paid. I followed the model of the American system. When I cancelled the check of the security guard who worked at the National Palace in Port-au-Prince, he threatened to kill me! He worked at the National Palace while his wife lived in Boston.

With all of these problems, there was some talk that I was going to be transferred to Chicago, and I decided to resign the post. The government owed me two months of salary that has remained unpaid until now.

These appointed officials are called upon to please two different groups with different agendas and different standards for those who hold public offices. On the one hand, they are considered by the diasporic community to be government officials—that is, part of a corrupt establishment that must be placed on notice to prevent ineptitude and enhance transparency and democracy. On the other, they are considered to be diasporans by the government—people who have not been socialized in the governmental culture of Port-au-Prince, who rely on friends in the diaspora rather than on classmates in Haiti, and who are less dependent on the government for survival and therefore more independent. They are placed in a difficult position to please these two critical constituencies.

Haitian American State Legislators

Recently, however, the informal aspects of diasporic politics have been supplemented by more formalized transnational elements situated in the hostland. Haitian Americans began to run successfully for elective office in the United States and thus to carry out homeland agendas from power bases in the hostland.

During the nineteenth century, there were a handful of Haitian Americans, mostly from South Carolina and Louisiana, who were elected to Congress and to state legislatures.[9] However, because they were the main plaintiffs in the *Plessy v. Ferguson* case in the U.S. Supreme Court and lost in 1896, they did not serve as either congressmen or state representatives until the very end of the twentieth century.[10] Beginning in 1999, however, Haitian American candidates began to win local and state elections inside and outside electoral districts with large numbers of Haitian American citizens. As reported by the U.S. Department of State during the George W. Bush administration,

> Republican Josaphat Joe Célestin, 44, defeated Democrat Arthur Sorey with 53 percent of the vote in the May 16, 2001 mayoral contest, while Democrat Jacques Despinosse, 55, won a term to the five-member council capturing 68 percent of the vote against three other opponents. . . . Célestin and Despinosse join North Miami's first Haitian American council member, Ossman Désir, and their election closely follows the victory in November 2000 of Phillip Brutus from Miami as the first Haitian American elected to the Florida state legislature. Voters in the Dade County city of El Portal elected a Haitian American mayor in 2000, and in 1999, Haitian Americans won a majority on the El Portal City Council.[11]

On July 6, 1999, Representative Marie St. Fleur became the first Haitian American to be elected to the Massachusetts House of Representatives. This victory was followed by the election of Phillip Brutus in 2000 to the Florida House of Representatives and in 2002 by that of Representative Yolly Roberson to the same legislative body. It is important to examine the candidates, the conditions that led to their victories, and their style of ethnic or diasporic politics. They are indicative of the overall trajectory that diasporic politics has followed in the United States.

Representative Marie St. Fleur, fifth Suffolk District In 1968, at age seven, she emigrated with her parents from Haiti to New Jersey and later moved and resettled in Dorchester, Massachusetts. After attending the University of Massachusetts at Amherst for her undergraduate studies and graduating from Boston College Law School in 1987, she served consecutively as a law clerk in the Massachusetts Superior Court, as assistant district attorney in Middlesex County, and then as assistant attorney general (under Attorney General Scott Harshbarger). She came to the House of Representatives as a result of a special election held during the summer of 1999 because of the abrupt resignation of Representative Charlotte Golar Richie, who held the position. Richie had resigned because she was approached by the mayor of Boston, Tom Menino, to serve as the chairperson of the Joint Committee on Neighborhood Development. Marie St. Fleur, who as assistant attorney general had been working in the trial division of the Office of the Attorney General and later as chief of the Unemployment Fraud Division, was tapped for the job by Representative Richie, who endorsed her candidacy. Since this was not a regular election cycle, a special election was held during the summer of 1999 with a group of strong candidates for the position. St. Fleur proved to be a superb campaigner-politician and won the contest (table 1.1).

The early endorsement by the departing member of the Massachusetts House of Representatives, as well as by the attorney general and by the mayor of the city, gave extra visibility to her candidacy, and she became known throughout the campaign as the "downtown candidate."[12] A young Haitian American strategist, with a degree in marketing from Boston College, William Dorcena, was recruited to serve as campaign manager for the 1999 legislative elections. As a *Boston Globe* reporter put it, he pounded "on every door in the 5th District" to ensure the victory of his candidate.[13]

Her victory was attributed by some observers to several factors. One was her involvement in community affairs and her service on

Table 1.1 1999 Special Election Results

Name	*Votes*	*Percentage*
(D) Marie St. Fleur	955	77
(R) Robert Fortes	210	17
(I) David Huggins	66	5

Notes: D: Democrat
R: Republican
I: Independent

Source: Carlos Monje, Jr., St. Fleur a big winner in fifth District. *The Boston Globe*, July 7, 1999.

community boards (e.g., Project Hope, the African American Federation, and the YMCA of Boston) which lend themselves to large community support. Two other factors were the campaign issues she raised in relation to housing, education, crime prevention, and punishment, and the employment needs of her district and her close relationship with State Senator Diane Wilkerson, who has been serving informally as her mentor. Also, "her main support came from a grassroots campaign that boasted 150 volunteers and campaign organizers in 15 of the district's 19 precincts."[14]

More than 50 percent of her electoral district is African American and the rest of the population is composed of smaller groups of Caucasians, Cape Verdeans, Latinos, and a few Haitian Americans. She owed her elections principally to the support she got from the African American community. Her electoral district is made up of North Dorchester and part of Roxbury. The campaign strategists focused their attention on voter turnout and spent a good deal of effort to energize her base of support. In the next two campaigns in 2000 and 2002, she largely maintained that base of support in the predominantly Democratic legislative district (tables 1.2 and 1.3). For example, during the elections of 2002, the *Dorchester Reporter* (October 31, 2002) endorsed her candidacy as "the tough former prosecutor who provides such a strong voice in the House."

Representative Phillip Brutus, District 108 A graduate from the University of Massachusetts (BS, 1982) and Suffolk University Law School (JD, 1985), he served for a while as assistant federal public defender in Miami, Florida. As a candidate in 1994 for a Dade County Court judgeship in Florida, he lost the race, but acquired much experience in campaigning. He was more successful in November 2000, when he became the first Haitian American elected to the

Table 1.2 Election Results 2000: Massachusetts House of Representatives (Fifth, Suffolk)

Name	*Votes*	*Percentage*
(D) Marie St. Fleur	4,098	73.5
(I) Althea Garrison	1,509	26.5

Source: *The Boston Globe*, November 9, 2000.

Table 1.3 Massachusetts House of Representatives Election Results: Fifth Suffolk State Rep. District

Name	*Votes*	*Percentage*
(D) Marie St. Fleur	4,037	68.0
(R) Peggy Chapparo	463	7.8
Blanks	1,433	24.1

Source: Massachusetts State Election, Boston Unofficial Results, November 5, 2002.

Table 1.4 Florida House of Representatives Election Results: District 108

County	*Reginald Thompson (R)*	*Phillip J. Brutus (D)*	*Jesus A. Camps (NPA)*
Miami-Dade	4,443	22,264	528
Total	4,443	22,264	528
Percentage	16.3	81.7	1.9

Note: NPA = No political association.

Source: Florida Department of State Division of Elections, November 7, 2000 Official Results.

Florida House of Representatives, receiving no less than 82 percent of the vote (table 1.4). His electoral district comprises Little Haiti, El Portal, Miami Shores, Biscayne Park, North Miami, and a portion of Liberty City.

The slight decrease in support for Representative Brutus during the 2002 elections (table 1.5) may be attributed to at least two factors: (1) The endorsement by the *Miami Herald* of his opponent, the Republican candidate, Val Screen, and (2) the effects of redistricting. According to the *Miami Herald* (October 16, 2002), "The new boundaries drawn by the 2002 Legislature have increased the diversity of this

Table 1.5 Florida House of Representatives Election Results: District 108

Name	*Votes*	*Percentage*
(D) Phillip Brutus	16,517	77.1
(R) Val Screen	4,919	22.9

Source: Florida Chamber of Commerce, 2002 Election Cycle.

traditionally black district. Where once the district was 59 percent black, it now has 45 percent black voters."[15]

Representative Yolly Roberson, District 104 In 2002, attorney Yolly Roberson became the second Haitian American to be elected to the Florida House of Representatives (table 1.6). A graduate from the University of Massachusetts-Boston (BSN, 1983) and the New England School of Law (JD, 1988), she was a public defender with the Committee for Public Counsel Services in Boston and later served as senior assistant attorney general in Fort Lauderdale. Her involvement in community affairs included the Miami City Attorney Selection Committee and the Florida International University Nursing Advisory Council. Her black majority district includes "African Americans, Jamaicans, Haitians and other West Indians" (*The Miami Herald*, November 6, 2002). Representative Roberson attributes her victory to "the help of a rainbow coalition" (*The Miami Herald*, November 6, 2002).[16]

Representative Linda Dorcena Forry, Twelfth Suffolk District After former House speaker Thomas Finneran who had been representing Dorchester, Mattapan, Hyde Park, and Milton in the *Massachusetts State Legislature* since 1978 abruptly resigned in 2004, he was replaced the following year by second-generation Haitian American Linda Dorcena Forry, who had been endorsed by State Senator Diane Wilkerson, State Representative Marie St. Fleur, the *Boston Globe, Boston Herald, The Boston Phoenix*, and by *Dorchester Reporter*, owned by her husband's family. She was sworn in on April 25, 2005, representing the Twelfth Suffolk District. She holds a BA in public administration from Boston College and at the time of the election was a candidate for a Master's Degree in public administration at the Carroll School of Management, Suffolk University. From 1996 to 1999, she served as legislative assistant, legislative aide, and then acting chief of staff for former state representative Charlotte Golar Richie (Fifth Suffolk District). Just prior to her election, she was employed as an official of the Department of Neighborhood Development, City of Boston.

Table 1.6 Florida House of Representatives Election Results: District 104

Name	*Votes*	*Percentage*
(W) Cedine Jean-Jacques		0.0
(D) Yolly Roberson	18,499	84.2
(R) Arlington Sands, Jr.	3,479	15.2
(W) Gary Smith	1	0.0
(W) Lenox Waciuma Wanjohi	1	0.0

Note: W = Write-in candidate (no political party)

Source: Florida Chamber of Commerce, 2002 Election Cycle.

For the Special Democratic Primary Election held in March 2005, she conducted a robust campaign with a specific focus on the following issues: education (creation of a new high school in Mattapan), housing (affordable housing for the poor), transportation (expansion of commuter rail stops in Mattapan and Dorchester), public safety (improving workspace at police station), health care (strengthening the capacity of Carney Hospital), parks (transforming the Neponset River into a river parkland), and recreational facilities (creation of a youth center). In March 2005, she won the Special Democratic Primary Election with 47 percent of the vote (see table 1.7) and the final election held in April 2005 with 93 percent of the vote, since she ran unopposed, without any major party challenger (see table 1.8).

Several factors contributed to her victory at the polls. According to a postelection assessment by her legislative assistant, Ken Donovan,

> "[She was elected because of her] experience in housing and constituent services at State and City level. Forry had broad appeal across the district, and worked to bring together groups in the district, from gay rights, marriage rights, immigrants, labor, etc. There was also a large contingent of liberals in the district (Milton, in particular) that made a decision, largely based on experience and Linda's lifelong residency in the immediate area to support her. In the end, the two other Haitian candidates focused strongly on the Haitian-American community (a small voting block in the district) and African Americans (a large voting block, but with traditionally low turn-out) and Linda was able to pull together high turnout demographics to put together her winning block." (personal communication, June 14, 2005)

In a moment of self-reflection, while addressing a Commonwealth Legislative Seminar, Representative. Forry attributed her 2005 victory "to

Table 1.7 Special Democratic Primary Election Results

Ward	*Linda Forry (%)*	*Stacy Monahan (%)*	*Eric Donovan (%)*	*Kirby Roberson (%)*	*Emmanuel Bellegarde (%)*
16	19.0	17.9	61.4	1.0	0.7
17	55.1	13.7	21.2	5.8	4.2
18	57.5	6.5	3.2	17.4	14.9
Milton	61.5	15.4	11.9	8.1	3.2
Total	47.1	12.7	24.5	8.8	6.7

Source: *Election Day Results* provided by Ken Donovan, Assistant to Rep. Linda Forry, June 14, 2005.

Table 1.8 City of Boston: Election Summary Report (April 12, 2005)

Rep. 12th Suffolk		*Percentage*
Number of Precincts	14	
Precincts Reporting	14	100
Vote for	1	
Total Votes	807	
Times Blank Voted	14	
Linda Dorcena Forry	757	93.80
Write-in Votes	50	6.20

a platform advocating for inclusion and coalition building among the diverse communities in her district." She did very well with the African American, Caribbean, and other minority and liberal white voters, but fared less well with the conservative white residential group in Dorchester (Ward 16), the major support base for losing candidate Eric Donovan.

Representative Jean Leniol Jeudy, District 10, Ward 3 (New Hampshire) Born in Jérémie, Haiti in 1958, he immigrated to the United States in 1981. A year later Jeudy married his wife, Elvire, and became a US citizen in 1995. From 1999 to 2004, he served as vice president of the Haitian Community Center of New Hampshire. He ran for a state representative seat in 2004, but was defeated at the polls. It was a close race in which his opponent garnered 50 votes more than he did. When Representative William Clayton moved out of Manchester Ward 3 in 2005, the governor and the Executive Council acted on the impetus and called for a Special Election.

Jeudy's campaign lasted about six weeks from late September to early November 2005 and he ran for two offices simultaneously, namely, state representative for Hillsborough County District 10 and selectman of Ward 3 for the City of Manchester, New Hampshire. He won the two contests on November 8, 2005 and on November 16, 2005, he was sworn into office by the governor. At the polls, he was the official Democratic Party candidate and collected 508 votes against his White Republican opponent, Robert M. Fremeau, who garnered only 322 votes.

Jeudy's victory was heavily influenced by his popularity throughout District 10 as a result of his reputable volunteer work and the television program he has been hosting through Community Television Access, but also because of his vigorous campaigning in the area and the logistic support from the Democratic Party. He has been actively involved in Ward 3 for the past 15 years as board member of United Way, board member of Manchester Community Television Access, Chairman of Community Health Board, member of the Manchester Steering Committee for Presidential Candidate John Kerry (2004), member of the Board of Greater Manchester Association Services Agency and producer and host of TV Palmiste. In 2002, he was the recipient of the Good Samaritan Award from the city of Manchester.

Illinois State Senator, Kwame Raoul, Thirteenth District Senator Raoul was selected by an 11-member Democratic Committee out of a pool of 7 candidates to serve as state senator for the Thirteenth District Legislative seat, replacing former State Senator Barack Obama who was elected to the U.S. Senate in 2004. Second generation Haitian American State Senator Raoul obtained a BA in political science from De Paul University and earned a law degree from Chicago-Kent College of Law in 1993. His previous work experience includes his service as Cook County prosecutor, senior attorney for the City Colleges of Chicago, the board of directors of the Cook County Bar Association and the Cook County Bar Foundation. He was not a novice to the Chicago political scene when he was appointed to the Illinois State Senate. In fact, he had previously lost three elections when he earlier ran for Fourth Ward Alderman in 1995 and again in 1999 and for the Twelfth District State Senate seat in 1996. He promises to focus his legislative agenda on issues of "public education, transportation, and health care." He was due for reelection in 2006.

Haitian American Municipal Officials

The most widespread Haitian American political penetration of the U.S. system has been felt at the municipal level. Several candidates have attempted to win municipal contests at various levels. As happens, some win and some lose. Here again, in some of the cases, diasporic support or lack of it has made a difference.

Haitian American candidates for mayors, city council members, or municipal judgeships have been elected in Illinois (the city of Evanston), New York (the city of Spring Valley), New Jersey (the city of Nyack and the city of East Orange), and Florida (the city of North Miami, the city of North Miami Beach, and the city of El Portal). The following tables identify the name, city, and office to which they were elected and the beginning and ending of terms in office (tables 1.9 and 1.10).

The majority of these elected municipal leaders have benefited from the support of Haitian voters in their communities and Haitian

Table 1.9 Haitian American Mayors and City Council Members

Josaphat Célestin, Mayor, North Miami, Florida, 2001–2005
Jacques Despinosse, Councilman, North Miami, Florida, 2001 to present
Ossman Désir, Councilman, North Miami, Florida, 1998–2003
Jean Monestime, Councilman, North Miami, Florida, 2002–2005
Marie Erlande Stéril, Councilwoman, North Miami, Florida, 2005 to present
Philippe Dérose, Council Member and Vice Mayor, El Portal, Florida, 1993– 2002
Philippe Dérose, Mayor, El Portal, Florida, 2000 (January–December)
Laura Charlemagne-Vancol, Council Member, El Portal, Florida, 2000–2002
Islande Salomon, Council Member, El Portal Florida, 1999–2001
Mariette SaintVil, Council Member, El Portal, Florida, 2002 to present
Philippe Dérose, Council Member, North Miami Beach, 2003 to present
Noramie Jasmin, Village of Spring Valley Board of Trustees and Vice Mayor, 2001 to present
Joseph Desmaret, Village of Spring Valley Board of Trustees, 2003 to present
Margareth Jourdan, Village of Spring Valley Board of Trustees, 1997–2001
Carl Henry Joseph, Village of Spring Valley Board of Trustees and Vice Mayor, 2001–2003
Démeza Delhomme, Village of Spring Valley Board of Trustees, 1999–2003
Daniel Jean-Gilles, Nyack Board of Trustees, 1988–1991
Lionel Jean-Baptiste, Alderman, Evanston, Illinois, 2002 to present

Table 1.10 Haitian American Judges

Fred Séraphin, Miami Dade County Judge, 2001 to present
Margareth Jourdan, Spring Valley Municipal Judge, 2001 to present
Sybil M. Elias, City of East Orange Municipal Judge, New Jersey, 2003 to present
Jacques C. Leroy, Administrative Judge for the Industrial Accident Board, 1988–1994, State of Massachusetts
Jacques C. Leroy, Judge, Trial Court of the Commonwealth, Springfield Division, 1994 to present

activists and community organizations that have organized voter registration drives on their behalf. The following example shows that not all of the attempts have been successful. A community leader in New York City reports the following:

> The last time that I lent my name to a flyer was with respect to the attempt by a Haitian American, Jean Vernet, who was campaigning to win a seat on the City Council of New York. I joined three or four Haitian community leaders in endorsing his candidacy and in asking people to vote on his behalf, but this was not an institutional support. He was seeking a seat on the City Council in 2001 in New York.
>
> Basically, what happened is that term limits were imposed on a number of members of the City Council, so a number of seats became vacant, which opened up an opportunity for people to campaign for them. Unfortunately, the seat he was seeking was held by Una Clarke, a Jamaican American woman, and what he failed to do, frankly, was to rely on the capacity of the Haitian vote. So Vernet had an endorsement from a number of Democratic Party leaders like Mayor Dinkins; he had the support of ACORN (Association of Community Organizations for Reform Now), a grassroots organization; he had the support of a number of other people; but he had unfortunately poohpoohed the Haitian vote. So Haitians did not go out in vast numbers to vote for him, and his closest competitor was the daughter of the City Council member: Yvette Clarke, Una Clarke's daughter. Una Clarke had distinguished herself in various communities: Jamaican American, Haitian American, and so forth. People did not see why they should vote for Vernet.
>
> Second, there were two Haitian candidates for that purpose. Jean Vernet was one of them, and Lola Poisson was the other. And apparently there had been disputes between the two Haitian American candidates. So that was it. This was in Brooklyn.

The shift from a primary focus on Haitian politics to a primary focus on American politics has been a major sea change since the late 1990s in the political behavior of the Haitian American community and accounts for this robust engagement in municipal politics.

The Trajectory of the Diasporic Political System

As the careers of these elected representatives show, Haitian Americans are going through a sea of change in matters related to diasporic political practices. After the period of euphoria that came with the collapse of the Duvalier regime, the period of political instability that followed, and the election and exile of Aristide, periods during which the diasporic community had invested most of its political capital in Haitian politics, the diaspora went back to the drawing board to reassess its practices. After the return of Aristide to Haiti in 1994, the disappointment about the performance of his government, a successful mobilization of the diaspora that nevertheless failed to lead to the restoration of democracy in Haiti, the split of the Lavalas Party that brought about a stalemate in Haitian governmental politics, and the immigration and welfare reforms in the mid-1990s that led many Haitian immigrants to become U.S. citizens, Haitian Americans have become convinced that the best alternative for them is to engage in politics in the hostland (United States) as a way of eventually helping Haiti (*The Miami Herald*, Haitian Americans Making Political Gains, December 20, 1999). This was the context under which the candidacy of Marie St. Fleur must be evaluated and why Haitian voters in Miami voted in large numbers for successful Haitian American candidates.[17]

The assimilation model has been placed by analysts in a polar extreme vis-à-vis the transnational model. This results partly from the different groups that have been researched, including individuals with different levels of participation in U.S. society, communities whose interests are hostile to or in harmony with those of the homeland, and differences in the length of time the research subjects have been in the United States. The feature that emerges from these polar positionings, however, is that the reality is more nuanced and that some assimilation and some transnationality is at work. It is not a situation of either one or the other.

The notion of ethnicity as performance sheds light on the problem. Transnationality plays a secondary and minor role in the political behavior of elected Haitian American officials, despite the fact that Haitian American voters constitute the political basis of their electoral support, at least in the case of the Florida elected officials. All successful Haitian American candidates there campaigned and won on the basis of issues pertaining to their local communities. Their communities wanted them to be their representatives and advocates on Haitian American issues, but not necessarily on Haitian issues.

The candidates fought their opponents fiercely, who wanted to portray them as interested only in Haitian issues. In fact, non-Haitian candidates have been in a better position to advocate Haitian issues than Haitian American candidates. The former can do so because they are not likely to be identified as single-issue candidates and also because Haitian American candidates are well aware of the political cost of such a posture. That's why transnationality is not the driving force behind these elected officials. Some of them have said so publicly. For example, "I'm campaigning in America as an American citizen. I cannot and will not run a campaign based solely on ethnic identity," says Brutus.[18] Representative St. Fleur made a similar statement: "sometimes I have to tell them that my main priority is the people in my District not the whole Haitian American community."[19]

However, the transnational component is not altogether absent, either, because some activists who represent political or civic constituencies do engage in political transnationalism. The fact that elected officials do not primarily engage in transnationality does not mean that the political process itself is not imbued with transnationality. It comes in via the following: (1) constituents who have a political agenda, (2) the decision of people to vote for a candidate as a result of the influence of friends who live in Haiti or in other diasporic sites, and (3) financing in the form of contributions from other diasporic sites made by people who are eager to see more Haitian American people elected to office. It comes in most fruitfully, however, in symbolic forms, as people help in order to have officials who are a symbolic representation of what the United States can offer to diasporans.[20] In this case, the domain of practice cannot be divorced from the symbolic representation that sustains and informs it. Transnationality is also the locus of tension and uneasiness between the leaders and the constituents—that is, the political orientation of the representative vis-à-vis the Haitian state may not totally be in sync with that of all Haitian American voters.

What must be stressed is the temporality of the manifestation of transnationality. It manifests itself in periods of crisis and in electoral periods and may remain dormant in between. Although Haitian American candidates do not campaign routinely on Haitian issues, they may at a time of crisis take a stance on these issues, as they may do for other issues concerning other ethnic groups they represent.

Furthermore, the question of leadership must be separated from the question of the orientation of the diasporic group vis-à-vis the homeland. Although a leader may adopt a position of neutrality out of respect for other constituents, the group is likely to push for a foreign policy that is sensitive to the homeland needs. Although the diasporic community may pursue ethnic politics for its domestic empowerment, it will continue to be transnational in regard to foreign policy vis-à-vis the homeland.[21] That's why an approach limited strictly to ethnic politics cannot account for both the hostland and the homeland aspects of diasporic politics.

During the centenary anniversary of *Plessy v. Ferguson* in 1996, the political consciousness and landscape of the Haitian American diasporic community shifted. This change was related to at least six factors. First, the Immigration Act of 1996, which barred noncitizen residents from benefits that until then they had enjoyed or that they expected to enjoy when they retired from their workplace, prompted many longtime legal immigrants to seek citizenship status. The year marked the beginning of a major shift in naturalization rates among Haitians in Florida and in the country in general.[22]

Second, the realization that political turmoil in Haiti was not likely to subside soon and that the possibility of influencing the course of events in Haiti was slim forced the diasporic community to reposition itself politically. This realization led to some disenchantment with the performance of the Lavalas Party and the Haitian government. Street violence and the split in the Lavalas Party that later led to political stalemate further undermined the possibility for direct political action in Haiti by the diaspora.[23]

Third, as a result of the first two factors, the diasporic community espoused the idea of actively participating in American politics as a way of advancing its agenda for better schools for its children, better health care for its sick, better housing for its neighborhoods, and more employment for its skilled and unskilled workers. All of a sudden, aided by the strengths of its voting members made possible by the 1996 Immigration Act, the diasporic community moved forcefully to vote for its own candidates for elective office. As one informant put it, "I don't think they are going to call us 'boat people' anymore. They are going to call us 'vote people.' We're voters."[24] In this new posture of the community, transnational politics in its homeland dimension takes a backseat to transnational politics in its hostland dimension. Transnationality is not the driving force of the politics of the elected officials, but it may come in during periods of crisis in the homeland or when pressed by the community to do so.

Fourth, the recent elections of Haitian Americans as state representatives have led to the reengineering of the architecture of the political leadership in the community. Since then, both the older leaders, whose main orientation has been toward the democratization of Haiti, and the activists who had imposed themselves on the community have been marginalized because of a lack of legitimacy. The new elected officials who have earned their reputations and positions through the polls have been identified as the recognized leadership of the diaspora. As Leonie Hermantin, the executive director of the Haitian American Foundation put it, "Before, any self-appointed person could come up and say, I am a leader. But now those who run for office and win are anointed as leaders. Now the Haitian community has elected officials; now we have stepped up to another level. Now to legitimize your leadership you either have to be on somebody's team so you are known to be in this person's camp, or you run for office."[25]

Fifth, the community has shifted its emphasis from street protests and its dependence on non-Haitian mainstream politicians to more formal organizations and to institution building for political action. There is a firm mission that is in view and reachable, plotting strategies on the ground for effective engagement in the American political process that could have as one of its dividends influence over American foreign policy vis-à-vis the homeland, as other ethnic groups have done in the past. This shift in the political orientation of the community was called forth by several analysts, activists, and politicians including Representative St. Fleur, who wrote in the *Boston Haitian Reporter*: "the reality is we have set roots here in every arena except in politics. It is past time for our involvement in American politics. . . . We must participate; we must do so now. . . . Every Haitian organization should get involved in registering people to vote, encourage people to attend citizenship classes, teach our children about civics and the importance of participation."[26]

Sixth, a new wave of younger Haitian American politicians who went to school here and earned their postgraduate degrees in law or in other professions have somewhat marginalized the older politicians who were hoping for a political career in Haiti.[27] These young professional politicians—in their thirties or early forties for the most part—are careerists who will do what it takes to win elections, have been socialized into mainstream American politics, are fluent in English, understand the mechanisms of the American machinery of government, and have only a "symbolic attachment" to Haiti, since they have already made the decision to live and pursue a political career in the United States. More American in their political demeanors than Haitian, they use mainstream strategies (using Anglo American and Jewish American lobbyists, conducting fund-raising events, engaging in coalition politics, seeking endorsements from well-placed political figures, associating themselves with the Republican or Democratic

Party, identifying the district where they can win on the basis of their analysis of the demographic composition of precincts, and conducting grassroots campaigns based on issues pertaining to the welfare of their district) to position themselves vis-à-vis the electorate and to deal with power brokers of their respective party affiliations. What this discussion indicates is that diasporic politics operates in an international universe comprising diverse sites of political action: formal, informal, and virtual political practices; activities geared toward local and transnational niches; and issues that are of concern to the homeland and the host country. In this integrated environment, at any given time, one site may engage in transnational practices while another may concentrate exclusively on local actions. In diasporic politics, it is not the case that all the political activities of the diasporic community are geared toward the homeland or other diasporic sites. Diasporic politics is undertaken in a plural universe, with political actions that may or may not have a direct transnational orientation. The capacity for transnationality may remain dormant in a site and may be reactivated at any time due to the influence of another unit in the universe. As we have noted, a crisis in the homeland may be the occasion for such a reactivation, or it may be the case that transnationality transpires through the political process, not by the activities of the elected leaders, but through the practices of the rank and file.

If we reflect on what we have seen in the case of Haitian diasporic politics, it becomes apparent that the course of diasporic politics follows a predictable trajectory. It usually begins with the first generation immigrants who maintain a strong identification with the homeland and organize their politics according to this vision. This orientation is aided by their socialization in the homeland culture and their marginal positions vis-à-vis the institutions of the host country. A singular manifestation of it is through *opposition politics* aimed at overthrowing the homeland regime (as in the case of Miami Cuban diasporic politics) or *alliance politics* aimed at consolidating the homeland government (as in the case of the support of the Haitian diaspora for the first Aristide administration).[28]

Diasporic politics then passes into the hands of the next generation, those who came at a young age or who were born here, went to school here, have been socialized in the ways of this country, have decided to live here for the rest of their lives, and are fluent in English. Although oriented toward U.S. politics, since they depend on the community for votes and since the community would vote for candidates who are sensitive to Haitian issues, they end up maintaining a balanced agenda pushing American issues while also bringing forth homeland issues that are of concern to the electorate.

Finally, with the passing of time, the American orientation becomes the central preoccupation, and the homeland appears on the horizon only if there is a political crisis there. The homeland is no longer a priority but rather a matter of symbolic attachment. This phase occurs in settings that no longer attract newcomers, and the relations with the homeland are not in an active mode. Haitian American diasporic politics is currently slowly making the transition from the first to the second phase.

Viewed more broadly, in the logic of the theory of diasporic globalization, cosmopolitan diasporic politicians are agents who constitute the global circuit of diasporic engagements, contribute to the maintenance of transnational relations, and operate both at the local and international levels. These varieties of practices indicate that this global process is not uniform, has multiple beats, with a peak season and less intense periods of border-crossing interactions, and has been made routine because of its ongoing performances.

2

State, Diaspora, and Transnational Politics

Embraced by new tentacles of the globalization process and the high-tech revolution, the states of the Caribbean are undergoing massive transformations in the conduct of everyday politics. This transformation is generated by a number of internal and external pressures that are both transnational and global in nature. Two such border-crossing practices will be identified and examined in this chapter to show their implosion into the states of the Caribbean and how they are reshaping their political identities: the transnational posture of local units (grassroots organizations and government agencies) and the diaspora's transnational maintenance of relations with the homeland (long-distance participation in local politics).[1]

In this chapter, state-diaspora relations are reproblematized in order to show how these are engendered through the process of immigration, diasporization, and transnational politics. To achieve our analytical goal of examining these issues and providing a frame of reference to understand the theoretical ramifications for the study of international relations (IR), this chapter first redefines and operationalizes the concepts of diaspora and transnationality and reconceptualizes state-diaspora relations by mapping identifiable models. Second, it examines a specific set of transnational connections with a focus on diaspora-grassroots relations. And third, taking stock of the widespread influence of the globalization process, it formulates an alternative way of framing the problem of the relations between states and diasporas.

This chapter analyzes five models of state-diaspora relations—the reincorporation model, the ethnic model, the economic model, the model of political opposition, and the transnational model—in the context of the history of Haitian immigration to the United States. It argues that these relations have contributed to a repositioning and reshaping of both the diaspora and the state. The multilayered dynamics and criss-crossing networks of these transnational processes will be examined in terms of the extraterritorial expansion of political constituencies and the rise of transnational grassroots organizations in an effort to show how international migration in particular and globalization in general have reshaped our notions of national territories and social identities.[2]

Issues for Analytical Observation

The Caribbean states did not develop consistent policies vis-à-vis their diasporas during the nineteenth and twentieth centuries.[3] The evolution of such policies depended on political circumstances at home or in the country of residence of the diaspora. There are several factors that influence these state-diaspora transnational relations: the size or importance of the diaspora, the extent to which the diaspora is creating a potentially embarrassing situation because of "illegals" or "undocumented immigrants" in the country of adoption, and whether the diaspora constitutes itself as the supporter of the homeland government or its foe—a government in exile, a liberation movement, or a movement of political resistance.[4] One may argue that state policies vis-à-vis the diaspora depend on the predicaments in which both entities find themselves.[5]

The state-diaspora problematic revolves around the resolution of three sets of issues and can be framed as an object of analytical investigation. These issues pertain to state transformation and the new political culture it generates, diaspora integration and its influence on the homeland, and the transnational nature of state-diaspora relationships. These variables are interlocked in the process that shapes their identities. Since they are not separated from each other, I will not engage here in a study of their impact on each other. Rather, I will concentrate on interactional processes that generate these transformations.

The first set of issues that I want to raise takes into consideration the reasons why a state gets involved with its diaspora beyond the mere question of emigration.[6] A state is involved in extraterritorial units to the extent that it sees a positive return for its population, whether in real or symbolic terms. How would a state benefit from such an engagement, since the population is living beyond its territorial borders? Why should a state intervene in a polity over which it has no control or jurisdiction? Why should a state allow another state to intervene inside its territorial borders? What would be the extent of that intervention for the sending state and the diaspora? What does the receiving state gain from a laissez-faire policy? Does such intervention require some complicity from the receiving state, which, in the process, undermines the legitimate basis of its territorial jurisdiction? Or does it just happen because such a process cannot be controlled or stopped?

I want to reiterate here that the concept of the state, or what it is supposed to represent, is problematic and cannot be taken as a given.[7] This is so because in the appropriated transnational practice of citizenship by a growing number of citizens, the nation continues to outgrow the state because of its diasporic tentacles.[8]

States maintain relations with their diasporas for different sets of reasons, sometimes against their will, such as when they are interpellated or forced to do so by the receiving country. For example, a state may get involved at the international level for the sake of its own reputation when asked to prohibit its citizens from illegally entering the receiving state. The impulse for involvement may be internal, as the state develops mechanisms for the channeling of diasporic money to the homeland, or the incentive may be external, as when there exists a diasporic political organization whose goal is to overthrow the regime. In the latter case, unless the state deals with such an issue, the result may be destabilization of the homeland government and collapse of the regime. The state may even go a step further by formalizing its relationship with the diaspora. That's precisely what the government of President Jean Bertrand Aristide accomplished by referring to Haiti's diaspora as its "Tenth Department," an addition to the nine territorial departments of the country.

The concept of diaspora has been transformed with the growth of return migration.[9] Once defined as the expression of population movement, displacement, and rerootedness, the concept of diaspora must now include the returnees, that is, those who once lived abroad. When a Haitian refers to someone as part of the "diaspora," he or she means one of two different things: either a person residing abroad or a returnee. This is not just an informal, semantic development. The Caribbean state has been in the business of officially dediasporizing some of its citizens. In the case of Haiti, a diasporan who has never renounced his or her citizenship needs only five years of residence in the homeland for complete dediasporization in order to be eligible for certain public offices. Those who at one point renounced their citizenship can never—even though they regain their Haitian nationality—be completely dediasporized to the extent that they are eligible for the post of president of the republic. Such individuals remain only partially dediasporized.

This point was forcefully put forward by a female diasporan who once served in the office of the Prime Minister Smarck Michel and later returned to resume her political activities in the United States. This informant, a keen opponent to the second Aristide administration, commenting on the inability of the Haitian parliament to pass a bill that would ease the dediasporization process, has the following to say:

> There was a presentation by some diaspora groups coming from the U.S. and Canada, and I know that Myrtho Blanchard had come down with them at one point. A lot of academics had joined them, some doctors' or lawyers' groups, I don't remember what it was. They had brought down a proposal, a bill, or a draft, and the government never acted on it. Then, when Aristide was coming back a second time, when Leslie Voltaire became minister of the Tenth Department, at that time, they hastily wrote a bill and made it into a law. . . . They did something regarding investment, but it did not stand for anything.
>
> When the former cabinet member told you that he had double nationality, he was lying! You may have double nationality from the Canadian side, but there is no double nationality in Haiti. Constitutionally speaking, there is no recognition of double nationality in Haiti. You can keep your foreign citizenship. For example, a Haitian American who rejects his American nationality and asks to regain his Haitian nationality has a problem if he has a problem in Haiti. He will not be considered an American by the American embassy. In contrast, if the Haitian Canadian does the same thing, he will have no problems with the Canadian embassy, because the Canadian government allows this to happen.

These developments simply mean that the category "diaspora" is resilient because it outlives the conditions that once exclusively defined it. Here, I use the extended definition of the concept because it gives a different twist to the state-diaspora issue. It defines two different things: the relations of the state with an extraterritorial diaspora and the diaspora as inclusive of the state. In this reformulation, *the state is reshaped by both internal and external diasporas*.

Just as states maintain relations with their diasporas for different reasons, there are a variety of reasons why a diaspora wants to maintain its connections with its homeland.[10] Some of these connections are symbolic, a way of maintaining the memory of the homeland. Others are practical, a way of helping the homeland in any way one can, as when, for instance, specific requests are made by family members or the government to help in the case of a disaster.

I see these relations as being shaped by the inward and outward goals of the diaspora. The goals are outward, from the point of view of the diaspora, in the case of a diaspora that constitutes itself as an opposition force to liberate the homeland or overthrow the government there. The goals are inward when the diaspora uses the homeland to reposition itself or achieve some political status in the country of adoption. The diaspora does so to maintain its identity apart from that of other groups.

The relationship between the homeland state and the diaspora articulates the process by which transnationality leads to globalization. State, grassroots, and diaspora strategies give us a glimpse of the inner workings of the process. These three actors are engaged in three different sets of transnational practices that turn what would otherwise be an incidental phenomenon into a sustained process. The state is engaged in border-crossing political practices, using the diaspora as a political constituency—that is, as a source of money for electoral campaigns through fund-raising or special donations, a source of technical knowledge to supplement what already exists in the homeland, or as a factor that influences voting behaviors and hence offsets the balance of local forces.[11] Such relations benefit state or government officials.

Local grassroots organizations engaged in transnational relations develop their own foreign policies as they link with other grassroots organizations in the United States or elsewhere and push their agendas, whatever they may be. These organizations either reinforce or weaken state practices. The presence of nongovernmental organizations in these local processes is the newest element in Caribbean politics. Not only do they connect with other NGOs, but they also connect with U.S. government officials who finance their activities or simply maintain contact with them. I imagine that the CIA has a field day with these grassroots organizations, who are always scrambling for funds from whomever they can get them, since the political and ideological persuasion of donors may not matter very much. NGOs do not necessarily have a noncapitalist agenda, but rather are concerned with specific issues such as human rights, ecology, gender disparity, and the implementation of democracy.

The diaspora is involved in these transnational relations through its financing of government projects, which makes the Ministry of Foreign Affairs compete with other agencies in the area of foreign relations; through its connection with grassroots organizations abroad, which enhances these organizations' chances of influencing government policies and practices; through its financing of local projects, which in turn affects local elections; and through its effort to raise the level of consciousness on human rights issues, which brings a new vision of democratic rights to the homeland.[12]

The following two cases give a glimpse of the sort of interventions carried out by hometown associations and larger nonprofit organizations in homeland affairs. According to a female activist informant,

> I know that some diasporans from Desdunes have established a very well organized hometown association that has existed for more than fifteen years. They do fundraising every year. They once came to visit with the Prime Minister's office and told us that they had been trying, with not much luck, to undertake several development projects in Desdunes. All had failed. We told them that their approach was unlikely to succeed and advised them that they needed to discuss the interest and feasibility of the projects with the community, to entice them to participate so that they would not believe that you are providing them with some kind of welfare handout or subvention of sort. And also you cannot establish a school or hospital without a government permit.
>
> So a lot of people, given the corruption level, milked the diaspora. When they were told very plainly what had to be done and what needed to be done, they had appreciated that very much. In fact, a couple of years after Smark Michel had left the government, they invited him to one of their annual dinners, and I went to the event with him. I was very impressed—that was in New Jersey. They were so well organized and I was so impressed by the level of organization, discipline, and mutual respect shown by the Desdunes Hometown Association.

In the second example below, the director of the National Coalition of Haitian Rights explains some of the accomplishments of the organization in Haiti.

> What we have been able to achieve in respect to Haiti is to have human rights violations put more at the center of political debate than it used to be. Part of what we have done has dealt with judicial reform, prison reform, and court reform. So what we have been doing is documenting the process in a significant way. We documented police reform. We issued a number of reports on police reform back in 1994 and 1995. We also sort of designed, or helped design, the rule of law effort back in 1995. One of the staff here in New York was hired as a consultant by USAID. He was contracted to come up with a judicial reform plan, and then in 2002 when I issued a report on *Restavek in Haiti*, it was seen as the basis upon which there would be, on the part of the U.S., an effort to stop what they call "trafficking in persons," which included children

being trafficked to work as domestics or to work the fields in the Dominican Republic, which is a major problem. So the essence of the report became the basis for a plan of action for USAID.

USAID did not even bother to meaningfully change too much of the report itself. They just turned it into a proposal. In a way, the effort has been more systemic, because the system in Haiti is, to an extent, far more resistant to change than it has been because of the dialogue one can engage in with the authorities in this country. It is a difficult dialogue that you can engage with Haitians back in Haiti, because they are not used to that dialogue. They are used to being in charge and not allowing much of an input from civil-society organizations, and then essentially, if they engage in a dialogue, the dialogue won't do much of anything.

Modeling Diaspora-State Relations

Understanding the relations between the diaspora and the state requires that we make operational specific models that can be documented from the history of Haitian immigration to the United States.[13] These data do not exhaust all the possibilities that exist, but rather reflect the conditions of a specific group of people.

The reincorporation model unveils a situation in which the sending state takes various measures to facilitate the return of the diasporic population, or some of its members, to the homeland. It does not matter whether the incentive for such a practice comes from one side or the other. This model reflects a situation in which *repatriation* is to the advantage of both sides or is the only available alternative. We have seen a recent example of the phenomena highlighted by this model on official efforts at dediasporization.

The reincorporation of the diaspora into the sending state implies that émigrés are willing to relocate to the homeland. In some cases, they may be forced to relocate. The point I wish to stress is not their willingness to do so, but rather the willingness of the sending state to welcome them. This is also true in terms of the logistics for the return of the émigrés. It does not matter whether the trip is arranged and paid for by the sending or the receiving state, or even by the émigrés themselves. The modality of the reincorporation may vary; that is, it can be a step-by-step or a mass phenomenon.

During the Haitian revolution (1791–1804), many refugees left the island and took up residence in New York, Philadelphia, New Orleans, Baltimore, and Charleston. President Jean Pierre Boyer invited these refugees to return home after the country won its independence. To help them out, he appointed American and Haitian agents to recruit returnees with the understanding that the government would pay for their trips, provide them with land, and help in their reintegration.[14] The state saw these refugees and prospective returnees as individuals who could help with the economic development of the island.

Another example of reincorporation occurred during the Clinton administration after thousands of Haitian asylum seekers who had been relocated at the U.S. Navy base in Guantánamo were denied refugee status and forced to return to their homeland against their will. Their repatriation, although monitored to some extent by international humanitarian organizations, was far less welcoming than it was in the previous example. Both cases, however, represent the repatriation model because of the state's willingness to accept returnees.

The ethnic model implies that the diaspora reconnects with the homeland for the purpose of strengthening its position in the country of residence. Here, the diaspora uses its connections to enhance its status as an ethnic group so as to claim specific rights (e.g., language rights) in its country of residence.[15]

In the ethnic model, the homeland is a symbol that helps define the group as an ethnic entity and gives legitimacy to the claim of ethnic identity. For example, in the Haitian American community of New York City, the struggle for bilingual education was fought for the purpose of giving youngsters the opportunity to have transitional instruction in Creole as an alternative to incorporation in an English-only classroom. This demand for bilingual education could not be made without reference to the language spoken in the motherland. While in the reincorporation model, the incentive for state-diaspora relations could come from either side, in the ethnic model, the incentive for maintaining a connection can come only from the diaspora.[16]

The economic model treats the diaspora as a source of foreign currency for the government or the homeland. Relations are maintained or nourished by the state for the purpose of extracting remittance money from the diaspora for the economic development of the nation.[17] The nature of the relations between state and diaspora is defined within the context of these economic realities and financial gains.

Sometimes, the government develops elaborate plans to make sure it gets its monetary share from the diaspora. For example, departure and arrival taxes are added by the state to one's travel expenses, and money sent to relatives is indirectly taxed through the manipulation of exchange rates. This diasporic money, which constitutes a significant sum, is needed to help keep things afloat, helps stabilize the financial markets of the country, and contributes to the survival of a good portion of the population via the monthly remittances received by individual households.

The political opposition model implies that the diaspora is seen by the sending state as an opposition force that must be silenced because of its potential to do harm to the government. It is materialized by the existence of a government in exile or by opposition groups in the diaspora whose aim is to overthrow the government. Such a government in exile can be either the legitimate government of the nation or one that is not considered as such by any state or international institution.[18]

Although, for example, Aristide was recognized as the legitimate president of Haiti while in exile in Washington, DC, the same cannot be said of Leslie Manigat, who was de jure, but not de facto, president while in exile in New York. The exile of President Leslie Manigat followed a logic different from that of President Jean Bertrand Aristide, which is why one succeeded in maintaining his position as head of state and the other failed. Shortly after the military overthrew the Manigat administration, the Reagan administration officially recognized the legitimacy of the new military junta headed by Lieutenant General Henri Namphy. The Bush and Clinton administrations, however, never recognized the postcoup civilian administration that replaced the Aristide government.

In this case, two politicians projected two visions of the Haitian state: One saw it as a *nation-state* and the other as a *transnation-state*. In Manigat's view, the diaspora was an *external entity*, while Aristide saw it as an *integral unit* of the state residing outside its jurisdictional territorial limits, but, paradoxically, comprising its "Tenth Department."[19] This is not the first time a country has recognized an overseas department—consider, for example, the status of the French Caribbean islands—but it is the first time that such a department has been squarely located inside the geographical and jurisdictional boundaries of another country (or to be more precise, inside more than one foreign country). This is why Aristide, while in exile, behaved as if he was inside the transnation, that is, in one of the departments of the state. In this rationale, he had left the territorial boundaries of the state but not the reconstituted spatial boundaries of the transnation. As such, he remained the de jure president of the transnation-state, and, in fact, the diaspora did its best to help him carry out his functions as president. As long as Aristide resided within the transnation, a coup leader could serve as a de facto, but not a de jure president of the state.

This understanding of the transnation-state sheds new light on the mutual relationships between the transnation and the state and forces us to reconceptualize the notion of exile itself. What does "exile" mean in this new regime of transnation? For one thing, it signifies that forcing a head of state to live outside the territorial boundaries of the state may not be enough to get rid of him or her. To accomplish that, a political leader must be pushed out of the spatial boundaries of the transnation, as well. While coup leaders may force a deposed president to move out of the territorial boundaries of the state, they do not have the power to prevent such a political figure from residing inside the bounds of the transnation. In this new logic, although a coup displaces the site of government, the coup leaders fail in their overall goal of replacing the government.

The definition of "political asylum," which used to have a universal meaning even though the conditions under which asylum was granted might differ from one country to another, is now fractured with diverse meanings. What is political asylum for the legal regime in the receiving state may not be viewed as such by the political refugees from the sending state. While refugees may negotiate asylum with the receiving state, backed by the political will of a transnation, they may refuse to permit the sending state to assign them such a status. After all, in the logic of the transnation, such a person is not in exile, but is internally displaced.

More often, opposition groups in the diaspora vie to liberate their country under siege by invading it, by influencing public opinion, and by spreading misinformation. In this adversarial posture, the diaspora and the state maintain tense relations, as in the case of New York Haitians vis-à-vis Papa Doc Duvalier and the case of Miami Cubans vis-à-vis Fidel Castro.[20] The diasporic community then becomes a spying ground, leaders are condemned in absentia, family members are imprisoned in order to silence opponents, properties are confiscated to prevent opposition leaders from returning home, and attempts at extradition are engineered to keep the opposition off balance. At the same time, the diasporic opposition tends to finance and support underground resistance movements in the homeland.

Finally, *the transnational model* implies the blurring of the boundaries between state and diaspora, the expansion of the nation, its transformation into a transnation, and the social normalization of border-crossing practices.[21] In this model, the diaspora may be constructed as a community, a state, or a province of the homeland. As noted earlier, the government of Haiti refers to its diaspora as its Tenth Department.

In this model, the state does not consider its diaspora to be outside its jurisdictional boundaries. It encloses it as an integral overseas part of the nation. People circulate, do business, occupy positions, or practice professions inside the transnation precisely because of the double allegiance they maintain to the homeland and the country of residence.

Unlike the other models we have examined, which distinguish between the diaspora and the state and see the two as separate entities, the transnational model projects them as parts of a continuum. In this light, state and nation do not coincide completely: the nation has outgrown the state or the nation is larger than the state.

Haiti: A Transnational Example

The Haitian case is worth analyzing since it involves a major attempt by a state to incorporate this transnational model into its governmental practice. Since the overthrow of the Jean Claude Duvalier regime in 1986, Haitian governments have tried different ways to integrate the diaspora into the daily life of the state.

The first attempt led to development of what might be called the *directorate phase*, which consisted in placing diaspora affairs under the aegis of the Ministry of Foreign Affairs. This bureaucratic arrangement implied that the ministry, which is already in charge of communications and transactions with outside regimes on behalf of the national government, would play a similar role as an intermediary between the government and the diaspora. The emphasis was more on helping and protecting Haitian diaspora interests abroad than on reintegrating the returnees at home. Since the Duvalier regime had been hostile to the diaspora, it was now time to show that the government cared for its displaced citizens. This model still recognized the separate identity of the diaspora. It effected integration within the state from a distance, with the state acting as a foreign entity.

The second attempt led to development of the *representative phase*, which President Aristide implemented in the beginning of his term in office. This phase opened the gate for the direct participation of the diaspora in the affairs of the state. In this phase, the representative was a special envoy from the state to the diaspora who reported directly to the president. This relationship fit the model of participatory democracy that Aristide was simultaneously implementing. However, this new and direct access to the president—in contrast to the previous phase, which peripheralized the office of diaspora affairs by locating it structurally under another ministry—lacked the necessary bureaucratic infrastructure to make it efficient and practical. It provided good public relations for Aristide, but it was not an efficient method as far as the diaspora was concerned because no formal mechanism was set up for the implementation of its policy recommendations.

Toward the end of President Aristide's administration, under pressure from the diaspora that stood solidly behind him during the years of exile in Washington, DC, the Lavalas Party government that Aristide headed inaugurated a new phase that would provide the infrastructure missing from the previous phases. This third attempt initiated the *ministerial phase*, which consisted of creating a cabinet-level ministry headed by a member or former member of the diaspora. Such a ministry would have three functions: it would coordinate diasporic contributions to the affairs of the state (economic aid, public policy formulation, technical support), give the diaspora a voice in the governance of the nation (by supporting policies reflecting the diaspora's views about human rights and the democratic orientation of the state), and protect the diaspora in general and Haitian refugees in particular, especially asylum seekers, who sometimes need the support of the government in order to succeed in their ventures. In this phase, state and diasporic interests have coalesced into an integrated vision of and policy for the transnation.[22]

The directorate phase had been too flawed to succeed or even to survive. The post-Duvalier governments had simply misread the intentions of the diaspora. The office was developed without consulting key players or leaders in the diaspora. In addition, it suffered from being located within the Ministry of Foreign Affairs because the views of the diaspora, a segment of civil society, were not always identical to the views of government. Within this structure, the office was unable to function independently and to represent the views of the diaspora. These intrinsic structural problems led naturally to its collapse because the directorate was unable to reconcile the views and interests of different groups with those held by people in different social positions within the social architecture of the transnation.

The representative phase was transitional because the infrastructure to carry out programs was nonexistent. The appointee was more a *rassembleur* (uniter) than an executive officer. Because he was an appendage to the National Palace, he lacked the independence necessary to develop the effective policies and legitimacy a non-officeholder needed in order to convince sectors of the diaspora that he could indeed deliver on promises, or even help diaspora interests make inroads into the social structure of Haiti. Aside from the lack of sufficient structure, the hopes that this model of representation created—the promises on which it could not deliver—contributed to its collapse.

The more recent ministerial phase is itself in search of a modus operandi. Its mechanisms of linkage with the diaspora are not fully operational. This phase has evolved internally. At the outset, the government attempted to establish a formal structure by selecting a leader in charge of the diasporic community in the United States who could coordinate the efforts of regional leaders located in areas with sizable Haitian communities. This imposed diasporic political structure created the problem of *nominal* versus *effective* leaders. Nominal leaders were ridiculed by traditional leaders who commanded constituencies. To this malaise were added logistical problems related to organizations, expenditures, accountability, regional competition, lack of direct access to the president and cabinet ministers in Port-au-Prince, and a general demobilization of the diaspora resulting from a lack of progress in managing state affairs and controlling public corruption in Haiti. Although the Ministry of Diasporic Affairs has been pushing for laws that recognize dual citizenship for diasporic Haitians, it still needs to work out a way of making its relationships with the diaspora practical, which is by no means a homogeneous entity.

As a corollary of the rise and importance of the diaspora, the Haitian diplomatic corps in the United States has lost its prominence. As diasporic leaders infringe on what used to be the prerogatives of the ambassador or the regional consul, latent tensions have developed between these government and grassroots entities.[23] This state of affairs has come about not only because diaspora leaders are pressing the diplomatic corps for action and want it to be accountable to them, but also because diaspora leaders have taken the initiative to contact American politicians on behalf of Haiti and without the knowledge of appointed officials. This is an era in which the country is traversed by two sets of foreign policies: the official foreign policies of the government and the unofficial foreign policies of grassroots organizations in their relations with the diaspora and other grassroots organizations in the United States, the European Union, and elsewhere.

A former consul general in New York City explains how he attempted to stay ahead of the diaspora activists and in some cases to neutralize them by way of co-opting them as social partners on behalf of the government.

> When I was in New York, the funny situation was that, for the first time, the office was actually visible both to the Haitian community and to the international community. Before, the Haitian Consul usually used to stay in his office—they never mingled with the community and the officials. So when I came in, during the year and half I was there, the office and country got on the map, because I honored many speaking engagements. I had many engagements with other countries that I honored. So I never had any problem with the community. I did not have any activists on my case.
>
> A person who would contact a senator on behalf of Haiti is perhaps the constituent of that senator. So you cannot stop that. For example, during my term as consul, I encouraged this kind of thing. By encouraging them, I showed them that I don't feel threatened, and as a government official when I would meet with them, I would say that "it would be good if you could include the Consul General in this."

The transnational model changes the dynamics of how the executive branch of government functions. Now, cabinet members maintain transnational relations with diasporic constituencies for the purpose of requesting money to finance projects undertaken by their respective ministries. Whereas formerly the Ministry of Foreign Affairs was the only office that specialized in transnational transactions on behalf of the government, the entire cabinet is now involved in such practices, as is a noisy segment of civil society constituted by grassroots organizations.

This practice also extends to elected officials. According to a former senator, a member of the Lavalas Party who served as secretary of the senate in mid-1990s,

> The candidates from the diaspora would be better off financially if they moved forward their electoral campaigns because they have more money than the rest of us and have more external contacts. They campaign both inside and outside the country. They travel to do fundraising in Miami and New York.
>
> That's the case of the last mayoral campaign in Cabaret with a certain Dacolo. He announced his candidacy, and the population did not know much about him and had never met him before. Since he brought some money with him, he promised the electorate more than he could ever deliver. Of course, he won the mayoral election in Cabaret. In fact, I was a victim of his victory. I was on my way to Gonaives, and the road was blocked by his partisans because his rival had submitted his dossier to the Electoral Council attesting that he was not Haitian, and the Electoral Council had dismissed his victory on constitutional grounds. His election was annulled, and the rival became, ipso facto, the new mayor. Immediately, the population took action by blocking the road

> for about a week. Finally the Electoral Council reversed its decision, and the diasporan was inaugurated as the mayor of Cabaret.

According to a former diplomat who had worked in the Haiti embassy in Paris, diasporans in France are able to entice some French legislators to support the activities of government officials in their region in Haiti. For example he reports,

> Diasporans from Aquin who reside in France have developed supportive working relations with Charles Pasquoi, a member of the French legislative assembly and the conservative caucus. With this connection, they have built a hospital, a school, and now they are trying to provide their regional city with electricity. There is a particularly active diaspora in Paris. Pasquoi is a member of UMP, the party of Chirac. He is a representative and has occupied very important offices. They have established friendly relations with him and he has provided them with his support and has helped them secure funds in various places.

A former legislator who now resides in New York as a result of the forced resignation of President Aristide sheds more light on the issue of transnational relations with diasporic constituencies:

> I know several colleagues who have received money from diasporans from their region, and who raised funds among the diaspora to undertake certain projects, such as the building of a school, construction of a running water system, the electrification of a village, etc. I particularly know one colleague from the Northwest Department who has always won elections, and no one can defeat him. With diaspora money, he established a community radio station and invested in a hospital. He was never living outside the country, but as you know, the Northwest is a bastion of the diaspora. Most of the residents have parents elsewhere and receive money from them. He could not have realized these projects without the help from the diaspora.

The five models analyzed above indicate multiple forms that the interaction between state and diaspora has taken over the years. Although the transnational model is predominant, it does not entirely negate the explanatory value of the others. At times, however, it transnationalizes aspects of the other models. The government has attempted to diversify its modes of interaction and to formalize its relations with the diaspora. However, since multiple types of relationships are involved in the process, one must recognize that there is a temporal factor in the hierarchization and expression of these forms. Some are more predominant in certain periods than others. For example, during President Aristide's exile in Washington, DC, the transnational form was not as prevalent as it is now, since Haitian American NGOs and diasporic politicians were unwilling to collaborate with the illegal de facto government in Port-au-Prince. More recently, the other forms of state-diaspora interaction have expressed themselves in a more transnational manner. So now, without losing their identity, there is growing transnationalization of some of their practices. In the same model, one may now identify the coexistence of both transnational and traditional forms of state-diaspora relations.

It is important to differentiate these models in terms of the interaction of the diaspora with the political society, the civil society, or both as constitutive of the state. The existence of these models also invokes the idea that the porousness of the state depends on the forms of interaction it maintains with its diaspora. While the state encourages all kinds of civic exchanges between the population at home and the diaspora and promotes particular laissez-faire economic policies because in the long run this benefits the homeland, it is unwilling to allow expatriate political opposition groups to undermine its activities. So porousness is not unidirectional, and it is sectorialized and temporized.

Diaspora-Grassroots Relations

The idea that diasporic grassroots organizations intervene in homeland political processes and influence their course of action merits fuller treatment to understand the conditions under which these might lead either to positive or negative outcomes or even how they might complicate the playing out of homeland domestic politics on the ground. The effects of diaspora-grassroots relations are not uniform and, as Zlatko Skrbis has argued,[24] ought not to be studied uncritically. They account for the organizational strength of grassroots groups, differently affect segments of the diasporic community, contribute to the repositioning of factions, help exacerbate tensions, and transnationalize old cleavages. Just as these relations may help solve domestic problems, they may also place obstacles in the resolution of local problems by complicating the ground rules with the injection of foreign contributions in terms of ideas, money, and interests.

So far, the scholarly literature on transnational relations has stressed only the positive effect of these border-crossing practices on the homeland in ameliorating human rights conditions, in enhancing prospects for democracy, and in advancing economic development, but has neglected to investigate the other side of the coin, that is, how diasporic intervention can reinforce cleavages, rather than eliminate them. For example, by siding with one sector of homeland society, the diaspora may shift the political balance from one group to another. Likewise, the government sometimes may prefer to keep a political problem as a domestic matter to be solved internally without bringing in outsiders and may view diasporic intervention as further complicating the crisis rather than solving it. After the fall of the Jean Claude Duvalier administration in 1986, General Henri Namphy, who headed the provisional government, was convinced that the diaspora would complicate matters and did his best to keep the issue of governance as an internal problem to be solved by domestic actors who understood the limits of what they could get, and not by the diaspora, which saw limitless possibilities for changing the face of the country.

Sometimes diasporic intervention is sought by the homeland government as a way of inducing the opposition to settle for less. Here, the diaspora is called upon to help solve a local problem opposing the government to a hostile sector of society. In the past, this role was sometimes played by the U.S. or French embassy, which was called to side with one group to the disadvantage of the other, and this was a productive means used by the U.S. government either to rescue a "friend in trouble" or to choreograph needed changes of direction in the political system.

Diasporic intervention has at times complicated life for the U.S. embassy. It is easy to bring the government and opposition together—without diasporic participation—to discuss matters of common concern, but with the diaspora, a "foreign" element is introduced, with foreign interests to be dealt with. This complication comes from the two ways in which the diaspora transnationalizes the local problem: the diaspora sides with one sector of society and therefore changes the political dynamics at the local scene, and the diaspora lobbies U.S. Congress against State Department or executive branch policies on behalf of the group it supports or the solution it favors. This new situation makes vulnerable the position of the U.S. ambassador if such an official does not side with the view of the majority of the diaspora. Since most ambassadors accredited to a third world country position themselves for the advent of a potential promotion to a more lucrative post, any open criticism by the diaspora of their performances or the policies of the administration they are called upon to implement may be a hindrance to their career advancement.

Diasporic intervention may also complicate life for the political party in office in the receiving country and can contribute a negative factor in the next electoral campaigns. In an interview on the CBS Evening News in December 2000, outgoing president Bill Clinton attributed the defeat of the democratic presidential candidate in Florida to the handling of the Elian Gonzalez case (perceived as mishandling by the Cubans). Ignoring the wishes of the Cuban electorate for not granting political asylum to the young boy (who was rescued on high seas as his mother attempted to flee Cuba) while following elementary principles of American law and a humanitarian agenda (by returning him to Cuba according to the wishes of his father) backfired on election day as Cuban Americans voted massively for the presidential candidate of the Republican Party.

On the basis of the Haitian materials discussed above, one may submit the following propositions.

- When the majority of the diaspora sides with the homeland government against the opposition, this factor may contribute to the isolation and marginalization of the opposition. During the electoral campaigns of 1990, Aristide's backing by the diaspora, despite hesitations by the Bush administration, was a factor in his acceptance by the American government and the defeat of the pro-Duvalier opponents.
- When the diaspora sides with the opposition, this may contribute to undermining homeland government policies and to the eventual downfall of the homeland government, if not to its isolation on the international scene. The René Préval administration suffered from this equation and could not accomplish much because of its paralysis as a pariah government.
- When the opposition is unable to operate at home because of repression, the diaspora may constitute the main opposition and undermine the activities of the homeland government through public demonstrations and its lobbying of Congress.

Diaspora intervention brings the domestic issue to the transnational level for its resolution. More often than not, however, the diaspora is split in its relations with the homeland: siding with both the government and the opposition, depending on one's political persuasion, or siding with the government on some issues and the opposition on others. That complicates the ground rules of diasporic politics, as has been argued in both the Irish and Israeli cases, in which the diasporas are very much involved in the resolution of their homeland political crises.[25]

Because the government and the opposition are each in the business of creating their own loyalist segment in the diaspora, diaspora-homeland relations tend to reinforce and exacerbate old cleavages, rather than eliminate them. Instead of remaining domestic, these cleavages now tend to be transnational, with each faction consolidating its own transnational bloc to oppose the other. This tendency of transnationalizing domestic political practices reinscribes local-level politics in the arena of transnational politics. The "local" in the transnational arena refers to three sites: the homeland as the initiating site for the performances of domestic politics; the homeland-hostland site in which a political issue is configured, as in the case of immigration and refugee matters, since the resolution of this depends on the collaboration of the sending and receiving country; and the diaspora as the initiating site for intervention in homeland affairs.

Diasporic diversity further complicates the transnationalization of domestic politics because of differences in styles of intervention, organizational makeup, and ideological orientation. The Haitian diaspora in France tends to be more of a leftist orientation, intellectualizes the ongoing political crisis, and sees the American contribution to Haiti in negative terms, while Haitian Americans are seen by the Haitian electorate as being more pragmatic and as welcoming a greater involvement of the United States in Haitian affairs. These political traditions evolved out of the experiences of different democratic practices in both hostlands (France and the United States) by Haitian immigrants.

Furthermore, in the nation-state, one speaks of regions, provinces, or departments to refer to the distinct population niches and traditions and the variety of sites. In the transnation-state, one speaks of different sites where the diaspora is inscribed and different national traditions.

The distinction made by Razmik Panossian between the state-centric interests of the state and the pan-national interests of the diaspora illuminates the relations between homeland and diaspora, in another arena—that of foreign policy.[26] The diaspora espouses the causes of Haitians wherever they live, and this is their most important priority. The government, in contrast, because it is called to provide leadership at the national level, looks at domestic issues as its priority. After all, governments are elected on the basis of their handling of domestic issues and not foreign issues unless it is a period of war or unless such foreign issues constitute a disgrace for the nation. The main reason why a government may not give priority to diasporic affairs is because they don't vote (or don't vote in significant numbers) in homeland elections and often, since they live in a foreign land, there is not much the government can do to help them in their everyday life other than exerting some diplomatic pressure on the host government that may or may not work on a long term.

Sometimes the diaspora is the main pressure group that forces the government to get involved in diasporic affairs and to produce results, tying its requests to its support of government policies. Sometimes, noting that the government does not have the effective means to intervene, the diaspora takes the lead on behalf of the government, as in the case of the plight of the Haitian braceros (agricultural laborers) in the Dominican Republic. Sometimes the diaspora withdraws its support if it does not agree with the government on domestic or foreign policy issues, for example, in the case of the Preval rapprochement with Cuba.

What emerges from this analysis is that these transnational relations must be seen in terms of issues (whether there is agreement or not between both parties), in terms of the bracketing of sectoral governmental activities (diasporans disagree on some governmental activities and agree on others), in terms of temporality (either side may change its position over time and thereby may shift its allegiance), and in terms of the location of the diaspora (country of residence) in the larger circuit of transnational relations.

The relations of the diaspora to the homeland have tended to be problematized in linear terms, seeing the diaspora as made up simply of migrants or their descendants. In reality, diasporic political groups are multicultural entities. James Goodman refers to them as "cross-national communities of conscience."[27] Participation in homeland affairs creates these politically motivated multicultural niches because it tends to attract nonmembers of the ethnic group as well. These other ethnic individuals are incorporated at various levels in diasporic grassroots organizations: as activists, as providers of financial support, as legal advisors, as lobbyists. This partly explains why the political ideology of these groups reflects in some aspects that of the hostland, because if it did not, these other individuals would not support the cause. It also explains why this hybridized diasporic ideology may be in tension with the homeland orientation. Here we have a multicultural niche where interethnic interaction is more intense and is accomplished for special political goals for which the rest of the population may have less at stake. These niches can be transglobal because the activities involved in the scheme communicate across national borders.

Once the different layers of transnational interaction are identified and discussed, it is important to explain the logic behind these occurrences and why they are not passing events, but are likely to become part of our everyday life. The mere presence of grassroots organizations could not itself change the order of things because there have always been voluntary political groups that did not share the view of government. In some cases, they were allowed to express themselves publicly; in other instances, not. What explains the success of these grassroots organizations is a shift in the way foreign policy is made. Ivo Duchacek explains this shift not only in terms of the interdependencies and the mass communication system that allow people to have complete knowledge of what is going on in the most remote corners of the world, but precisely, and perhaps as a consequence of the above, because of "the expansion of the field of foreign policy from the traditional concerns with status and defense into economic, social, cultural and environmental issue-arenas."[28]

This expansion has led to the enlargement of the group of foreign actors with which a state must deal and opens the door for grassroots organizations to access foreign officials. State officials maintain contacts with grassroots diasporans for leverage in dealing with foreign government and as potential members of government in the future. These grassroots organizations are constructed as an important element in the equilibrium of interstate relations.

What is important is not the fact that a foreign government maintains contact with an entity other than the seated government to maintain equilibrium. That has been a common practice because foreign governments, "accredited to the recipient state, have always maintained overt or covert contacts with the second national 'voice'—that of an opposition that has a reasonable chance of acceding to power at the next elections."[29] What is new is the direct and open interaction of foreign governments with grassroots diasporan organizations to show displeasure with the behavior of the homeland government and also to channel financial aid to these groups openly, with the knowledge of state officials and as a publicly avowed and thus popularly endorsed policy, despite objections by the homeland government in the name of national security and the principle of sovereignty. During the Aristide and Preval administrations, instead of filtering foreign aid through the central government, the United States, Canada, and the European Commission dealt directly with Haitian grassroots organizations that help to reengineer the balance of forces in the country.

For example, more than one grassroots organization is known by government officials to have bigger operating budgets than some of the ministries of the government. According to Frantz Voltaire, Prime

Minister Malval's chief of staff,

> It is evident that some NGOs have more money than ministries of government. Take, for example, the case of the Ministry of Agriculture and the NGO "FOKAL" (Fondation Connaissance et Liberté) financed by the Soros Foundation . . . Once I did an evaluation for OXFAM of an NGO they finance at Petit Trou de Nippes. The money that this NGO receives cannot be compared with the budget of city hall or the mayor's office. If you are poor, it is more productive to request help from the NGO than from the mayor. This difference does not depend on the local authority, but on the generosity of OXFAM. As an external evaluator paid by OXFAM, I assessed the budget of City Hall to be about $1,000 per year, while the NGO had something between $3 to $5 million for three years. The NGO has jeeps and an entire infrastructure of support.
>
> The problem that I see with this is that the mayor should be the coordinator, and then they could put their resources together. This is not done in Haiti because foreign donors are afraid of the rampant corruption in the government. These bureaucratic expenses do not realize much in the end because of the lack of synergy between projects and actors on the ground and between the foreign donors and the local government.

For Georges Anglade, who served in the Aristide cabinet in 1995, the annual budgets of the Ministry of Environment, the Ministry for the Welfare of Women, and the Ministry of Diasporic Affairs had each a budget of less than $1million per year, while the yearly operating budget for FOKAL (Fondation Connaissance et Liberte) was more than $1 million. One former senator interviewed extends this comparison to NGOs controlled by political parties, as well.

> The founders of most of the political parties each have an NGO. Sometimes there are two NGOs in the same household, one headed by the husband and the other by the wife. They receive money from overseas donors who finance their operations or activities. These donors are headquartered in Northern Europe, in Denmark or Norway, the European Union in general, Mexico, and the U.S. For example, the NGO created and headed by the general secretary of the Haitian Socialist Party receives its funding from the French Socialist Party. These NGOs were created by the heads of the political parties. Perhaps, the only exception to this is Leslie Manigat. I cannot say for sure that Manigat has an NGO.

This new policy of foreign governments to interact directly with local grassroots organizations leads to two consequences for the state that highlight its transnational character. First, it empowers the grassroots organizations at the expense of the central government and repositions them in such a way that they can make demands that it cannot fulfill. Therefore, it causes a weakening of the central administration. At the same time, it allows the grassroots organizations access to outside allies, the possibility of networking with external forces (those of the diaspora, foreign governments, and foreign grassroots organizations) for the sake of moving the democracy project forward.

The transnationality of the state is highlighted in these processes because the state is the local site where these transnational transactions occur, the site where transnational actors engage in their border-crossing activities, and the reconstructed site that allows foreign intervention in the everyday management of affairs of state. In other words, the local government's relations with its civilian population are no longer exclusively domestic, but are reconstructed as a transnational issue because of the de facto intervention of foreign actors with transnational interests, either on their own or at the invitation of local grassroots organizations to help them carry out their progressive human rights agenda. Grassroots organizations and diasporic organizations are engaged in a relentless effort to uphold human rights and democratic principles, even in circumstances where it might be more beneficial to the central government to do otherwise.

The diaspora-grassroots connection has truly become a third sector, locating itself between the public sector (the government) and the private sector (the bourgeoisie). The presence of this third sector displaces the government-bourgeoisie relationship because it has its own political project that does not coincide necessarily and fully with that of either of the two sectors. By attacking both the bourgeoisie for its lack of empathy with the poor and the government for its inefficiency and corruption, this third sector appropriates an alternative space in which to discuss state matters on behalf of civil society. Both the state and the private sector are readjusting themselves to the diaspora-civil society alliance and the watchdog role played by the diaspora-grassroots sector.

We have seen how the diaspora, with its alliance to civil society, was influential in the return of exiled President Aristide to Haiti and how the diaspora made it difficult for the bourgeoisie to sustain its relationship with the military, which in turn led to the disbanding of the military.[30] It is also worth mentioning that the bourgeoisie, which was until recently the main political player because of its ability to finance and control presidential elections, has become only one of many players, because diaspora money now defrays a good portion of these expenses. Lately, mounting criticism of governmental corruption launched by the diaspora-civil society alliance has led to the downfall of some of the officials, including cabinet ministers, in the Aristide and René Préval governments.

For example, a diasporan political activist explains how various presidential candidates have sought financial backing from the diaspora. He does so by focusing on the evolution of the practice in one U.S. city, Chicago, where he has been living for the past 30 years.

> After 1986, just about all the political parties came to Chicago at one point or another. Everybody was testing the grounds. The first politician to come to Chicago after 1986 was Marc Bazin. He had a big meeting at one of the local universities to expose his platform. He convinced some people, but unfortunately a lot more people were not convinced. After Bazin, Leslie Manigat came and did the same thing. He convinced some people, and most people were aloof towards his discourse. Others came, Hubert De Ronceray came, Victor Benoit came. They might have had a little fundraising here and there, but that was not a general practice until 1989, with the coalition that was going to put Aristide in office. There was a major fundraising drive that took place. There was a dinner, a raffle, there was a contribution drive. That was one of the first actual drives to raise money to send to Haiti for that, and this was essentially the only thing of any magnitude that I can remember. But to say that politicians would come and raise money here, they found some supporters to give them money without a doubt, but it was not something that was done as a matter of routine or fact until Aristide became a presidential candidate.

The presence of this third sector challenges the status quo, not simply because of the transnational relations in which it is engaged, but because it has the ear of the American government and politicians and of multinational agencies sympathetic to this sector's efforts, who at times provide it with a podium from which to promote its agenda for democracy and human rights in Haiti.[31] Part of this sector's appeal to the larger population results from the fact that it does not seek profit for itself (as in the case of the private sector) or popularity (as in the case of government officials), but rather is perceived to be advocating a cause for the common good of the nation. *This is the first time in Haiti that a third sector has existed whose role is to make government accountable to its people*. In light of this, one may argue that democracy will continue to root itself in Haiti precisely because of the existence of this third sector.

Although state-bourgeoisie relations are considered necessary because of the complementarity of their activities, especially in the area of employment, the state sometimes uses its relations with the diaspora to marginalize the bourgeoisie, as occurred in the early years of the Aristide administration. In view of this, the diaspora can be seen in terms of the expansion of political constituencies. It is used as such by politicians who have established their satellite political bureaus in New York and Miami, where they raise funds for their electoral campaigns.[32]

Conclusion

In this chapter I have attempted to briefly delineate models of state-diaspora relations in the history of Haitian immigration to the United States. This discussion has examined how these models have evolved, their strengths and weaknesses, and how they have in turn reshaped relations between the government and the private sector. I think we are now in an era in which democracy can no longer be imposed from above by the elite, as some Haitian governments had attempted to do in the pre-Duvalier era, because the role played by grassroots organizations and the diaspora—two important arms of civil society—can no longer be ignored. Haiti is moving toward more, not less, democracy, and the diaspora is certainly a major player in this new order of things.

Revamping the question of international relations in terms of the role of civil society—as a way to explain or engineer the transformation of the state under the international regime of globalization—is useful on one level, but not another.[33] It is useful in the sense that civil society can be used as the site for the transformation or redefinition of the state. However, to separate civil society from political society by defining them as playing separate roles in the construction of the state is to ignore the many levels on which the distinction between the two is blurred and the fact that they are equally involved in various forms of transnational relations because their interests are intertwined.

These models are not presented to unveil the genealogy of state-diaspora relations or to imply that they are mutually exclusive, but rather to identify the multiple forms of border-crossing practices. As diasporic communities promote their own democratic projects for the governance of the economy of the homeland, some individuals are constructively engaged in helping the Haitian government, while others are actively involved in undermining its policies and practices. Some use their connections to the Haitian state to consolidate their identity in the host country, while others, although living abroad, consider themselves to be still inside the Haitian transnation. In this context, the state is readjusting itself under the pressure of these transnational flows as it undergoes its own transformation.[34]

The cases analyzed above point, on the one hand, to the unsettled character of deterritorialization and reterritorialization and to the fluid boundaries of national territories, and, on the other hand, to the respatialization and transnationalization of social identities. This issue of transnational space destabilizes any fixed conception one may have of the "modern Westphalian," "postcolonial," or "postmodern" state, which has been a central feature in theories of international relations.[35] State and nation have been decoupled through international migration and the rise of diasporic communities. While the state continues to exist inside its legal and inherent jurisdictional territories, the nation has expanded to include what had been extraterritorial sites, which have now been converted into transnational sites. Within this phenomenon, one may further say that diasporas contest, by their daily practices, the identification of their offshoot communities as being outside the homeland, and they reinscribe them in the transnational identitary structure of the transnation.

This new social transnational practice has a number of ramifications for the framing of international relations. One may speak of the implosion of the field of international relations as it searches for a new identity, that is, as it proceeds to redefine its object of study. The field is based on the existence and recognition of distinct entities such as the state, the territorial articulation of the nation with the state, the sovereignty of the nation-state, and the government as the formal locus for extraterritorial relations. However, the rise of diasporic communities has blurred these distinctions and has made the boundaries more fluid.[36]

As international relations are being heavily influenced by and sometimes collide with transnational relations, the categories of analysis change and so do the assumptions. The state has been defined as a sedentary phenomenon, but the diaspora is intrinsically an entity in a state of motion. To reconcile these different sites, some have attempted to reconceptualize the structural location of the state by paying attention to the globalization process. In this new effort, the state is theorized as being in "decline," as being "modified" by globalization, or as being "transformed" by it, or observers have used the Gramscian concept of the "extended (expanded) state" to account for these twists in international relations.[37]

The Haitian data provide details of these border-crossing practices as they affect Haiti's relations with the United States and, by extension, with other countries as well. As noted, many of the grassroots organizations involved do not have an ideological agenda and, influenced by pragmatism, follow guidelines from foreign donors that shape the orientation, content, and outcome of their projects.[38] Local grassroots organizations are engaged in transnational relations not only with diasporic communities, but also with their foreign counterparts and agencies of foreign governments. In this sense, one may say that "nonstate actors have become significant international actors."[39]

The rise of transnational communities has reshaped the identity of the state and has repositioned it in the larger context of global politics.[40] We are witnessing a shift from international to transnational politics or from state-centered to transnation-centered political practices.[41] The shift from nation-state to transnation-state calls for a reconceptualization of international relations because of the existence of new sets of assumptions, new interests at stake, and the reterritorialization of the transnational space of the transnation. Therefore, transnation-state-centered political practices are the new modalities of the world order, resulting from the implosion of the globalization process engendered by transnational flows such as, for example, immigration, diasporization, information technology, and financial markets.

The fact that the nation extends beyond the state's borders accentuates the distinction between nation and state. The territorial equation between the two is the primary basis upon which the system of states was constructed, and it justifies the boundaries of the relations between states in the international arena. Given the existence of the transnation as a mode of interstate interaction, I see the following ramifications in the repositioning of this basic unit of international relations.

- The decoupling and recoupling of state and nation expand the spatial and intranational parameters of the state into another state in order for the first state to interact with the diasporic tentacles of the nation. The relations are ongoing, affect diverse aspects of national life in both the sending and receiving states, and the receiving state may not be able to stop them. As a result of these practices, relations between states cannot take territorial boundaries as the marker of national boundaries. These boundaries have expanded beyond the territorial limits of the state.
- The existence of diasporas is now a factor to be reckoned with, because a diaspora may affect the state's conduct in managing its international relations.[42] Sometimes, under pressure from this contingent and with a view toward securing the diaspora's vote on election day, a receiving state develops favorable or unfavorable policies vis-à-vis the sending state.[43]

- In matters of international relations, the diaspora produces transnational political actors who help the sending state to access politicians in the receiving state, or the receiving state to understand the ways of the sending state, and who potentially even serve as go-betweens for the two states.
- The preoccupation of the sending state with the well-being of the diaspora may become a factor in the formulation of its international relations with the receiving state.
- The transnational model implies a constant flow of relations between the two countries. A major area where international relations between states are affected is in the domain of foreign aid. The total amount of "remittances" sent by a diaspora has become one factor that is used by the World Bank to gauge the ability of a state to pay its foreign debt and to determine the level of foreign aid it is eligible to receive.[44] The total of remittances is construed here as the portion of foreign aid given by a diaspora that is factored in to decrease the amount underwritten by a donor nation. In the logic of the receiving state, remittance money is money given by civil society to a foreign state.
- The diaspora becomes crucial in shaping domestic policies of the sending state because it influences various sectors of civil society.[45] It is an entity that remains outside the physical boundaries of the territorial state, but that appropriates and uses its right to intervene in the sending state's affairs.
- Pressures on the direction of the state's domestic policies migrate among constituencies residing inside and outside the legal boundaries of the state.
- Increasingly, international relations are becoming relations between transnation-states instead of between nation-states because of diasporas that may play a role in the conduct of foreign policies.[46]
- As a consequence of the above, international-relations analysts must reproblematize their units of analysis as they are influenced or even reshaped by the border-crossing practices of diasporas.[47]

The rise of the transnation-state has led some to speak, perhaps prematurely, of "the end of the nation-state,"[48] the "postnational moment,"[49] "a new cosmopolitanism, after internationality,"[50] or "postinternational politics."[51] Instead of envisioning the apocalyptic vanishing of the nation-state, one should perhaps take stock of this transformation of the nation-state and reproblematize the role of this unit in international relations.[52] A partial perspective that sheds light on this new dynamic is provided by Christopher Ansell and Steven Weber in regard to the issue of sovereignty, which they analyze from the standpoint of an open system rather than from the traditional closed-system perspective.[53] In so doing, they undermine "the implicit assumption that there is a zero-sum relationship between states and globalization—that what global processes gain, the state necessarily loses."[54]

To account for the existence of the state under the assault of globalization, they focus their investigation on the "porousness of boundaries," defining it as a central issue to be explained if we are to understand the elastic way open systems work. By "porousness," Ansell and Weber mean "the existence of fluid and multidimensional boundaries, in contrast to the solid and one-dimensional borders that constitute the ideal-typical sovereign state that fits comfortably in closed-systems theories."[55] Taking some insights from organization theory, they rightly argue that "the boundaries of organizations depend upon the nature of the transactions that are taking place. And presumably those boundaries can move and reconfigure themselves as the nature of the transaction changes."[56]

This approach to interstate relations indicates that porousness of boundaries may lead to the transformation of the state, but not necessarily to its collapse. How this change may proceed depends on several types of transactional relationships. A number of variables are implicit here: the hierarchy of scale of these relations (volume and intensity), the sectorialization of relations (geography of points of anchorage), the multiplicity of temporalities (permanent relations, incidental relations depending on events or periods of the year), and the content of the transaction (which can be either very important or of only passing significance).

In this flexible scheme, the state constitutes itself inside boundaries that can expand on occasion by including its diasporic tentacles in order to meet the new dynamic required by the nature of specific transnational transactions and relations. This logic has always been at work when a state joins forces with another state to accomplish acts beneficial to both or when a state develops an independent strategy to achieve its own goals. The view of the state as an open system presents it as a more "flexible" entity capable of reinventing itself or of readjusting itself to meet new challenges in the international arena. Such a view provides some insights as to how the diaspora fits into this redefinition of the state.

3

Diasporic Lobbying in American Politics

Ethnic lobbies stir up deep animosities. Influentials who deal with foreign policy issues see them as a bother. Politicians group them with single-issue gadflies who see the world with blinders. Worst of all, ethnic lobbies have an aroma of being un-American, if not anti-American. They may imperil the country from within because their attachment to another country could undermine the national interest.

—*Keely (1995: 212–243)*

Diasporic groups and individuals have participated in the performances of American politics ever since the birth of the republic because the mainstream politicians were all diasporans of European descent. This, however, is not the historical angle through which diasporic politics will be studied in this chapter. The focus here is on the contemporary period, a time when the Anglo majority constructs itself as mainstream and the first generation nonwhite immigrants as engaged in ethnic and diasporic politics. Such hegemonic construction of social reality wrongly implies that the mainstream seeks only to achieve the common good while diasporans are solely interested in the welfare of their ethnic communities. This categorization brings its own set of analytical problems, because the United States is a fundamentally diasporic nation. The distinction is better made between Creolopolitans (those who have been here for several generations, but who do not actively maintain relations with families in the ancestral homeland) and newcomers who are very much involved in ensuring the welfare of the homeland.

Diasporic lobbying therefore implies three different processes: the willingness of the diasporan to engage in politics in the hostland on behalf of the homeland (whether to help, undermine, or consolidate the political regime of the homeland), the interaction of the diasporan with hostland political actors and institutions, and the interaction of the diasporan with homeland political actors and institutions, directly or indirectly, and as individuals or a group. This interaction is sometimes induced as the result of an initiative by the hostland, undertaken on its behalf to convey its views to the homeland regime. These three sets of processes form the content of diasporic political engagement and establish the infrastructure that maintains and channels this activity. We reserve the term "ethnic politics" for those processes engaged in improving the local conditions of the immigrant group and "diasporic politics" for those processes that serve both the ethnic group and the homeland—that is, those processes that influence the political regime of the hostland for the benefit of the homeland and that influence the politics of the homeland for the benefit of the hostland and the diaspora. While "ethnic lobbies" are the staple of the former, "diasporic lobbies" are an important engine of the latter.[1]

Different approaches have been used in the study of diasporic political lobbying. It has been seen either as a passing component of ethnic politics or as an intrinsic characteristic of diasporic political practices. It is a passing component of ethnic politics when lobbying is undertaken solely at specific moments of crisis of the homeland political regime because the political context in the hostland would not allow it otherwise or simply because the ancestral homeland is temporarily under foreign occupation. In contrast, lobbying is an intrinsic element of diasporic politics when it is undertaken on a continuing basis as an ingredient that glues the various transnational and local components of diasporic politics. Its ebb and flow is shaped by the political context of the hostland and the stability or crises of the homeland government.

There are several ways we could frame the lobbying question: by investigating the diasporic lobby group as an organization, focusing on its internal structure and on "the process by which public interest groups reach decisions concerning their issue priorities and their lobbying tactics,"[2] by investigating the formation and lifespan of the lobby group, the causes of its extinction, and the way in which lobbying reshapes the content and orientation of American foreign policy,[3] by studying lobbying as the activity of an interest group and comparing it with that of other interest groups,[4] by focusing on regulatory mechanisms that police such activities, or by seeing diasporic lobby groups as necessary factions that are the glue of grassroots American democracy.[5] These perspectives may indeed shed light on various aspects of the architecture of the problem. However, since my interest here is in globalization, the focus of this chapter is on how lobbying implodes the political boundaries of the nation-state—how it transforms diasporic lobbyists into informal state agents and relocates their political activities inside the transnational arena of the transnation-state. The shift here is primarily in the identity of state-diaspora relations, rather than in their consequences for American domestic and foreign policy.

Three Moments of Haitian American Lobbying

The three principal moments of Haitian American lobbying in American politics correspond roughly with the administration of Duvalier "Pere" (1957–1971) and "Fils"(1971–1986), the immediate post-Duvalier era (1986–1991), and the exile years of President Jean Bertrand Aristide in Washington, DC (1991–1994). They differ from each other in terms of style, demographic participation, and emotional intensity. During the Duvalier era, government lobbyists worked under cover to prevent the open hostility of diasporic opponents. These were often individuals who had worked in some capacity in the government (in the civil service, the military, or the paramilitary) and were either dispatched for damage control or to advocate the cause of the regime in Washington governmental circles along with paid American lobbyists (lawyers such as African American Ron Brown, who later served in Bill Clinton's cabinet and died in a plane crash).

Because of the secrecy under which they operated, these government-sponsored lobbyists had very little support from the diasporic community. In any case, they were not recognized by the diasporic community, nor did they play a leadership role in that community, which was asking for the removal of both François and Jean Claude Duvalier from office. It was precisely because the community had its own grassroots lobbyists that they were able to undermine the work of the government lobbyists and to project a bad image by publicizing the human rights abuses of the homeland government. Because of that lack of strong connection with the diasporic community, these lobbyists, who were an extension of the homeland government, could not develop independent stances on issues without being isolated from both groups—the government and the diaspora.

In an attempt to develop alternative lobbyist groups that would serve as counterweight to diasporic grassroots lobbyists, the Duvalier governments facilitated the formation of progovernment diasporic lobbyists in both the United States and Canada. These *sponsored lobbyists* had their own protest groups, organized to counterbalance the protests organized by the opposition in the diaspora, and their own radio programs, which attempted to change the opinions of the diaspora, but sooner or later they were denounced by insiders, which made their coexistence with the diaspora less easy to manage as their covert operations were uncovered. They had both active and reactive strategies, depending on what they were defending or opposing.

The second moment in the history of Haitian American diasporic lobbying corresponds to the immediate post-Duvalier period (1986–1991) during which lobbyists provided a modicum of support to the military government in the hope that it would organize general elections to return the country to civilian democratic rule. Unlike the previous period, during which the lobbyists and the diasporic opposition were in opposite camps promoting different agendas, lobbyists became more malleable, willing to support the efforts of the government on some occasions and voicing their dissident voices against it when they disagreed. A prodemocracy lobbyist coalition began to take root, including grassroots organizations working hand in hand with formal lobbying organizations. Some activists were recruited to work inside these organizations and in local city administrations in New York, Boston, and Miami, and private foundations provided logistic and financial aid. During this period, there was a trend toward the formalization of grassroots organizations and active lobbying by grassroots leaders in Washington, DC.

During the exile of President Aristide in the United States (1991–1994), these lobbyists became organized and professional. As the case studies produced below will show, forming coalitions became a modus operandi to establish linkages. Some lobbyists were directly connected to the pro-Aristide effort and were part of the government-in-exile team, while others worked on their own behalf to promote democracy, and not exclusively Aristide, so that they may continue to pursue their human rights agenda. These coalitions were made possible because some were interested in helping Haitian refugees and were convinced that it was time to fuse these forces and to organize rallies that supported both causes: asylum for Haitian refugees and the return of President Aristide to Haiti to complete his term in office. Several

American NGOs also wanted to help the cause and networked with these groups either by providing them logistic aid (lawyers) or by financing their undertakings.

A mixed type of coalition comprising Haitian and non-Haitian sympathizers became a reality during this period. This form of coalition led the Haitian membership to reciprocate by participating in non-Haitian lobbying activities as well. A multicultural lobbying coalition works to the extent that it implies reciprocity. The network has enlarged itself to include newly formed NGOs and non-Haitian supporters and has secured the help of key individuals and groups in Congress such as Senator Kennedy, Congresswoman Waters, and other members of the congressional Black Caucus.

Of course, in these coalitions, "the free rider problem" persists as "different groups shoulder different amounts of responsibility."[6] When one disaggregates the coalitions, one finds the following components: "the coalition core . . . made up primarily of the founders," "players," who "tend to be specialists who join a coalition for tactical reasons," and "peripheral groups who tend to tag along with the rest of the coalition for nonpolicy incentives."[7] Although this description portrays well the structure of formal coalitions, as we will see, informal coalitions among diasporic lobbyists tend to display more ad hoc forms of composition depending on the issues and the availability of players.

Two Case Studies

An interview with Jocelyn McCalla, the energetic director of the National Coalition for Haitian Rights, with its headquarters in New York City, details the involvement of the organization in a major lobbying effort on behalf of Haitian refugees.

> Well, the major thing that the coalition was involved in, which started shortly after Clinton was elected to office back in 1992, was drafting a three-page document that was submitted to the Clinton administration to deal with the Haitian refugee crisis, and by extension, the Haitian political crisis itself. So the document was achieved through two major consultations, one of which was a conference call that lasted about two hours, where forty organizations were involved. There were a lot of organizations there from the mainstream that function like voluntary agencies, such as Church World Services, the Joint Immigration Refugee Service, the U.S. Committee for Refugees, the National Immigration

Forum, and some labor union leaders. Otherwise, there were the people and organizations that have been at the forefront of the founding of the National Coalition of Haitian Refugees, what was then the Emergency Coalition for Haitian Refugees and now has become the National Coalition for Haitian Rights, but we also had a number of Haitian Americans there.

So it was a two-hour phone call and there were a lot of papers that were being circulated among the people. Some had various and lengthy propositions. Others were of the same sort, and pulling it all together was my job. At some point, after two hours of conversation, it was clear that if everyone had his say, you would come up with a document that was too broad in scope. And despite the fact that Clinton in his campaign had promised to change the policy toward Haitian refugees and be friendly to democracy in Haiti, there was very little indication as far as I am concerned that this was going to be the new administration policy. So to make sure that it was something that the new administration could swallow, it had to be clear that we needed to get a single document. It was my duty, my job, to bring everybody into order and make sure that we were going to have a very concrete document.

I drafted the document and circulated it, and we had a second conference call and agreed on it and submitted it to the Clinton administration in December, before the Christmas holidays. We met with the Clinton guy in charge of the transition to the Clinton administration, the fellow who eventually became the head of the USAID, Bryan Atwood. We met with him and other aides, and at the first meeting there were twenty-five people and he said the plan was good and that he thought that Clinton could go for it, and then he said he was sure that Clinton would go for it.

And then we met with him in January, about a week before Clinton's inauguration, and he said I am sorry, but Clinton is not going to go for the plan and he is going to announce that he is going to maintain the interdiction policy and is not going to give safe haven to the Haitian refugees in Guantánamo and so on—that it was best to return Aristide to power and he was not going to open the floodgates, because as far as he was concerned, a lot of Haitians were waiting for this to happen. He empathized with their plight and therefore they were still preparing something.

What the State Department and the Department of Defense told him was that there were at least one hundred and twenty-five thousand Haitians who were ready to flood the shores of Florida, and that if he wanted to doom his presidency, he could work with them, or reject them. So he decided to reject them, and he had to get Aristide agreements, and there was a joint statement made then.

Frankly, the coalition—almost all the people who came together to push for that, because of the particular agenda they wanted to get through to the Clinton administration—did not want to get on the administration's bad side as it was coming in. There was, I would say, lukewarm support for the standard that was advocated, which was, let's take a strong stand about this and let's go out there and pillory the administration. The reversal was far too much of a betrayal to let it stand.

Although the coalition did not fall apart, I would say that during the first six months of the Clinton administration, the support was really lukewarm, so we had to build the support up again, meaning that there were a lot of activities like meetings using the coalition partners, like the U.S. Catholic Conference, the Church World Services, and people who have offices in Washington, and talking to the Haitians and making sure they understood what we were fighting for. And we tried to get consensus on this issue. We had a lot of meetings with the White House, the National Security Council, and the Immigration Service, because the head of the Immigration Service was Doris Meisner, who had been opposed to the idea when she was an interim immigration commissioner back in 1980 during the transition to the Reagan administration. You must remember that Reagan was the guy who opposed the immigration policy.

In 1994, we eventually succeeded. The plan that was put forward was essentially what the Clinton administration bought into in 1994 after the momentum had been built so much that the Black Caucus took some leadership on this issue, including fellows like Randall Robinson, who was rising in the ranks. We worked with all of these people to get it done.

The key thing was making sure that Guantánamo was going to be used as a safe haven and that people fleeing Haiti would be going to a safe haven. The advocacy group would impose a moratorium, insisting on refugee processing at Guantánamo for six months, a period during which the Clinton administration would have to come up with a response to Haiti's political crisis. So Guantánamo was opened up as a safe haven back in June and early July, and then marines intervened in Haiti in September 1994. That was one of our major lobbying efforts.

The second case study that reports an interview with Harry Fouché, a Chicago activist and former consul general in New York during the second Aristide administration, provides an example of lobbying efforts undertaken by Haitian Americans on behalf of the implementation of democracy in Haiti. This cosmopolitan politician was involved in lobbying efforts both as a grassroots organization leader and an overseas employee of the Haitian state.

Before 1986, people were reluctant to talk about anything concerning Haiti because of the fear of the possible retaliation that could be taken against their families back home. But there was always a group of people that felt it necessary to denounce the exaction of the Duvaliers, and speak out against the dictatorship. After 1986, as Haitians were coming out of their shells and wanted to be part of the larger group that wanted to build the country, reshape society, there was a need to do something, to allow people to effectively work together. One of the things we did was form a Haitian Patriotic Committee in Chicago. . . . There were about five people on the committee.

Once we formed the group we found that there was a lack of sources of information to let our people know what was going on in Haiti, even though at that time there were two Haitian radio stations in Chicago. They used to say, "We don't do politics." So we created a radio station that was all news about what was going on in Haiti. The radio was becoming more accepted by the community.

Then we formed a committee, a support committee for another committee in Haiti called Konbit Solidarité. That's when I first met Aristide, in the meeting of Konbit Solidarité. So with the Konbit Solidarité we were able to effectively link our group to the country. We linked the people here who wanted to make a contribution to their country—the group in Haiti was involved in that kind of things, rebuilding the schools, building new schools. This is something I thought was good for the community. The idea was to capture the energy that was present in the diaspora and get people to respond to the needs of their country.

Of course, in the process, politics was always involved. Politics would determine what course the country would take. In 1987, when the election was drawing blood, the whole group that was formed to do charitable work in Haiti became a political group. Even people who in the past did not want to get involved in Haitian politics, when they saw pictures of people shot down in polling places, they said, "No, this is not acceptable. We are not going to tolerate that." So we gained more momentum with our movement, and up until 1990, politics was our prime objective because of the turmoil in the country. After Manigat was put in by the military, there was a mobilization against that. We said that we will not accept that, and the pressure was mounting against the military and the Manigat government, which never gained any acceptance, or recognition from the international community, as you remember. So we were part of that movement.

During the first coup in 1991, some people had access to the Internet through industry (it was not widespread then), but telecommunications played a major role. I was involved in a group that was called the "Tenth Department." What that group was, in essence, was an ad hoc diaspora association of Haitians, and what I did when I became the general secretary of that group was establish linkages with different Haitian communities, whether they were in Europe, Canada, the Antilles, or the United States. I established telephone trees, for example, and a system where I would have regular telephone conference calls once a week. One teleconference could include someone from Canada, somebody from Paris, somebody from Haiti, somebody from New York, somebody from Chicago, somebody from St. Louis, somebody from Los Angeles, and somebody from Miami. So we would have anywhere from twenty to thirty people on the line. This was during the time of the first coup. The conversation was about the return of Aristide and the mobilization throughout the diaspora to combat the coup and try to reverse it. That in effect was the reason why the issue remained on the front burner for the diaspora. One of the things we tried to do was not just go for Aristide supporters, but all Haitians, at that time of good will, thought that it was a bad idea to accept this fait accompli—no matter what bad politics was the motive of the coup.

Lobbying American politicians was important of course. You need to remember that in addition to these teleconferences, there were also regular demonstrations scheduled and taking place in Washington, Boston, Miami, and New York. So as a result of these frequent trips to Washington, we developed a sort of affinity for some members of Congress, so each time we would come in, we would be welcomed by Charles Rangel of Manhattan or maybe Billy Martini from New Jersey. There would always be a congressman or congresswoman that we would meet with.

This soon developed into more formal lobbying. For example, we would have, on any given day, a Haitian lobby in Washington whereby we had people flying from different cities and meeting in Washington and then going to visit their different congressional delegations. Someone from California would visit the California delegation with the group; someone from New York would do the same with his congressional delegation. This type of thing took place as a result of our lobbying. In these groups, sometimes we had individuals from California, Miami, Detroit, St. Louis, Boston, and Chicago who flew in in the morning. Each one paid his expenses from his own pocket, and that was the beauty of the whole thing—whether it was the plane tickets, telephone calls, hotels, people paid for their own expenses. It did not evolve into a formal organization.

After Aristide returned, some people felt there was a need to transform it into an external arm or extension of the political party that Aristide was operating in Haiti. I was always against that. I said there was a difference between a political party and this larger diasporic movement. Some people organized a coup against me, and I would say to some extent they succeeded. I withdrew from the group, and the many people who believed in my way of doing things also withdrew, and that's how the thing collapsed in 1995 after the return of Aristide to Haiti.

Another dimension was the church. The churches responded very well, Catholic or Protestant, through campaigns, and provided support

> for the reconstruction of the country, and support for the overthrow of the coup of 1991. This was really good. On any given Sunday, I would begin my day as early as nine in the morning and would visit three or four churches and not get home until ten or eleven at night.
>
> I do not want you to get the idea that we were mouthpieces for Aristide. We met Aristide in the movement, he did not bring us to the movement. The movement existed before Aristide. Aristide showed more courage than most people in terms of keeping the course, despite whatever mistakes he may have made. This is what we need for the country, addressing the plight of the illiterate, and the poor in the country, the kinds of things that we did not get from the other traditional candidates. The response was good during the period from 1991 to 1994 when he returned. After he returned, things went quite a bit down, and then as you can witness during the second Aristide administration, the diaspora cooled off a bit in terms of responding to events in Haiti. I can tell you from recent events, with the removal of Aristide, the response of the diaspora has not simply been lukewarm, but almost nonexistent.

Political Protest and Lobbying

Diasporic political protest is a means, a pressure mechanism, or tactic used by any ethnic group to back up formal lobbying in the resolution of a problem that directly or indirectly affects the community. It is employed to call public attention to a specific issue at home or abroad and is meant as a call for redress and a support mechanism to facilitate the work of formal lobbyists. The Creole and French phrases used by the community such as *anbasadè san kravat* or *ambassadeurs du béton*, meaning street protesters (literally "tieless ambassadors" or "street ambassadors") very well express the deep meaning attributed to such actions by the diaspora. These street ambassadors are supposed to negotiate a solution to a cause—national or international—that is dear to the diaspora. For example, *The Miami Herald*, August 23, 1994, reports the occurrence of a march organized by the Haitian American community of Miami:

> The march was organized by the local Haitian political activists and Creole radio personalities to protest the Clinton's administration's wavering actions toward Haiti's military coup leaders and refugee detentions at the Naval base in Guantánamo, Cuba, and at Krome Detention Center.
>
> The demonstration backed up traffic on Northeast Second Avenue and Biscayne Boulevard between 54th and 79th streets for more than five hours.

Similarly *The New York Times*, October 12, 1991, published an article entitled "50,000 Haitians March in Manhattan in Support of Ousted Aristide."

> Tens of thousands of Haitian demonstrators spilled into lower Manhattan from Brooklyn today in a spirited demonstration of support for ousted President Jean Bertrand Aristide.
>
> Clogged by more than 60,000 demonstrators—the police estimate—the streets of the financial district were virtually paralyzed for most of the afternoon. Marching groups split like amoebas into independent pockets of chanting, flag-waving enthusiasts.

These protests are undertaken either exclusively by the group or a coalition including sympathizers. One such protest is described by *The Miami Herald*:

> The march, organized by a coalition of local Haitian and African American groups, set out at 2 P.M. from Bicentennial Park. Waving signs that read "True Democracy, Not Hypocrisy" and "Aristide or Chaos," the Haitians walked along Northwest Street while chanting and singing. They hooked back to Bicentennial Park for a rally that ended peacefully at dusk.
>
> Other sponsoring groups included the NAACP, Véyé-Yo, Jhuti Maat Sphere, Boycott Miami and the Haitian Refugee Center.

These demonstrations were undertaken to resolve a local and national problem, as in the case of the plight of Haitian refugees in the United States; an international problem, as in the case of the reinstallment of Aristide to the office of the presidency in Haiti in 1994; or a problem confronted by the diaspora group in another country, as in the case of Haitian labor migrants in the Dominican Republic. Thus, in a brief note under the headline "Haitian American Protest," on November 20, 1999, *The Miami Herald* reported, "Haitian Americans picket the Dominican Republic Consulate on Brickell Avenue in Miami on Friday demanding an end to what they said are daily forced, mass deportations of Haitians from the Dominican Republic." These protests and their meanings in terms of what they are supposed to accomplish are another way of understanding the global parameters of diasporic politics.

Forms of Diasporic Lobbying

The phenomenon of diasporic lobbying does not have a monolithic form. It comes in various shapes, and it is necessary to explain the architecture of these shapes in order to understand the multifaceted nature of these nodes of diasporic politics. These forms seem to oscillate between the formalization of the entity as a formal group and the multiple informal shapes it may take. Many of these lobbying groups emerge for a specific purpose and either move to a dormant state or else disappear and reappear in a different form, with a different leadership and a different agenda for action.

Diasporic lobbying is involved at one level or another in coalition politics. Therefore, it might be more appropriate to refer to it as "diasporic coalition lobbying." Forms of lobbying are dialectically related to forms of coalition building. Coalition lobbying may occur at both the community level and the national level. In this instance, one is the extension of the other.

The term "diasporic coalition" refers to two different domains: *intergroup coalitions and intragroup coalitions*. We assume intragroup coalition as a given, although, of course, no coalition is without its internal cleavages. The focus here is on explicating forms of intergroup coalition. The diaspora may struggle with its problems at the local level and then find out that an intergroup coalition is the best way to move the agenda ahead or find out that others who want to help are endorsing its cause. The national level thus adds complexity to the local level by enlarging its ramifications so as to accommodate allies.

Diasporic lobbying may include coalitions on the ground that support a specific issue but that do not seek national allies because specific members of Congress who are already aware of the issue and sympathetic to it have been targeted for action. This happens when a local community is seeking help from their congressional representative that will benefit the representative's district.

Diasporic lobbying appears as a formal, permanent structure or as an informal, ad hoc organization. Groups that are formally organized tend to do better in lobbying matters than those that are not. Some level of efficiency presupposes some formal organization. For example, Vered Talai has found that although Armenians in London have several voluntary associations that attract the active participation of members, the looseness of their organizations has rendered them less effective in terms of building strong networks between associations for lobbying purposes.[8]

After an issue is resolved, a formal lobbying agency may add another item to its agenda. These are structures with multiple vocations, capable and willing to deal with a different mix of issues. By contrast, the ad hoc organization interested in a single issue tends to disappear when the issue is resolved. The single-issue coalition therefore must be differentiated from the multiple-issue coalition. Some issues are by nature *coalition issues*, such as an immigration bill, while others are not—for example, the effort in the late 1960s to legalize marijuana use by Rastafarians was an issue that mostly concerned that group of Jamaican immigrants. Of course, units in a coalition do not enjoy the same status. Some are more central than others in relation to issues of parity and subalternity.

Both formal and ad hoc lobbying often depicts the party involved as a *victim*, appealing either to the law (to redress the undemocratic or repressive situation) or to *compassion* (if the country is unduly taxed to do something, as when a homeland is placed in quarantine for a natural epidemic over which it has no control). These appeals are the stuff that diasporic lobbying is made of. Diasporans are also involved in lobbying when their homeland is seen as the villain. Here, lobbying is undertaken for damage control in order to prevent further erosion of international confidence and to prevent alienating the sympathies of friends. While the first type is active, the second by its very nature is reactive. Its shape depends on the level or intensity of public outrage.

Until recently, these various forms of lobbying have entailed mostly face-to-face relations in interactions with the coalition, with additional telephone calls and the use of the fax machine as a way of conveying *alert messages*. With the appearance of the Internet, a new means to contact coalition members and to negotiate propositions was made possible. The Internet has given rise to another form of lobbying, *virtual diasporic lobbying*. This type of lobbying is the process by which immigrant actors (individuals or groups) establish a coalition through online communication for the purpose of achieving a specific goal. Such an Internet coalition is most likely to be transnational, because it may include individuals in the homeland, in the diasporic site where the project is initiated, and in other diasporic sites as well. This form must be distinguished from the other forms in which the Internet is used only as an addendum, but in which Internet use does not characterize the identity of the coalition.

The Internet has changed the parameters of the lobbying process because it allows an expansion of the space of interaction, participation, and action, allowing people in different sites to plot out strategies, including people who, because of the constraints of distance, otherwise could not participate, and providing access to officials, to various media for publicity, and to a podium from which issues can be explained. It also forms a virtual community with actors located in noncontiguous physical sites whereby individuals from one site may influence the outcome of the lobbying process. Residence in the place of protest is no longer a requirement to be a leader or participant in that network. In such a virtual setting, activists in the homeland with computer access may exert more influence on the path of the lobbying process in the hostland than residents who are not online.

Diasporizing the Policy-Making Process

Lobbyists are mediators, the point of contact between the diasporic community and the American government in matters affecting both U.S. foreign policy and the homeland policies of states such as Haiti. They are at the center of a mechanism of exchange. What they exchange has value for both sides: the gift necessitates one in return (countergift).[9] In this instance, the gift from the lobby group may be money, or a financial contribution to a campaign, or the promise to do so in the future, or simply the promise to deliver the ethnic vote on Election Day. The countergift that brings some balance in the relationship is the promise to influence policies to the advantage of the group, including its homeland. Two types of lobbying therefore must be distinguished from one another: active and passive. In the former, exchange and counterexchange are part of a simultaneous process, that is, a gift is given or promised for the performance of a specific and immediate task. In contrast, the latter form entails a permanent bond whereby gifts are given for a general purpose and to maintain trust between the parties. It is implied, however, that in due time, benefits would ensue.

Even the active relationships between a politician and an ethnic group may not always be active, since an ethnic issue may arise as a result of a crisis in the homeland. Once the crisis is resolved or subdued, that relationship may shift to a dormant phase. The rhythm of the relationship is cadenced by the rhythm within which homeland problems arise. This is a clear instance whereby the relationship between the ethnic community and the dominant political system of the hostland is regulated by events in the homeland. An exclusive focus on the hostland to understand this pattern would have yielded an erroneous conclusion. Lobbyists not only link the two together, but also prioritize the issues in terms of their central or peripheral importance and in terms of strategies of action, whether to attempt to resolve the entire problem at once or whether to approach it incrementally.

Three modalities can be identified in the ways in which the gift-countergift exchange mechanism functions in diasporic lobbying. In the *no-strings-attached scheme*, the gift is given in good faith with the expectation it might yield benefits in the future for the group. It is given with the purpose of maintaining good rapport with the other party. In *the focused gift scheme*, it is given for the performance of a specific task, and it is understood that it might or might not result in a benefit for the group. What is asked is that the congressperson do his or her best to achieve a specific outcome, knowing full well that the issue is not the only game in town. For example, the congressperson may submit an immigration bill, but there is no guarantee that it will pass as is. The *post-performance gift*, finally, is given only if the task is performed. In this light, referring to the United Kingdom, Sajal Lahiri and Pascalis Raimondos-Moller write, "The lobbyists make political contributions to the political party in power, and the amount they contribute is contingent upon the policy that the government adopts."[10]

Lobbyists wear different hats when they serve as mediators between the hostland and the homeland, the diaspora and the homeland, and the diaspora and the hostland. These are different jobs and may require different skills of negotiation.

When the diaspora seeks the support of the hostland government, either on behalf of the homeland government or to overthrow that government, it turns to diasporic lobbyists. As representatives of the community speaking on its behalf, the lobbyists may make proposals and seek the goods sought by the community. For example, they lobby Congress against the homeland government if the goal of the exile group is to change the direction of American foreign policy vis-à-vis that regime. Miami Cuban efforts, as well as Filipino strategies during the Marcos regime, reflected this lobbying reality. Here, the role of the lobbyists is strategic. They become the voice of the community and their informally appointed spokespersons.

Lobbyists play this role not only because they are mandated to do so by the community or self-mandated, but also because they are recognized by those they seek to influence. The connections between the sending and receiving parties complete the trajectory of the process of the institutionalization of the status of the lobbyist. The lobbyist must be recognized or legitimized as such by the group that it represents and by the group with whom it is called upon to intercede.

Although lobbyists may influence members of Congress because of the votes they can deliver on Election Day, there are other factors that help shape the outcome of congressional votes. Bruce C. Wolpe and Bertram J. Levine mention among others "pressure from party leadership, logrolling and deal making with other members, the quest for higher office, and a genuine desire to make effective public policy."[11]

When the hostland seeks the support of the diaspora for its policies toward the homeland or simply wants to convey a clear message to the homeland government after regular diplomatic channels have failed, as in the case of the results of the legislative elections in Haiti in April 2000, the hostland government itself seeks out the lobbyists as unofficial messengers. The role of the lobbyist in this case is to convey to the homeland government the seriousness of the position of the hostland government and the foreseen negative consequences of their lack of cooperation or stubbornness. In this instance, not only does the hostland government recognize an individual as a lobbyist and thereby legitimize his or her position, but it also seeks out the lobbyist's help for the performance of a government function. A typical example of this type of undertaking is provided by Lawrence H. Fuchs: "During the most critical hours of negotiation between the United States and Israel over the withdrawal of Israeli troops from the conquered Sinai desert in February 1957, Secretary of State Dulles called eight leaders of philanthropic non-Zionist Jewish organizations to his office. He attempted to persuade them to use their influence with Tel Aviv to bring an Israeli retreat."[12]

Of course, lobbyists who target the diaspora do not just help advance the agendas of the hostland. They also play an important part in advancing the domestic policies of the homeland. When the homeland seeks the logistical support of the diaspora for its policies and its financial support during electoral campaigns, it turns to the lobbyists. The support of the diaspora may enhance national support for homeland candidates and policies or at least serve as a backup supporting the actions of the central administration. The population may be in a better position to accept governmental policies if these have the blessing of the diaspora. Diasporic support of government policies gives some indication that something good might perhaps result from them.

The Boundaries of Diasporic Lobbying

Until recently, diasporic lobbyists were prominent in influencing three policy arenas of the hostland: foreign relations, immigration, and refugee policies.[13] The success of such enterprises is often explained in terms of election politics, that is, congresspersons "see the demographics of their districts as central to their electoral chances."[14] This ethnic intervention on behalf of refugees has been noted in the case of Jewish refugees. Sharon Stanton Russell notes that "[a]fter the Second World War, American Jews formed the Citizens' Committee on Displaced Persons to pressure the U.S. Congress for legislation allowing the resettlement of Holocaust survivors in the United States."[15] The Jewish lobby went further than that by way of influencing the U.S. Congress to incorporate the Jewish refugee question as an intrinsic component of relations between the United States and the Soviet Union. Indeed, Aristide R. Zolberg rightly remarks that "the well-organized Jewish groups in the United States persuaded foreign policy decision makers to incorporate Jewish emigration as a condition for improved relations with the Soviet Union."[16]

Requests by local communities concerning their homeland are factored into the mathematics of representation. Unless these needs are met, a candidate risks not being able to capture the diaspora's votes. This stretches the congressional candidate's agenda and explains why some take a vigorous role in foreign policy. Sometimes what is important is not the overall size of the population, but its ability to contribute financially or its concentration in a specific state or major city, which can tip the balance in the electoral process.[17]

In the beginning of the twenty-first century, however, foreign relations, immigration, and refugee policies are no longer the exclusive arenas for diasporic lobbying. Human rights, the environment, and the relations of the homeland with other nations or international bodies that may have no direct bearing on the hostland are now also primary arenas where lobbyists are engaged.

In addition to noting the policy areas where diasporic lobbying attempts to help shape agendas, it is also possible to study diasporic lobbying not from the standpoint of what it sets out to accomplish, but from what it does to or for diasporic groups. For Yossi Shain, who initiated this line of thinking, diasporic lobbying also facilitates the integration of disenfranchised groups into U.S. society and politics.[18] Their grassroots participation is a form of integration as they make their interests known to the larger system.

Official and Informal Diasporic Lobbyists

Official diasporic lobbyists are formally recognized lobbyists paid by a foreign government to represent the country abroad. Their job consists of projecting a positive image of the government and advancing its views in diplomatic circles, Congress, and the executive branch of government. They are registered at the U.S. Department of Justice as agents of a foreign government and are known as such in their capacity as lobbyists (tables 3.1 and 3.2).

Table 3.1 U.S. Law Firms Retained by the Aristide Government, Haiti (2001–2002)

Law Firm	*Location*	*Amount of Money*	*Duty*	*Periods Covered*
Burton V. Wides, P. C., #5278	Washington, DC	None reported	Assisting government of the Republic of Haiti, Ministry of Foreign Affairs	None reported
Dellums, Brauer, Halterman & Associates, LLC, #5442	Oakland, CA	$210,000.00	Lobbying Congress and U.S. government on behalf of Haiti	Six-month period ending December 31, 2001
		$180,500.00	Same	Six-month period ending June 30, 2002
Downey McGrath Group Inc., #5411	Washington, DC	$75,000.00	Lobbying U.S. government and assisting foreign principals	Six-month period ending February 2002
Global Market Solutions, #5475	Washington, DC	$30,000.00	Lobbying U.S. government and providing strategic advice and media relations	Prior to February 25, 2002 registration
Kurzban, Kurzban, Weinger & Tetzeli, P. A., #4604	Miami, FL	$355,849.50	Serving as general counsel to foreign principal in the United States	Six-month period ending June 30, 2001

		$514,606.64	Same	Six-month period ending December 31, 2001
		$600,634.01	Same	Six-month period ending June 30, 2002
Levy, Michael #5420	Osceola, WI	$9,500.00	Monitoring human rights matters and exchanging info on human rights, security and reform	Six-month period ending September 30, 2001
Patton Boggs, L.L.P., #2165	Washington, DC	$292,322.58	Lobbying for multilateral and bilateral lending to Haiti	Six-month period ending December 31, 2001
Ross-Robinson & Associates, #4992	Basseterre, SC W. Indies	None reported	None reported	None reported

Source: U.S. Department of Justice, Report of the Attorney General to the Congress of the United States on the Administration of the Foreign Agents Registration Act of 1938, as Amended for the six months ending June 30, 2001 (December 31, 2001; June 30, 2002; December 31, 2002)
2001
http://www.usdoj.gov/criminal/fara/SemiAnnualReportsToCongress2000-2003/June30-2001.pdf [pp. 107–108]
2001
http://www.usdoj.gov/criminal/fara/SemiAnnualReportsToCogress2000-2003/December31-2001.pdf [pp. 107–108]
2002
http://www.usdoj.gov/criminal/fara/SemiAnnualReportsToCongress2000-2003/June30-2002.pdf [pp. 105–106]
2002
http://www.usdoj.gov/criminal/fara/SemiAnnualReportsToCongress2000-2003/December31-2002.pdf [pp. 100–101]

Table 3.2 U.S. Law Firms Retained by the Préval Government, Haiti (1999–2000)

Law Firm	*Location*	*Amount of Money*	*Duty*	*Periods Covered*
Arent Fox Kintner Plotkin & Kahn, PLLC, #2661	Washington, DC	$30,000.00	Lobbying Congress to rebuild country and maintain government security	Six-month period ending February 18, 1999
Burton V. Wides, P.C., #5278	Washington, DC	$45,000.00	Lobbying to obtain aid for stability and development	Six-month period ending April 30, 1999
		$45,000.00	Same	Six-month period ending October 31, 1999
		$41,000.00	Same	Six-month period ending April 30, 2000
		$39,000.00	Same	Six-month period ending October 31, 2000
Kurzban, Kurzban, Weinger, & Tetzeli, P. A., #4604	Miami, FL	$317,387.90	Foreign principal's general counsel, seeking removal of ash dumped by the City of Philadelphia	Six-month period ending June 30, 1999
		$288,115.12	Same	Six-month period ending December 31, 1999
		$302,483.28	Same	Six-month period ending June 30, 2000
		$328,849.09	Same	Six-month period ending December 31, 2000
Levy, Mike, #5280	Osceola, WI	$21,011.31	Monitoring human rights matters, and exchanging info on human rights, security, and reform	Six-month period ending June 30, 1999
		None reported	Representing on human rights, U.S. assistance, elections, media coverage, and territorial claims to Navassa	None reported

Continued

Table 3.2 Continued

Law Firm	*Location*	*Amount of Money*	*Duty*	*Periods Covered*
Ross-Robinson & Associates, #4992	Washington, DC	$45,000.00	Dealing with publicity and the media re political and economic stability	Six-month period ending February 28, 1999
		$46,117.45	Same	Six-month period ending August 31, 1999
		$45,339.69	Same	Six-month period ending February 28, 2000
		$33,000.00	Same	Six-month period ending August 31, 2000
Sandler & Travis Trade Advisory Services, Inc., #4699	Washington, DC	None reported	None reported	None reported

Source: The U.S. Department of Justice website at <http://www.usdoj.gov/criminal/fara/fara1st02/country/haiti.htm>.
U.S. Department of Justice, Report of the Attorney General to the Congress of the United States on the Administration of the Foreign Agents Registration Act of 1938, as amended for the six months ending June 30, 1999 [December 31, 1999; June 30, 2000; and December 31, 2000]
1999
http://www.usdoj.gov/criminal/fara/SemiAnnualReportsToCongress1997-1999/June30-1999.pdf [pp. 118–119]
1999
http://www.usdoj.gov/criminal/fara/SemiAnnualReportsToCongress1997-1999/December31-1999. pdf [pp. 116–117]
2000
http://www.usdoj.gov/criminal/fara/SemiAnnualReportsToCongress2000-2003/June30-2000.pdf [p. 108]
2000
http://www.usdoj.gov/criminal/fara/SemiAnnualReportsToCongress2000-2003/December31-2000. pdf [p. 108]

Because many of them are lawyers or work in a legal firm, they consider the foreign government as a client, one among others. This is a contractual arrangement for a service and for an agreed-upon amount of money. In a few cases, they may do it on a pro bono basis for a limited period of time provided that their expenses are reimbursed. This is the exception, and not the general rule.

In contrast, informal diasporic lobbyists are not paid by the homeland and are engaged on the basis of their citizenship rights. They lobby as American citizens urging the government to uphold democratic principles. They do not see themselves as agents of a foreign government, but as upholding intrinsic citizenship rights, an obligation imposed on them as taxpayers. They do not see themselves as professional lobbyists, but rather as activists advancing a good cause. Informal lobbyists cannot succeed without the help of key congresspersons representing their districts.

Although in the recent past, the formal lobbyists for the Haitian government were Anglo and African American lawyers connected with well-known law firms in Washington, DC, Haitian American lawyers have recently joined the fray. They either do pro bono work or work for a negotiated fee. This legal and formal lobbying work is carried out either in Haiti or in the United States, as reported in the following two cases. *The Miami Herald* of November 9, 1995, quoting U.S. Justice Department records reports that "Mildred Trouillot, a Haitian American attorney and registered lobbyist living in Haiti, receives about $10,000 a month." While living in Haiti, Trouillot described her lobbying work for the *Miami Herald* of December 2, 1995: "From offices in Haiti, I have notified members of the U.S. Congress of the progress of political and security conditions in Haiti since the restoration of democracy on Oct. 15, 1994, in an effort to continue constructive relations between the U.S. and Haiti. In Haiti, I advise the government on agreements with the U.S. government."

Haitian American lobbyists have done pro bono work on behalf of both the Aristide government and the Haitian refugees. Their work in this area has not remained unnoticed by the mainstream media, as is the case in this piece by Doreen Hemlock in *South Florida Sun-Sentinel*, June 1, 2001.

> How did three women—all in their 30s, all born in Haiti, raised in the United States and graduated from South Florida law schools—manage in just three years to develop a law firm with five attorneys, a total of 10 employees, billings close to $1 million and offices in Miami Shores and Boynton Beach?
>
> Indeed, it was on a lobbying trip coordinated through the Haitian American Lawyers Association, when the three women came up with the idea to form a practice together. The trio—all solo legal practitioners then—shared a hotel room to cut costs as they lobbied in Washington, D.C., for a bill granting residency to tens of thousands of Haitians in the United States. The women became such good friends, they opted to pool their resources permanently, setting up shop in Miami Shores in 1998 to handle primarily immigration cases.

The role of the official lobbyists is to lobby Congress to enact laws favorable to their client country and to prevent sanctions against possible excesses of the client government. They work by means of financial contribution to electoral campaigns. These gifts are given to ensure that the causes of the foreign government will be promoted and protected.

Lately, however, the official lobbyists have enlisted the aid of the unofficial ones. They want the unofficial lobbyists to contact the congressperson for their district, to promote the cause in their community, and to participate in protest actions to keep the pressure on Congress. As the director of the National Coalition for Haitian Rights puts it,

> The protests we participated in have obviously been many over the years. I would say there were a number of rallies that were held in Washington, DC back in 1988 in support of the adoption of the Haitian Refugee Fairness Act which essentially had to do with providing legal immigrant status to the Haitians who had been screened in from Guantánamo Bay, Cuba as refugees with credible claims to asylum, and who remained in limbo because their asylum claims did not go anywhere. So the push was for the Haitians to be offered permanent legal status. So we participated in a number of rallies and lobbying efforts in Washington and Miami in that regard.

When grassroots organizations ally their forces with formal lobbyists, it strengthens the position of the foreign government and makes it a bit easier for the formal lobbyists to lobby on its behalf. The official lobbyists either formulate the issues around which they should fight or else inform the grassroots organizations about their legal strategies so as to keep them hewing the party line. Although informal lobbyists can help formal lobbyists to achieve their goals, they can also undermine their work if they are in opposition to the practices of the homeland government.

When official and grassroots lobbyists hold different views vis-à-vis the government, members of Congress find themselves being lobbied by two different sides. Formal lobbyists are less likely to perform well in this environment because congresspersons think in terms of electoral votes to be earned on Election Day. A foreign government must wage an uphill battle to succeed if the diaspora is against its practices. Here is another example of the centrality of the diaspora in the relation of the homeland with the U.S. government.

The relations that the grassroots organizations maintain with the homeland also influence the relations with the official lobbyists. The informal grassroots organizations do not operate in a neutral environment. They are aware of the official lobbyists and take measures either to reinforce and help them or else to thwart them.

The presence of informal lobbyists presents a challenge to the homeland government. This is not only because it seeks to consolidate and augment diaspora money, but also because of the extra amount of money it must pay lobbyists to prevent or counterbalance hostile and negative diasporic propaganda and the undermining of its legitimacy abroad.

Official and informal lobbyists each have limitations in what they can accomplish. Official lobbyists do well when the homeland they represent has the support of the hostland government and the diaspora, but do poorly when the homeland has neither source of support. Informal lobbyists do well with the member of Congress who represents their district, but have less access to other members. John P. Paul has shown that mostly congresspersons who represented areas with Greek concentrations voted consistently against the Turkish invasion of Cyprus and for the embargo on arms sale to Turkey.[19]

It is also important to report that formal lobbying for third world governments has been recently *racialized* as efforts are undertaken to select nonwhite lobbyists for the job, as well. In the Haiti case, this trend began with the Duvalier regime with its hiring of African American lobbyist Ron Brown and has become a routine matter, with Randall Robinson and Ron Dellums serving as members of the group of lobbyists on behalf of Haiti during the Aristide and Preval administrations. The congressional Black Caucus has played a key role in opening up that area to black lawyers. According to *Miami Herald* of December 23, 1992, citing again Justice Department records,

> Brown pleaded Haiti's case about 60 times a year, principally with members and staff of the Black Caucus, the House of Foreign Affairs Committee, and liberal Democrats. . . .
>
> Haiti was the first big client Brown brought to Patton, Boggs and Blow, the aggressive Washington law firm known for lobbying on behalf of unpopular clients. Fauntroy and the Black Caucus had urged Haitian officials to drop white lobbyists then handling the account and hire a black lobbyist, according to congressional aides.

Lobbyists as Activists

Although there are some studies of ethnic lobbies, no effort has been expanded yet to distinguish the different types of such groups as one does in the case of formal lobbyists. For Andrew Stark,[20] formal lobbyists can be divided into the following categories: "(a) lawyers, accountants and other professionals, who may from time to time make representations to government on behalf of their clients; (b) lobbyists in the employ of business organizations, chambers of commerce, boards of trade, professional associations and labour federations; (c) full-time lobbyists . . . in the employ of individual corporations, unions or other private interests; (d) so-called 'hired guns,' that is, third-party lobbyists who, for remuneration, represent clients before government; and (e) paid lobbyists for voluntary, single-interest or non-profit organizations typically referred to as 'public interest' or 'ideological groups.' " In this nomenclature, he totally ignores the reality of ethnic lobbying.

The distinction drawn by Alicja Iwanska[21] and followed by Yossi Shain[22] pays attention to the internal composition of the ethnic group and identifies three different types of lobbyists and political activists. They refer to " 'core members' or organizing elites who are intensively active in diasporic affairs; 'rear guard members' or past diaspora activists who have drifted away; all other 'silent' members whom diaspora elites, host governments, or home governments consider as potential recruits for diasporic politics."[23]

These typologies pay attention to what lobbyists do and to their status but for lobbyists in the diasporic community, it seems important also to develop a typology based on the genesis of their calling. One can then distinguish the *generative lobbyist* from the *regulative lobbyist*. The generative lobbyist emerges from the ethnic community as a political entrepreneur, a self-made lobbyist who enters the fray on his or her own to intervene on behalf of a cause. In contrast, the regulative lobbyist is appointed to head an organization and is paid by a third party for a cause that it supports or is paid by either the host or homeland government to counterbalance the political activities of another group whose philosophy or goal they do not share. Such protégé lobbyists may not be paid, but their work is facilitated by the government that solicits their actions. The regulative lobbyist is an extension of a hierarchical power structure and is controlled or influenced from above.

Different types of lobbyists intervene on behalf the community they think that they represent. It is important to focus on these types in order to understand their mode of operation and their location in the globalization process.

The *volunteer lobbyist* is the most common type—an individual who is engaged in lobbying for the sheer pleasure of helping others. Some do it on a part-time basis while they are full-time employees in their regular jobs. They do not expect any financial returns from their engagement and act on a volunteer basis. They activate their participation whenever a good cause needs their help. They may belong to an ad hoc organization that may collapse once the crisis is solved or simply volunteer their work in an NGO that lobbies on behalf of the local community, the homeland, or a foreign country.

The *entrepreneurial lobbyist* (self-employed) is an individual who opens his or her own shop and who sustains the organization through volunteer work by others, government subsidies, foundation grants, and aggressive fund-raising. This money is used for overhead, expenses, and the leader's salary. The organization, which may start as a one-issue entity, may expand as a way to generate income to sustain itself. The expansion that is needed in order to generate income may turn it into a moneymaking enterprise. Expansion in other areas of lobbying effort or refocusing the organization from refugee resettlement to human rights in the homeland may take place, especially if refugees are no longer a problem.

The *hired-gun lobbyist* in the context of diasporic political representation, unlike the formal lobbyists who are paid by their clients, is often not hired by his or her client, but rather by a sponsor institution. It may be an independent institution that the lobbyist is called upon to administer or a lobby unit within a larger structure. While fund-raising takes place, it is however not central to the operation of the unit as, in the case of the entrepreneur lobbyist.

While these different lobbyists collaborate among themselves for the common good, sometimes they are on different sides of an issue, but they also compete with each other, because they tend to target the same source for fund-raising.

One distinction made by Stark is important, however, because it sheds light on diasporic modes of intervention. He distinguishes direct lobbying from indirect lobbying. He sees direct lobbying as the situation "in which lobbyists contact the officeholder," while indirect lobbying occurs when "lobbyists initiate mass-mailing campaigns to public officials, especially politicians, with the hope of pressing them in a particular direction."[24]

What distinguishes the lobbyists of the diaspora from the rest of the diasporic population is that members of Congress are more amenable to listen to them than to other people because of their status as folk representatives, the ethnic votes they can deliver on election day, and the damage they can do in their diasporic communities to the reputation of a congressperson, thereby undermining his or her ability to be reelected.

The Tactics of Diasporic Lobbying

It is important to distinguish between *cold* and *hot* lobbying because they differ in terms of the intensity of the lobbying and the means used to achieve the proposed goal. Cold lobbying consists of contacting elected officials in the hope of changing their minds or influencing them on specific issues and is a long-term commitment. Hot lobbying is done for an immediate result and is accompanied by mass demonstrations, not only to put pressures on policy makers, but to attract public attention so that the media may find the issue newsworthy and to attract resources and sympathizers. Because of its intensity—and because of the inability to maintain that level of intensity for a long time—it aims at a short-term goal and conducts many activities at once to achieve that goal. In cold lobbying, facts are presented to convince the interlocutors, but in the hot lobbying there is a tendency to exaggerate or distort facts and to highlight the worst scenario in order to show the urgency of the situation. Cold lobbying puts the emphasis on the process, while hot lobbying is more concerned with immediate action.

However these two types cannot be easily separated, because one may transform into the other or the same diasporic lobby group may pursue both strategies at the same time. Lobbying might be cold at first to test the waters, but if no action is forthcoming, hot lobbying may be adopted to press the issue. Vice versa, one may start with hot lobbying and decelerate the pressure to cold lobbying once the desired outcome is in progress. Each type requires different organizational management of the lobbying group in terms of resources, membership participation, and strategies of action.

The Internet has been used lately by diasporic lobbyists as an instrument for the consolidation of their effort, to spread the news about their grievances, to request action from their sympathizers in terms of resources, to inform the public, to reach their congressional representatives, loading their e-mail with statements prepared by the headquarters of the operation, and to maintain contacts and develop strategies with homeland activists and hostland sympathizers and organizations. In contrast to the telephone and regular mail, e-mail reduces costs and provides direct access in real time.[25]

What we might call *lobbying in the dark* also takes two forms. Lobbying in the dark is lobbying for a cause that diasporans would prefer not to support, but that must be supported because of their allegiance to the homeland. In the first of its two forms, the lobbying reflects diasporic attachment to the homeland, but not to the eccentricities of any particular government, and reflects public, not private or in-group sentiment. While publicly the diasporans support the government, they may also actively send signals to the government of their disapproval of its practices. But such in-group sentiment is not for public consumption.

The second form of lobbying in the dark derives from the first. It is lobbying to protect the reputation of the country because there is no better choice available. The best example here is the attitude of the Jewish lobby groups vis-à-vis the human rights of displaced and returned Palestinians. Some lobby hard for Israel while recognizing in private (and sometimes in public) the legitimate claims and aspirations of the Palestinian people and their rights for a secure homeland and disagreeing with some Israeli air strikes within Palestinian territories and the killing of innocent lives.

Lobbying in the dark is a cause of division within the lobby group itself because it divides them into hard-liners and moderates, that is, those who would continue to lobby for the government no matter what (extremist or radical patriotism) and those who would do so provided that the government readjusts its policies to meet common standards of democratic politics.

Lobbying in the dark is different from the more common types of lobbying, *positive lobbying* and *negative lobbying*. By positive lobbying, we mean the action taken by activists to ask officials of the hostland government to engage in activities they consider being beneficial to the people. For example, the Bush and Clinton administrations were asked to support the return of Aristide to Haiti during his exile in Washington, DC. In contrast, in negative lobbying, officials of the hostland government are asked to stop doing beneficial activities they were engaged in vis-à-vis a foreign government or to adopt a negative stand vis-à-vis this government, for example, to prevent it from getting a loan from the IMF or World Bank or, in an extreme situation, to embargo the country. In the 1960s, lobbyists asked the American government to suspend its foreign aid to Haiti or to make Jewish emigration from the Soviet Union a cornerstone of U.S. foreign policy in relation to this other superpower.

Diasporic Lobbyists as Cosmopolitans

New transnational classes are emerging that do not necessarily duplicate local class categories, but instead operate across national borders.

They are cosmopolitans. The diasporic lobbyist is an ideal type of cosmopolitan politician because his or her political arena spans borders. Transnationalization sometimes relocates individuals in different class positions in comparison with what they once occupied at home. Thus, members of these new transnational classes may be at variance with national class positions both at home and abroad. Heretofore, social class has been defined within the context of the nation-state and is compared with units inside that unit. Transnationality adds a new dimension to that definition with a new point of comparison by expanding the universe outside the nation-state. As transnational cosmopolitan politicians, diasporan lobbyists may influence both hostland and homeland policies. It is therefore important to identify specific areas where the diasporic lobbyist's interventions have been felt.

Diasporic lobbyists account for the expansion of funds for congressional races and therefore play a critical citizenship role by actively participating in the election of U.S. representatives. They do so in the name of their communities and on behalf of the homeland. They want their member of Congress to be not only the representative of their community, but also a strategist on behalf of their country. For this group, voting, which is supposed to be a *national act* because the voter belongs to a nation-state, now becomes for some a *transnational act* for the benefit of a transnation-state. The congressional candidate also relies on the largess of the transnation for his or her election because the money received may be from the homeland and transmitted by lobbyists. In the same way that homeland governments give money to official lobbyists to help congressional candidates in their fund-raising activities, they also use diasporic lobbyists to channel money to congressional campaigns.

Diasporic lobbyists elevate their status by serving as middlemen between their homeland government and the United States, by interceding on behalf of their homeland or on behalf of the United States as a go-between individual. This status elevation is marked by the invitation they receive to attend official gatherings and sometime a Ministerial Cabinet post in the homeland government. The cosmopolitan status is reaffirmed by the ease with which they navigate through two different governments.

Diasporic lobbyists integrate three political communities in a single transnation, provide specific services to each, relate to each differently, and occupy a unique position that cannot be filled by any other agency. The diasporic lobbyist thus operates in three different political spheres at once. By means of the lobbyist's services, the homeland gets political access to U.S. officials, the diaspora gets its voices heard through its lobbyists, and the U.S. government gets its message transmitted to the homeland government when regular diplomatic channels fail to accomplish the same.

Until recently, diasporic lobbyists were concerned with influencing the homeland through their pressure on politicians in the hostland. Their local politics was circumscribed, and engaged only the homeland and the hostland. What is new is the global network in which they are connected. They now target other governments that are capable of influencing homeland politics.

This new international profile of diasporic grassroots lobbyists came about through their network with other diasporan groups and international sympathizers with their cause. In a sense, one may speak of an international coordination without necessarily an international headquarters of operation to assess local and extranational outputs.

What we see here is a redrawing of the space of diasporic lobbying interaction with agendas that are worked on via Internet communications and with modes of intervention decided not by the local group, but in interaction with extralocal entities. The Cuban American National Foundation, by directly lobbying foreign countries—such as governments in Latin America and Europe—brought an international dimension to the situation of Cuban exiles in Miami.[26] Likewise, Haitian American groups were able to keep some pressure on Canada, France, and the European Commission until the return of Aristide to Haiti. This was done in collaboration with diasporic groups and local sympathizers in Canada, France, Belgium, and the United Kingdom.

In short, diasporic lobbying groups are now moving into a new, transnational dimension. Jackie Smith[27] argues that transnational social movements organizations (TSMOs) provide a number of services to their groups: distributing information on relevant issues, coordinating on strategies for local action groups, representing their interests in international organization forums, and monitoring homeland compliances with international standards. Most diasporic groups are not formally organized, with a central headquarters and subsidiaries distributed in key countries and the homeland. We have seen a different deployment of transnationalism, one that is more informal and decentered. The local organization that raises an issue seeks the help of other, similar organizations. Instead of hierarchy, there is more equality as the source of initiative, for an action may migrate from one group to another or from one country to another.

There are different levels of transnational involvement. The National Center for Haitian Rights lobbies for Haitian refugees in the United States, but it is also organized transnationally in the sense that it has a subsidiary in Port-au-Prince and coordinates actions with associates in the Dominican Republic. Its alliances for action are carried out not only with Haitian groups but also with other sympathizers. Here, again, one may speak of degrees and moments of participation. It serves as a central coordinating mechanism and sometimes solely as a node in a network as when pro-immigrant activists call on diasporic groups to help undermine the implementation of restrictionist immigration policies.[28] These distinctions pertaining to temporality and degree of involvement help us to understand better the mechanism of operation and how different cycles and circles of transnationalism may traverse the same site.

The transnational linkage between the headquarters in New York and the subsidiary in Haiti shows how the central office is able to influence the course of things in Port-au-Prince through its proxy. It also shows how this linkage provides some external protection so that the local office can carry out its mandate without being harassed by the government. As the director of the National Coalition of Haitian Rights puts it,

> One of the reasons why NCHR has been able to function in Haiti is because of the international connection. The fact that what we say in the States has some weight, and we have been able to communicate our opinions and past statements to both high level officials in the U.S. at the UN and OAS. We have this history of association with a large number of organizations with far larger membership than we were taking our positions and so on. This is probably why our representative in Haiti has never been arrested. There was an attempt on his life in 2000. The branch in New York provides some protection. If they take our associates to jail in Haiti, there will be someone in New York to make enough noise for their liberation. This kind of symbolic protection, no doubt, energizes our people to be more forthcoming in bringing human rights violations to the attention of the international community.

Transnationalism is unavoidable when issues become part of a larger policy agenda that also addresses a problem that concerns a diasporic group and whose solution is perceived as dependent on the larger network. Jewish lobbying on behalf of the emigration of Jews from Soviet Union necessitated the collaboration of Jews in Canada, the United States, Israel, and various countries of Europe. Harold Troper[29] has found that the effort on behalf of Jews in Syria did not parallel that on behalf of Soviet Jewry. His interpretation is that although the Soviet Union might give in to protests, Syria would not, and therefore that transnationalism on behalf of a cause is more likely to happen if the argument over the issue is perceived to be winnable.

Diasporic Lobbyists and the Breakdown of Political Careers

Diasporic lobbying has contributed to the breaking of political careers in three crucial areas. The most obvious and the most studied is its contribution to the overthrow of the government or of specific cabinet members. Lobbyists do not directly and alone overthrow regimes, but expose political corruption and thereby undermine the popularity of a government and create obstacles for the government at home among homeland population and abroad in the international community. This is why homeland governments pay attention to lobbyist efforts and in some cases develop their own lobbyist groups to counterweight those of the opponents.

Diasporic lobbyists also have caused the abrupt end of political careers among official representatives of the homeland government. Although lobbyists tend to work hand in hand with such officials, they also sometimes defend alternative views and thereby undermine the effectiveness of these individuals. Diasporic leaders have in the past requested the transfer or dismissal of officials whose politics they dislike. The following case recounted by a Chicago activist informant illustrates one aspect of that power.

> There was a problem in the Haitian consulate in Chicago that was purely administrative. The problem was that there was somebody named to the office, and the person was functioning, but in the midst of his administration there were some employees who felt that there were slighted by him, both in terms of the way he treated them and also in terms of not receiving their pay. The government did not pay these people. What happened in the course of the first Aristide administration, a lot of the time, was that complaints the general population would have for the government usually didn't go to the government officials, but rather to activists that were perceived as being very close to the government. In that case, there were indeed a group of activists. I was one of them. I was really the main person, so those charges/complaints came to me. What I did was compile them and send them to the authorities (Aristide,

the minister of foreign affairs and other members of the cabinet. I had nothing to do with the gentleman who was consul. I went straight up).

At that time Aristide was in exile. When time passed and nothing happened, I upped the ante. I said, "Listen, if there is a charge of corruption and you people are not doing anything to substantiate what is going on, if indeed there was a case of corruption, they should take action, or if there was nothing, they should come up and say that they investigated it and there was nothing." There were also charges of sexual harassment in addition to embezzlement. So in any case, at the end of the day, I also told Aristide and the other cabinet ministers, "If you are somewhat ambivalent about dealing with this thing, I have some evidence that there is some wrongdoing. Maybe my place is not alongside you people. If you look at corruption in the government and you are not doing anything about it, then I am on the wrong side."

So a group of people came from Washington, and they shut down the consulate office. A lot of people attributed that to me, when in fact I don't think that's true. The consul did not lose his job, he was simply transferred to another post. And the office reopened three or four months later with a new person who was not from Chicago, but rather from Haiti.

Diasporic lobbyists have also contributed to the demise of their own political careers because of the polarization of the community they create by their actions. *A lobbyist is by definition a partisan who operates on behalf of a faction*. Winning other factions to his or her cause may not be high on the lobbyist's political agenda because the idea is to sell a political platform or a specific policy. More often, the lobbyist is selling it not to a diasporic faction but to the hostland government so that it may help the homeland government. The demise of the lobbyist's political career may be due to divisions, frictions, and conflicts attributable to his lobbying efforts.

Lobbyists, Hostland, and Homeland Governments

Lobbyists operate in three arenas: single (hostland), transnational or binational (homeland), and compound arenas (which include these two and more). Different explanations are provided on the reasons why they follow one path or another. For example, Shain has argued that the involvement in homeland affairs is often carried out in order to better position themselves "to mobilize their political communities for empowerment inside the United States."[30] But he also found that they must operate under specific structural constraints in order to succeed in their efforts. For example, "they must justify their actions in terms of American national interests and values, answer to their U.S. ethnic compatriots, and prove their loyalty to their home country."[31]

Participation in homeland affairs creates its own set of problems, because diasporic lobbyists may not agree with homeland policies or hostland policies vis-à-vis the homeland, thereby finding themselves in a no-man's land. Agreeing with one and trying to help change the policies of the other is one thing, but being at odds with either side requires a different posture in this arena.

According to Myron Weiner, diasporic lobbyists may be harmful to U.S. foreign policies in two major ways.[32] Pushing the United States to adopt democratic and human rights principles in dealing with the homeland may create tensions between the United States and the foreign government. And such demands, according to his argument, are likely to generate "conflicts within Washington over how we should weigh human rights against strategic considerations."[33]

Fuchs identifies two areas in which lobbyists have influenced American politics:[34] the role played by foreign policies in influencing the voting patterns of ethnic communities and the interests that members of Congress take in shaping foreign policies that are advantageous to homelands of their ethnic constituents.

Ethnic lobbies bring the race issue to the foreign policy debate to the extent that racial considerations may shape the outcome. Here, considerations of strategic interests are interpreted as racial, especially in regard to non-European countries. Clinton's foreign policy vis-à-vis Haiti was addressed by the congressional Black Caucus as intrinsically located inside the American domestic racial issue.[35] Strategic considerations could not be disentangled from racial considerations.

Diasporic lobbyists seek out members of Congress with the same ethnic background whether they represent their district or not. These individuals are natural allies and are usually targeted to help the cause. For example, the Irish congressmen such as "Speaker O'Neil, Senators Edward Kennedy and Daniel Patrick Moynihan, and Governor Hugh Carey of New York" were lobbied by ethnic lobbyists on behalf of Ireland during the administration of Ronald Reagan.[36] Similarly, Arab American lobbyists sought out the help of Arab American politicians such as "Representatives Marie Rose Oakar (D-Ohio) and Nick Joe Rahall (D-West Virginia), Senators Abdnot (R-South Dakota) and George Mitchell (D-Maine), and Governors Atiyeh (R-Oregon) and Sununu (R-New Hampshire)" to influence the shape of U.S. Middle

East policy during the Reagan administration.[37] Likewise, John P. Paul has shown that Greek American congressmen such as John Brademas (D-Indiana), Paul Sarbanes (D-Maryland), Paul Tsongas (D-Massachusetts), Gus Yatron (D-Pennsylvania), and Louis Bafalis (R-Florida) "generated, coordinated, and lobbied for the embargo legislation [because of Turkey's invasion of Cyprus] from the introduction of the first embargo resolution in September 1974 to the embargo's reversal in October 1975."[38]

The members of Congress who have been active on behalf of Haiti and Haitian Americans have been mostly from Florida, New York and Massachusetts, as we have seen—states with large concentrations of Haitians. In this endeavor the Haitian case follows the patterns found elsewhere. African American members of Congress through the Black Caucus have been sympathetic in the name of racial solidarity.

The ethnic lobby phenomenon is not peculiar to the American political process, but it is found in other democracies as well. The Kashmir lobby in England is a case in point and displays characteristics similar to those found in the United States. According to Patricia Ellis and Zafar Khan, "Analysis of the membership of the Kashmir Group, by constituency and political affiliation in 1995, showed that not only were the majority of the Group Labour Party MPs, but that many of these members represented constituencies with relatively large Pakistani/Kashmiri communities."[39]

The Haitian lobby expresses the three characteristics of the architecture of diasporic lobby. First, it engages in politics in the hostland on behalf of the homeland (whether to help, undermine, or consolidate the political regime of the homeland): It is made up of members of the ethnic group who attempt to influence parliamentary politics in the country of residence and the homeland. It is heterogeneous, however, because different factions tend to propose different agendas (opposition versus loyalist politics). Second, the diasporans interact with hostland political actors and institutions: Their lobbying targets and enlists for its support representatives from hostland states that house concentrations of the immigrant group, whether they directly or indirectly represent such districts or not. It also seeks the support of representatives of same ethnic background from other states. It is ethnic-led, not ethnic-exclusive, because it comprises nonethnic sympathizers, as well, and it is made up of paid lobbyists (pro-government) and unpaid lobbyists (opposition and pro-government activists). Finally, the diasporic lobby interacts with political actors and institutions in the homeland, directly or indirectly, and as individuals or a group: The lobby is influenced in one way or another by politicians in the homeland, whether those in the government or those in the opposition.

Perhaps the most visible effect of the role of ethnic lobbyists vis-à-vis their homeland is that lately they have become the new missionaries of American democracy there.[40] In some cases, they are extensions of American foreign policy because they believe democracy is the best hope for their country and go even further by preaching it to their own compatriots in the homeland.

The Temporalities of Diasporic Lobbying

Diasporic lobbying has its own temporal cadence, with dormant periods interspersed with periods of intensity. Congress is able to maintain its balance in the foreign policy arena precisely because these diasporic demands are not quotidian affairs, but rather arise at specific periods. Diasporic lobbying is more intense in periods of crisis in the diasporic community because this may affect the relations between the homeland and the hostland: in the homeland because help from Congress may be sought to resolve the problem (political turmoil, disaster, an electoral campaign, and in the relations) between the two countries because the lobbyists may be called upon to serve as go-betweens by either side.

These forms of lobbying intervention are done to deal with the urgency of the crisis and are expected by all parties involved. Some issues that also call for diasporic intervention remain dormant, to be taken up in due time. The presidential campaign period has become a cherished moment to resurrect such issues. As an intense lobbying year for diasporic citizens, an electoral period provides the diasporic community and the homeland an occasion to present their preferences as a package to be addressed in order to secure their votes, and it is the best time for would-be immigrants to show up at the hostland's gates, as happened in the cases of the Cubans and the Haitians during the 1992 U.S. presidential campaign. Candidate Clinton was able to play up that issue against his opponent, George Bush, Sr., and in the process scored some votes among Haitian Americans and Cuban Americans throughout the United States. The electoral year thus enhances the visibility of diasporic lobbies because they are more astute and forthcoming in asking for specific favors, and at the same time, American foreign policy is thrown off balance because diasporic requests are taken more seriously than at other times.

The Life Cycle of Diasporic Lobbying

In addition to having its own temporal cadence, diasporic lobbying has its own life cycle. This depends on a series of variables: loyalty to the homeland, the existence of a crisis in the local community that compels action at the national level, as in the case of an influx of refugees, the transitory or permanent character of such a crisis, and the ability for fund-raising to prevent the collapse of the core group. If we assume that individuals engage in lobbying to help with a crisis and that they tend to be committed to the welfare of their countries of birth and of residence (homeland and hostland), we may then examine two important aspects of the life cycle of diasporic lobbying: the fund-raising cycle and the effects of competition for resources with similar groups.

Fund-raising is necessary to pay for the basic expenses of a lobbying operation because the work of unpaid volunteers is not enough to reach long-term objectives. Few volunteers have the means to pay for such expenses year in and year out. External funding then becomes a means of survival. Fund-raising becomes central when formalization is necessary. Formalization requires space (rent), administrators (managers and secretaries), and expenses (office materials and overhead). Many one-purpose groups disappear at this level because they are unable to move their operations from informal to more formal types of lobbying, which may require pursuing additional or new objectives. Those operations that survive often must enlarge their missions to include other activities, such as shifting from concentrating on homeland crises whenever they occur to becoming a diasporic community-services center that caters to local needs.

Such shifts in orientation require fund-raising to enable the organization to survive during periods when there is no homeland crisis that could bring volunteers, a sense of urgency, and money. Lobbying organizations that succeed in fund-raising not only have the opportunity to engage in other types of work and to network with other organizations, they can survive during the period between crises and deal more efficiently with a crisis whenever it occurs. Usually if an organization fails to raise the needed money, that is the end of it. The period between crises and the way in which diasporic lobbying organizations adapt to such periods thus are important factors in the life cycle of these organizations.

So are the extent of their proliferation during crises and the consequences of that proliferation in the periods in between. This phenomenon can be understood by using a resource competition approach.[41] During a crisis, goodwill and resources can be plentiful, and this may explain why diasporic lobbying organizations proliferate. During the in-between periods, however, they must compete for scare resources. The best-organized ones are more likely to survive than the others. Some cease to exist because they are one-purpose enterprises, and at the end of a crisis they disappear, while others fail because they are not able to shift from one organizational level to another or are led to bankruptcy by their competitors. Others cease to exist even before a crisis is solved because of internal problems such as ideological dissention, poor finances, or poor management.

Transnational Rival Blocs

Lobbying does not always lead to a unity of purpose, but sometimes results in rivalry because of competition for resources, different ideologies, or simply different methods used to attain the same goals. Friendly competition or hostile rivalry occurs when groups with similar agendas compete for resources in order to survive or to undermine their rivals. In a period of crisis, different groups may emerge and receive equal treatment by the homeland headquarters of the operation (whether the government or the opposition), but in a moment of stability, the headquarters may side with one group to facilitate its growth or to represent its voice abroad. Splinter groups either must then coalesce with the chosen group or else reconnect with a different group in the homeland.

Local rivalries and competitions sooner or later will expand through transnationalization. These transnational blocs are multisite operations that seek to strengthen the headquarters, and the relations of headquarters with other groups are mediated and fueled by diasporic tentacles that can either facilitate matters or else complicate things on the ground.

The existence of transnational rival blocs attests to the role of diasporic lobbyists in homeland political affairs and to the extraterritorial extension of homeland politics. A recent illustration of such a practice may help us to understand its importance and the parameters of transnational politics. In Haiti, during the electoral campaigns in 2000, an opposition coalition Convergence Démocratique sought to boycott the presidential elections held in November of that year because of the presumed allegiance of the Electoral Council to the governing party. They sought help from the international community (the Organization of American States, the European Union, the United Nations) and from specific countries such as the United States, Canada, and France and enlisted diaspora lobbyists to help intervene with their respective governments. This was also an election year in both Canada and the United States, and the Clinton administration refrained from officially supporting the party in office in Port-au-Prince.

Both factions sent key members of their party or coalition to seek the support of the diaspora. Both used diasporic lobbyists to plead their causes in Washington, and both sought diasporic support to strengthen their position at home. Alliance with a segment of the diaspora population was seen as a sine qua non for success. Each used three forms of intervention to sway the diaspora to their side of the dispute: The party in office sent representatives to Miami to hold press conferences, while the opposition coalition sent representatives to New York and Washington to enlist new sympathizers to their causes. Both used diasporic radio programs and newspapers to spread their messages in their respective diasporic communities. Finally, both sent delegations accompanied with diasporic lobbyists to Washington to negotiate on their behalf. In addition, the opposition was able to target a specific group in the diaspora—academicians and technocrats—who in alliance with Haitian academics in the homeland issued similar statements against the undemocratic tactics of the party in office.[42]

Because of the work of the diaspora, political conflict thus becomes transnational, no longer bound within the geographical borders of a single nation-state. Because diasporic actors have their own agendas in addition to the agenda of the party to which they subscribe, the conflict becomes exacerbated. The party in office sees its reliance on the diaspora as a way of strengthening its position in relation to the opposition, and the opposition uses a similar strategy to achieve similar goals.

Conclusion

Diasporic lobbying cannot be understood outside its historical and sociological context because similar activities may be seen differently by different interpretive communities. In the nineteenth and early twentieth centuries, this type of lobbying was seen as a lack of loyalty to the state. Since the collapse of the Soviet Union, it has been viewed as a way of advancing the causes of democracy and human rights abroad. The act of lobbying itself is interpreted differently by the public whether the lobbyists follow the government policy or oppose it, whether it is undertaken in a period of war or a period of stability, whether the lobby is large and influential or small and insignificant, and whether the issue being addressed is of strategic importance or not in the context of U.S. foreign policy. Despite differences in ideology, ethnic Americans view lobbying favorably as a necessity of democracy.[43] For example, in the words of Keely, "ethnic lobbies serve as a useful voice and can even be a corrective to conventional wisdom. They certainly can claim as much right to present views about the national interest as any Americans."[44] Shain makes a similar claim when he states that "the participation of ethnic diasporas in shaping U.S. foreign policy is a truly positive phenomenon."[45] Diasporic lobbying, of course, is just one form of transnational lobbying and does not exhaust the subfield because not all transnational lobbying is diasporic. No matter what one thinks of this phenomenon, however, it is a social reality to be reckoned with.

This chapter has remapped the landscape of diasporic lobbying by identifying lobbyists as affecting and carving out a transnational niche inside American politics. It suggests that this field of political activity affects the diasporic community because of the type of leadership it provides. It also affects American politics because of the pressure it exerts on elected officials and because it influences policy formation. It serves as a point of contact between the homeland and the hostland: it affects the homeland directly through interactions with homeland political actors and institutions and indirectly through their political activities in the hostland.

4

Virtual Diasporic Public Sphere

The Haitian American case analyzed here provides a full picture of the trajectory of diasporic politics, from the political activities of diasporans in the hostland to their becoming government officials in the homeland. The fall of the Aristide administration and his departure for exile on February 29, 2004, set the stage for a new chapter in Haitian diasporic politics and caused a reversal of fortune in a most visible way. The former president, Jean-Bertrand Aristide, became a diasporan, while a diasporan, Gérard Latortue, who was living in Florida, was offered and accepted the job of prime minister of Haiti.

Former president Aristide did not exit Haitian politics, but reconnected to it from a diasporic base, and Gérard Latortue did not exit diasporic politics, but reconnected to it from a homeland base. The dynamics of this transnational version of local politics thus are best understood and captured by the metaphor of "circulation" rather than that of "exit" and by the metaphor of "repositioning" rather that of "exile." Diasporic politicians return to the homeland, and homeland politicians may find themselves living in the diaspora, either by their own choice or after having been forced to do so by events over which they have no control.

The terrain of operation of both homeland and diaspora politicians is transnational or even global because of their ability to relocate from one site to another, because the homeland sees the diaspora as a reserve army of talent, and because the diaspora sees the homeland as a natural target in the trajectory of its political engagement. Politicians circulate through the circuits and nodes of transnational local politics to allow the political system to revamp itself, to abide by the law of supply and demand, to reposition themselves strategically within this transnational space, or because of a political crisis in the homeland.

The spatiality of this newer form of political engagement and activism establishes a disconnect between the state's fixed boundaries and the nation's flexible territorial expansion. In this circulation, politicians may find themselves inside the expanded nation, but not necessarily inside the state, yet still able to reenter the state at any moment. Diasporic politics both reflect and are an expression of this territorial expansion of the nation. Becoming a diasporan in another country or returning to the homeland to occupy a position entails the crossing of the state's boundaries but not of the nation's boundaries.

The peculiarity of the Haitian political system is that it has been characterized by its fundamental transnational nineteenth-century feature: the central role of the diaspora in engineering coups d'état—with the help of one or more foreign governments—and in overthrowing the sitting government. This caused the displacement of the deposed leader, repositioning him in the circulations of transnational diasporan politics. This historical feature of the political system continues to this day to feed the mechanisms of governmental succession.[1] It is a political tradition that has become ingrained in the political culture of the nation and that is exploited at times by foreign governments that want to overthrow an unfriendly regime. The 2004 invasion of the diasporan rebels coming from the Dominican Republic, occupying strategic towns in Haiti, paralyzing potential government responses to recoup the territory, and causing the forced resignation of President Aristide is a concrete episode of the centrality of diasporic politics in the functioning of the homeland governmental process.

The Diasporic Public Sphere

What I will call the diasporic public sphere is the political arena where the diaspora expresses its political views, discusses its project for the homeland and the diaspora, interacts with hostland and homeland government officials and politicians, and reflects on its contribution to society.[2] This public sphere, which permeates the spatiality of the transnation, uses various means of expression, ranging from gossip, to diasporic media (ethnic television, ethnic newspapers, ethnic radio), to public gatherings and discussions, as well as the Internet (web sites, chat rooms, e-mails). It has both online and off-line dimensions that feed each other, that sustain and expand the sphere of interaction from the local to the global both formally and informally, and that differentiate the diasporic public sphere from other public spheres.[3]

Diasporic politicians listen to the ebb and flow of communications in this public sphere to legitimate their actions, to test the itinerary of their engagement, and to tap into ideas flowing through this circuit and obtain constant feedback in order to readjust their trajectories. The diasporic public sphere is not exclusive to the diaspora, since some homeland individuals participate in this exchange, as well. But this public sphere intends also to influence events in the homeland, as newspapers have been doing as the most visible expression of diasporic views on homeland affairs. This sphere is neither separate from nor identical to the homeland public sphere because of its transnational nature. It mingles audiences from both sides, yet some issues are germane to one side and may not have direct relevance to the other side.

In the months of stalemate preceding the forced resignation of Aristide, the diaspora was very active promoting immediate change in Haiti along the lines of the policies formulated by the OAS and later endorsed by CARICOM, the Bush administration, and the United Nations. The last road map prepared by the OAS proposed that Aristide should complete his term in office, that he should replace the corrupt leadership of the National Police, and that he should disarm the armed bands that were terrorizing the population and preventing the holding of fair elections in Haiti because of objections from the opposition.

The diaspora was divided on the stalemate, sometimes blaming the government and at other times the stubborn opposition. A public opinion poll taken by Bendixen and Associates between February 12 and February 18, 2004, with a sample of 600 Haitian Americans who resided in New York, New Jersey, Connecticut, Massachusetts, and Florida, states with strong concentrations of Haitian immigrants, concluded the following:

> Asked whether they approved of President Bush's handling of foreign policy toward Haiti, a very small percentage of respondents (9 percent) said they approved and a larger percentage (33 percent) said they disapproved . . .
>
> Of those aged 18–29, almost half (46 percent) said that Aristide should resign and a smaller number (39 percent) said that he should serve out his term.
>
> Among those aged 50 and above, the opinions are quite different. Only one-fourth (25 percent) said that Aristide should resign, and a clear majority (64 percent) said that he should serve out his term.
>
> Of the Haitian-Americans who were polled in English, a slight majority (55 percent) said that Aristide should resign and a smaller number (35 percent) said that Aristide should stay in office.

> For those who were polled in Creole, the results were reversed. A majority (58 percent) said Aristide should serve out his term. A smaller percentage (27 percent) said that he should resign.[4]

The diasporic public sphere is fed not only by those who live abroad but also by those who reside in the homeland. In some cases, these are dediasporized individuals who had returned home and resumed their activities as if they had never left. For example, one such individual, in an effort to sway the opinion of the diasporic community, published an op-ed piece in a very well-known French Canadian newspaper published in Montreal, *Le Devoir*, on February 17, 2004. In it, he documented and explained the violence inflicted by the armed gangs of the regime, the corruption of the National Police, and the continuing deterioration of economic conditions of the country. He concluded by saying that "Aristide, the last dictator of Latin America, must go" to prevent atrocities similar to those of Rwanda.[5]

Contesting Hegemony in the Diasporic Public Sphere

Achieving hegemony for the constructed, dominant view of the diaspora in matters pertaining to the strengthening of the democratic process in Haiti is an ongoing project of the diaspora. The views of the diaspora are not homogeneous because they correspond to cleavages in its midst. The claim to speak for diasporic opinion thus is always contested in the diasporic public sphere.

For example, some were for and others against the forced resignation of Aristide. In this case, as in others, part of the project of participants in the diasporic public sphere is to persuade others of the legitimacy of their claims so that the diaspora can be of one voice on a given issue. This requires a form of proselytism, enlarging the basis of support for the view of one side at the expense of the others.

It also requires enlisting the cooperation of those who do not participate in the diasporic public sphere to help in homogenizing this socially constructed dominant view so that it can be established over all other claims made by dissidents. Persuading the congressional Black Caucus to side with the pro-Aristide group, for example, subalternized the voices of dissidents for a while.

However, doing so also produces new divisions in the diasporic public sphere. The recruitment of the congressional Black Caucus by the pro-Aristide forces created some resentment among some members of the diaspora community. This is a recent development and concerns only the overthrow of the Aristide regime, but more broadly, it refers to public representation of Haitian interests vis-à-vis the refugee situation in Florida, where these two voices have always been in harmony.

The anti-Aristide dissidents have voiced their concerns about the one-sided position of the congressional Black Caucus and have raised the question about who is best equipped to authentically represent the voices of the majority of the diaspora concerning the political direction of the homeland. These opinions were recently expressed in a meeting attended by the Haitian American diasporic leadership in Miami.

> Leaders of South Florida's Haitian community met behind closed doors over the weekend and denounced some members of the Congressional Black Caucus for their ties to departed Haitian president Jean-Bertrand Aristide. . . . Saturday's meeting was held at the North Miami Office of state Rep. Yolly Roberson, the third such recent gathering among the area's Haitian community. . . . Those who attended the meeting said Miss Roberson, a Democrat, emphasized that Haitians in the United States "must take our case into our own hands.". . ."She asked that members of the community call Maxine Waters and tell her what we want," said one person in attendance.". . ."If we can do that, she said, we can be a powerhouse. Otherwise, they are free to say what they want, which isn't fair.". . . François Leconte, president and CEO of Minority Development and Empowerment, a Broward County outreach program . . . said in an interview . . ."it is time that we come up with national representation that speaks for Haiti instead of going through other elected officials."[6]

The contest over the representation of Haitian American voices in the American public sphere continues to be a matter of concern for members of the community, since the views of non-Haitian elected officials might not be the orientation they hope for the homeland. In this light, Paul Barthole, who has been serving as vice chair of the Haitian Community Services of South Dade filed the following in *The Miami Herald*,

> from Randall Robinson . . . to Reps. Charles Rangel, D-N.Y, and Maxine Waters, D-Cal., to Jesse Jackson, we get strident support for Aristide. . . . Their views do not reflect those of most Haitians and Haitian Americans. A recent informal poll conducted by Radio Carnivale in Miami reveals that the vast majority of its listeners in Miami-Dade County and over the Internet are ecstatic with Aristide's departure and the initial performance of new Prime Minister Gérard R. Latortue.[7]

Contesting the claim to the hegemony of diasporic opinion in the diasporic public sphere allowed Gérard Latortue to develop a political base in the diaspora that he successfully used to promote his interests in homeland politics. He had been a talk-show host in Florida, which gave him a podium to criticize the Aristide administration. Through the show, he developed an attentive audience and was able to deliver his anti-Aristide message directly in his televised commentaries and indirectly by means of the guests he invited. Not being officially a representative of a political party, even though he served earlier as minister of foreign affairs in the Leslie Manigat government in 1989, he projected to the listening audience the image of an objective outsider and experienced administrator. Here is how his tenure as a television journalist was portrayed in the mainstream U.S. media.

> Over the past year, Latortue had become a prominent voice among Haitians in South Florida. He debuted on the air in March 2003 with the launch of the Haitian Television Network of America, or HTN, a 24-hour channel offering French-, English-, and Creole-language programming. One of Latortue's shows, "Revue de la Semaine," was a political round table on Haiti, "a sort of Capital Gang."... The other, "L'inviter," is "like Larry King"... featuring weekly guests in one-on-one interview format.[8]

This was a political maneuver to position himself strategically in the eventual collapse of the administration, which served him well. The television show provided him with a political basis of support, a laboratory where he could try out his political ideas on people, and a community in which he could make his presence and interests known to the homeland.

The audience was not simply local—the Miami area—but became transnational because of visitors who listened to the show while sojourning in Florida, because of the discussions it raised in the community, because of the taping of some programs, which made their way to Port-au-Prince, and because of the diasporic alternative it provided to the country in search of change.

One year before he assumed the position of prime minister, Latortue began in earnest his campaign for the job with appearances before the Chambre de Commerce et d'Industrie, to which he presented a conference at the Kinam Hotel on February 3, 2003, followed by a focus interview with him on the private sector and international cooperation, and on March 13, 2003, he delivered a presentation in Washington, DC, in which he extolled his views on the political and economic development of Haiti. The Haitian visit was aimed at reconnecting him with the bourgeoisie, and he discussed things of common interest in an effort to appease their fears, while the Washington visit was to present and justify his plan of government before the Bush government and representatives of international organizations. From February 2003 to February 2004, his politics evolved from the goal of serving as prime minister with an independent agenda under President Aristide to advocating the departure of Aristide as the only viable solution to the political stalemate and the success of his future administration.

Events helped Latortue consolidate his anti-Aristide position. On December 5, 2003, Aristide's armed bands invaded the State University of Haiti and broke the legs of university president Pierre-Marie Michel Paquiot. Indeed, since the beginning of 2003, the diaspora had become very disappointed with the chaos brought about by the Aristide regime and began a series of street protests in Miami, New York, Washington, and Paris. For example, they staged a protest on October 17, 2003, before the Haitian consulate office in Miami. According to Patrick Eliancy, "the protesters carried posters with slogans hostile to the Haitian government and President Jean Bertrand Aristide. 'Aristide must go,' they shouted."[9] Although these protests did not attract large crowds, they were an embarrassment for the regime, since they called for the removal of Aristide from office. Latortue is quoted having said in reference to these demonstrations that the protesters were hoping "the echoes will go to Gov. Bush, and he will advise his brother," thereby endorsing the objective of the street protesters. Thus, the dissatisfaction among diasporans against the Aristide administration was already substantive and growing. As one report puts it, "since December, Haitians in South Florida have been drumming up support on radio and television stations, and conducting weekly rallies. Some traveled to New York to demonstrate in front of the United Nations on Martin Luther King Jr. Day. . . . The latest protest in South Florida was conducted Friday at the Broward County Federal Courthouse. . . . Three other organizations—Patriots United for democracy in Haiti, PATRI and the Haitian American Republican Caucus—have been organizing demonstrations at the Torch of Freedom in Miami."[10]

"Reserve Army" of Talent

The success of Latortue in repositioning himself as Haitian prime minister from the status of diasporic talk show host underlines the way in which, in the circuits within the diasporic public sphere, the diaspora, in addition to being a source of remittance for the homeland, is also seen as a reservoir of talent to be tapped into in due time. What was new from the Duvalier regime to the Aristide regime was that there came to be more fluidity in the way in which this flow between the country of origin and the diasporans took place. For example, diasporans who were appointed to cabinet and as ambassadors returned, in some cases, to their country of diasporic residence after their terms in office in the homeland.

In the case we have been examining, both the government and the opposition had asked for a neutral prime minister, preferably from the diaspora, to resolve the political stalemate they were in. In an unprecedented move, the American embassy also called for a diasporan to fulfill that role. In his last speech to the Chambre de Commerce Americaine d'Haiti, on July 9, 2003, in Port-au-Prince, U.S. Ambassador Brian Dean Curran encouraged the audience "to seek new leaders, preferably among your qualified professionals (trained in the best American and European universities) to facilitate the emergence of a new generation of politicians and to prepare a better future for your country."[11]

Without the U.S. embassy preparing the way, the choice of a diasporan as prime minister probably would not have happened. Thus we can see that it is not only the Haitian political class that accepts the diaspora as part and parcel of the political process, but also foreign embassies such as those of France and the United States. U.S. embassy officially recognized the transnational character of the Haitian political process, validating and encouraging diasporan participation. In reaching this new threshold, the Haitian political system expressed the coalescence of its two poles, as individual politicians migrated back and forth to unlock the process, to bring new life to it, or to complicate local relations.

Prime Minister Latortue explained how he remained a diasporan, despite his presence in Port-au-Prince to head the government until the next presidential elections was to take place, by making a distinction between his permanent homeland—that is, Haiti—and his permanent home in Florida. He did so to mark a break with the old way of doing things in Haiti and to show that there is a more efficient, more productive, and more rational way of conducting the business of government.

There is much at stake here for diaspora-homeland relations. Latortue's success as prime minister is likely to enhance that relationship, and his failure may negatively affect it. He defines his engagement as a "mission" with the double French meaning of the term: that is, both a short-term project and a specific goal to be attained. Here is how he put it in a response to a question posed by a *New York Times* journalist: "My career is behind me. To me this is like a mission. It is like the UN sent me for two years to do something. This is how I look at it. When it is done, I will go home."[12]

What this latest crisis of the Haitian political system indicates is that the circulation of diasporic leaders or their positions in the transnational circuit can be mapped out and studied. It shows that the diaspora is a niche that occasionally provides the homeland with technicians to staff the ministries and government agencies, with politicians to revamp the system when no insider is found to be adequate for the job of reconciliation of the nation with itself, with diplomats to represent the country in their hostland, with liberation fighters or mercenary soldiers to unseat a legitimate or illegitimate regime, with lobbyists to advance the causes of the government, with analysts to provide policy recommendations to the administration, and with negotiators for conflict resolution between the government and civil society and between the government and entities in the hostland.

In their political engagement with the homeland, diasporic politicians return to the homeland for the duration of their terms in office and relocate to their diasporic residences after they have completed their assignment or after a coup d'état, or reintegrate into the homeland as dediasporized citizens, a status change that is required to occupy certain positions such as running for a parliamentary seat, or conduct their political activities in the hostland, as is the case of the political party Union Nationale des Démocrates Haitiens, headquartered in Miami.

Changes of government in the homeland often bring with them changes in the informal political leadership of the diaspora. This is so because individual partisans of the new regime are called upon to have more visibility in the diasporic community, are endowed with more responsibility to enlarge the basis of support of the government, and are questioned by diasporans to provide the rationale of government policies and practices. The processes of repositioning and circulation in the diasporic public sphere that we have just examined no doubt will continue to underlie these changes.

IT and the Diasporic Public Sphere

The use of information technology has brought a new development in the way in which the Haitian American diaspora sustains, expands, and consolidates the transnational public sphere where its political views are expressed. One may speak of the virtual dimension of the public sphere, which coalesces with both its formal and informal aspects. Information technology complicates our understanding of the working of the public sphere because it provides diverse routes used by the people to communicate among themselves.

The use of IT by the diaspora has evolved over time, going through different phases. For example, during the crisis of the overthrow of the first Aristide government in 1991, the main means of communication of the diaspora were the Haitian American radio and television programs, traditional telephone calls to each other and loved ones in the homeland, Haitian American newspapers, and, before the embargo, audiocassettes in which information and strategies of resistance were exchanged. During the second crisis, in 2004, the use of audiocassettes to communicate with the homeland had disappeared, since there was no fear for censorship. By 2004, Haitian American television and newspapers had become truly transnational, with offices or subsidiaries in Port-au-Prince and a strong readership in both hostland and homeland. In addition, two new modes of communication have been added to the mix: the Internet and the cell phone. I asked a Haitian American cyberactivist who played a leading role in the cyberspatial political debates during the crisis that led to the resignation of Aristide to assess the use of the Internet in the U.S.-based Haitian diaspora. In the following interview, she provides an assessment of the situation:

> Among the most active sites used by the diaspora to discuss Haitian politics during the last crisis are Corbet, Moun, HaitianPolitics, and haitipolicy.org. I work for the Haiti Democracy Project, which curates haitipolicy.org. It was the main reference for people who were seeking up-to-date and accurate information on Haitian politics and the chief opponent to Aristide on the Net. I was in charge of the site, providing information, analyses, and also circulating from time to time statements that came to us from other cybersites. I was responsible for the visit of Mr. Pasquiot, the rector of the State University of Haiti who was beaten up by the Aristide partisans, to Washington D.C. to meet with Noriega and other government officials and to participate in the congressional hearings on the atrocities of the brutal Aristide regime.
>
> I must say that there were many Haitians at home and abroad who participated in these chat-room debates. There was a level of sophistication in their analyses that I had not seen before. It was at a higher level, and people were more politicized, because a lot of those who have

> been involved in these debates wanted Aristide out. These were people who were engaged.
>
> The Internet is everywhere in Haiti. Access is not a problem. The Internet can be accessed in almost every neighborhood in Port-au-Prince. For the sites that I consulted, English was the language used, but from time to time, there were Creole phrases or even long statements or debates in Creole. Not everyone could join these conversations, because most of us cannot write properly in Creole. Government officials did not take part in these online debates, at least they did not identify themselves as such, even though anyone was welcome to participate. However, there were opposing views, individuals who were pro-status quo and others pro-change. I remember having a heated exchange over the net with Ira Kurzban, the main lawyer who lobbied on behalf of Aristide. Of course, there were parallel networks.
>
> There is a multitude of sites that appeared during the Aristide regime. One can think of the consulate and embassy sites, the pro-Aristide NGO Haiti Reborn, which has its own site with the same name. I did not waste my time checking on their Web sites. I was too busy carrying on the banner of the opposition. I limited my time to serious things, and I had no time for junky Lavalas stuff. I had seen Aristide in all of his dimensions.

I also asked the former consul general who served in the consulate in New York City to provide his own assessment of his use of the Internet during the last Haitian crisis:

> I think some people used it during the last crisis, but I would not say that it was the primary means of communication among the political activists. I am somewhat ambivalent about how effective it was. Some people use it, but a lot of people don't—that is the reality. In particular, I used a number of Web sites, I exchanged letters with people, but I do not do chat rooms. I use a variety of Web sites. For commentaries, I use Haiti en Marche; some times I use Véyé-yo. I also use Haiti Progrès, sakapfet.com, metropolehaiti.com and other Haitian Web site outlets maintained by different radio stations throughout the U.S.
>
> There are issues in terms of dissemination of information and exchange of information. I use the Web for that. Just to have sterile discussions—I don't do chat rooms. At the New York consulate there was a Web site. The Web site was very moribund when I got there. I stimulated it, and it did have a lot of information. For example, when the president traveled to New York or elsewhere, I would make sure I had information about the trip and put the information on the Web—whether there were speeches, pictures. Also for example, we would get certain information from the Web site of the Ministry of Information or

> National Palace reporting on an event that has taken place in Haiti—for example, information about the president of a foreign country who visited the country or a major public works project that was completed. So we would go there, and if it were something people in the New York area needed to know, I would put that on my Web site, as well. There was a time when some public housing scheme was built—three thousand units of housing. I thought that was important, and I put that on the Web site.

The use of the Internet has become pervasive as a means for the sustenance of the diasporic public sphere. It was used to communicate with the homeland via e-mail in order to inform about newspaper articles that had appeared in the foreign press that gauge the view of the U.S. government on the crisis. Sometimes the text of the article was sent out as is, other times a French translation was needed and provided. Sometimes research on the Internet had yielded additional information that was pasted in and sent via e-mail or simply posted on a Web site. Much of this kind of research was done in the diaspora and was provided as a service to the homeland. One may even speak of a division of labor whereby the Haitian side did the street protests and the diaspora side did the Internet research, because it was more costly or simply not convenient to do so in Haiti as a result of the constant blackouts experienced by the residents of Port-au-Prince. Some political organizations prepared editorials—a tactic used by most of the political parties—that they posted on their Web sites for everyone to read. Others just used the spam technique to reach their audiences.

From around 6 PM until midnight, participants in various forums or chat rooms that I accessed as a passive onlooker discussed their political views on the nature of the homeland political crisis. Some of the views expressed were pro-Aristide and others anti-Aristide. Some presented constitutional or philosophical arguments, while others documented with plausible information the accomplishments or failings of the government. In analyzing the content of these exchanges, it is difficult to know if the participants were living in the United States or Haiti. I assume that because of the cost of connection in Haiti, more participants from the United States than in Haiti daily took part in these forums.[13] While some of the chat rooms and forums (chat@HaitianConnection, chat@Sakapfet.com, chat@HaitianLink, Brikouri.net, chat@Haitiforum, salon@intervision2000—which refers to itself as the "i-teledyol national" or E-gossip national network—Portail Universitaire Haitien.org, windowsonhaiti.com, and intermediahaiti.com) use either French or English, but from time to time a

Creole speaker intervened to bring a little spice to the conversation with some flowery language in discussing the political crisis.

The Internet was used not only by the politicians and the common people but also by the rebels. The chief of the rebellion, Guy Philippe, said in an interview with a U.S. journalist broadcast on CNN that it was by using the Internet that he learned of or received an order from the U.S. government not to enter Port-au-Prince immediately with his ragtag troops so that further negotiations for Aristide's resignation could be pursued. During the entire ordeal, anti-Aristide individuals sent countless numbers of negative articles (published in European, Canadian, and American mainstream newspapers) to various members of the diaspora to sway their positions on the issue. These messages were sent and distributed through various subscribers' e-mail lists that I had an opportunity to access and read. Other lists sent out both negative and positive opinions expressed by the membership or published in the mainstream press. Cidihca.com belongs to this last category.

During the entire crisis, sakapfet.com, metropolehaiti.com, and the Agence Haitienne de Presse Web site were probably the most popular sites for news on Haiti used by the Haitian American diaspora because they daily updated the news they offered. The Miami-based sakapfet.com was the leader of the pack because it updated its Web site more than once daily and added news items with pictures, when available, as events unfolded in Haiti.

It must be recognized that not all the groups that used computer-mediated communications voiced opinions for or against Aristide. Some entered the debate as objective observers who wanted to provide a way of resolving the contentions between the opposition and the government. The National Organization for the Advancement of Haitians (NOAH), headquartered in the Washington, DC area, posted an open letter to the leaders of Haiti on its Web site on December 29, 2003: "We propose the parties in the current conflict in Haiti engage in a mediation process lasting 30 days using the one-text mediation procedure. If an agreement is not signed within 30 days, we propose that the next step be a binding arbitration process lasting another 15 days. NOAH, for its part, will put together a 12-person group to conduct this mediation and if necessary a binding arbitration."[14] This led to a sharp reply from a Haitian American netizen, who wrote back saying, "how can we be assured that this is not yet another elitist initiative excluding a true representation of the voice of the vast majority of Haitians from the internal affairs of the Republic of Haiti? . . . I do mean to praise you for your sense of citizenship and organizational responsibility, but your present initiative invites a serious analysis of yet another 'democratic' undertaking, amid the graveyard of other failed experiments."[15]

Deposed former President Aristide also made use of IT to speak to his supporters in Haiti and the diaspora and to the world while he enjoyed temporary residence in the Central African Republic. Using a cell phone, he conveyed the following message to a "Haitian journalist in the United States working with a radio station in Berkeley, CA." In this recorded address broadcast on KPFA on Friday, March 5, 2004, he says,

> During the night of the twenty-eighth of February, 2004, there was a coup d'état. One could say that it was a geopolitical kidnapping. I can clearly say that it was terrorism disguised as diplomacy. . . . We know there are people back home who are suffering, who are being killed, who are hiding. But we also know that back home there are people who understand the game, but will not give up because if they give up, instead of finding peace, we will find death. . . . I know it is possible that all Haitians who live in the Tenth Department [the diaspora] understand what tragedy lies hidden under the cover of this coup d'état, under the cover of this kidnapping. I know and they know if we stand in solidarity we will stop the spread of death and we will help life flourish.[16]

Likewise, the cell phone, in the aftermath of the coup, has been the primary mode of international communication for people who live in remote villages in Haiti or who are in hiding. Some use it to report about the postcoup violence in their areas, as happened in the case of the mayor of Milo, a village in northern Haiti, who called a California radio station from his hiding spot to detail the atrocities committed by the rebels. Others use it to inform relatives in Haiti and abroad of their whereabouts. Still others use it to request that Haitian radio stations in New York, Boston, or Miami spread the news. For example,

> Jean Kernazan, a radio producer on Radio Soley in Brooklyn, home to the largest [Haitian] community in the United States, says he's spending hundreds of dollars weekly on calls to cell phones in Haiti. . . . Many callers, from Haiti, in order to save money, place quick calls and ask to be called back. . . ."To put it simply," Kernazan says, "the expense of these phone calls to Haiti is driving me to the poorhouse, but they are worth every penny."[17]

I think that the Internet, with its diverse forums and audiences, has led to a fragmentation or Balkanization of the Haitian American diasporic public sphere while it has also contributed to its globalization. Every evening, diasporic Haitians around the globe using one of these chat rooms discuss and share information on the political direction of the homeland and on other matters as well. There is a new Haitian diasporic political culture that is emerging, a culture that is facilitated by IT and that serves as one of the central mechanisms in the reproduction of the diasporic community.

Digital Communication Hubs

The architecture of this *virtual diasporic public sphere* begins to emerge when we recognize and analyze the existence of digital hubs that serve as the central nodes in its networks. The transformation of certain sites into digital hubs used by less well-known sites, by sites with very limited membership, by partisan sites that belong to political groups, and by other entities tells us much about the centrality of these nodes. These are strategically positioned sites with good reputations in terms of the ability to assess incoming information from less well-known sites for accuracy and appropriateness before it is rerouted through the network. And, of course, they provide a service to the senders and the receivers. For example, cidihca.org and haitipolicy.org function as digital hubs.

Once information reaches these hubs, it may be either discarded or distributed to any of the existing lists or to a newly fabricated list to meet specific needs. The Ministry of Information Web site also functions as a digital hub that distributes information to various audiences. Here information is collected from various cabinet ministries and posted for public consumption and specialized information tailored to meet the needs of government officials including diplomats is packaged and sent out via e-mail.

These digital hubs have a membership or subscribers list that is international, not simply local or national, that is educated and influential, and therefore that is capable of influencing public opinion. At the same time, they enable their users to exploit or access other networks and downgrade or upgrade the circulation of information through sites that users normally do not access.

A digital communication hub is thus a virtual site that is located at the intersection of several networks and that fulfills a double function, filtering information according to its authenticity, accepting some and rejecting some, then relaying the filtered information received from other organizations and individuals to the network it controls. In a similar fashion, it also distributes news from the membership to partner networks. Digital hubs move information in every direction: up from below, down from above, and laterally. They provide members access to other lists and also prevent access if in the judgment of the virtual hub manager the information should not be distributed because of its presumed inaccuracy, because of its partisanship, or because it may undermine a rival structure. Censorship is therefore one of the roles of the hub manager.

The following statements excerpted from two interviews explain the centrality of digital hubs in the distribution of news items during the recent Haitian crisis and how publics that are separated off-line mingle online. A diplomat explains how he was able to receive information from both the government and the opposition on a continuing basis:

> I certainly used the Internet when I was working at the embassy in Paris throughout the recent crisis. Various people e-mailed me all kinds of documents. They came from the Aristide government officials, but also from sources in the opposition. For the most part, these documents were relayed to me by third parties. For example, someone in Washington close to the opposition e-mailed me documents received from the opposition or critical of the government. These documents did not come from the government, but from other sectors, such as the opposition, and contained propositions put forward by the Convergence Démocratique. The Groupe de 184, which knew my e-mail address, also sent me materials. They have their own site. Most of these opposition sites posted materials on their Web sites and sent out documents with alarming news that had nothing to do with reality.
>
> These documents for the most part originated in Haiti and were sent to well-known Haitian sites outside the country for widespread distribution throughout the diaspora. Webmasters in charge of lists that are known to be neutral and objective in their reporting on Haiti received these documents and distributed some of them to their membership.
>
> These e-mails functioned like a laboratory where decisions had to be taken on whether to distribute or not distribute them. I know that within the government, the Ministry of Foreign Affairs and the Ministry of Information sent me via e-mails information and documentation for my diplomatic work. These documents were mostly about recent initiatives of the government concerning, for example, meetings with OAS, negotiations with the opposition, and disinformation put forward by the opposition. That was information for the consumption of the diplomatic corps. Sometimes I was forced to ask the officials in Haiti "What should I say about these allegations by the press or opposition?" For

> me, that was not always a problem. I held the Francophony and UNESCO portfolios. With the UNESCO, I could intervene and dialogue with the delegates. That is, I had an opportunity to provide a reply or correct a misunderstanding. That was not the case with the Francophony portfolio. Access was more restricted with this group, and I knew that they were preparing something against the government. The first international attacks to overthrow the regime came from the Francophony group. They held a meeting in Canada with the participation of France and the U.S., and they agreed to start a movement to overthrow Aristide.

I also asked a manager of a digital hub to provide his assessment to see how he characterized the architecture of the communication network in which he works.

> As a Webmaster for the Cidihca list, I receive daily information from various sources, and I relay them to different people in the Cidihca network. Haitians use the discussion groups as they do with the *telediol* [gossip]. Among the best-known sites used by the community for news and analysis are Dalyvalet, Carlfombrun, renaudbenodin. Many individuals use the internet as a *telediol.* There are several discussions groups, and they circulate their gossip on the Internet. There are a lot of informal groups composed of Haitians on the Net. They literally intoxicate themselves with it. In my case, I select the information before I distribute it to the list, but many use the net as a virtual *telediol.*

What one learns from the use of these digital communications is that the diasporic public sphere is enhanced, expanded, and fragmented by IT—that IT is a mode that facilitates transnational contacts. It provides a central means for the exchange of ideas, for the distribution of political documentation, and for spying on the activities of the opposition or the government. Digital hubs are cornerstones in the deployment of this digital communicational infrastructure.

Diasporic Politics and the Remaking of Homeland Politics

A period of crisis leading to the overthrow or resignation of the government is a privileged moment that exposes the working of diasporic politics' various components, including relations among diasporic actors and with the homeland, the contribution of the diaspora to the unmaking and remaking or reconstituting of the homeland's political system, and the relations of diasporic leaders with hostland politicians. In the Haitian case, the system exploded and reconstituted itself as a result of the diaspora's role, with one of its members called upon to fill the position of prime minister. Yet the political views and practices of the diaspora have a distinct rationale that is different from that of homeland views and practices because of the double loyalty of its actors to both the country of origin and the country of residence.

Regime change in the homeland necessarily brings about change in the composition of the diaspora's political leadership because the same actors are unlikely to reappear with the same access to homeland authorities and to the diplomats who officially represent the country. For example, Aristide's supporters are now in the opposition and no longer enjoy a cozy relationship with the national government. A new set of individuals is now lobbying on behalf of the Latortue government and are invited to attend public events at the embassy or to meet with visiting officials from the homeland. The relationship of these newly constructed leaders seems to result more from friendship and regions of origin in Haiti than from ideology. Diasporan activists from southern Haiti were by and large the most prominent among the Haitian American leadership that supported the Aristide administration.

Regime change also affects the leadership structure of some diasporic NGOs, since some of these leaders may be invited to work for the government at home or abroad. For example, on April 12, 1994, *The Miami Herald* reported that "Rolande Dorancy, a vocal advocate for the rights of Haitians fleeing poverty and political persecution, has resigned as executive director of the Haitian Refugee Center to take a job with President Jean Bertrand Aristide's government in exile." As discussed earlier, the Haitian Community Center in Manhattan was similarly affected during the presidency of Ertha Trouillot when the director was appointed consul general of the Haitian Consulate in New York. The circulation and repositioning of political figures thus continues.

In this process of remaking the homeland government, there is much politicking that goes on in the diaspora to establish contacts with the new leaders, to stake a claim on informally representing the new government abroad, to influence the nomination of diplomats who will serve in the country of residence, to undermine the position of competitors, and to regroup so as to assert one's newly acquired authority. The remaking of the homeland government thus explains the remaking of the diasporic political leadership that is engaged in political activities on behalf of the homeland. However, the portion of the diaspora leadership that is more oriented toward the assimilationist integration of the community may not be directly affected by these changes, but is not likely to be totally immune to the long-term ramifications of such events.

What emerges from the analysis above is that diasporic politics must be distinguished from both homeland and hostland politics, that it adjusts itself to regime change in the homeland, that its identity is constructed out of its interaction with both the homeland and the hostland, that it must be distinguished from the international relations between both or conducted by either the hostland or the homeland, and that it is performed within the context of the diasporic public sphere, which legitimizes its actions.

5

Dediasporization: Homeland and Hostland

The literature on international migration usually identifies three aspects of the phenomenon: (1) *forward motion*, with a focus on its causes and consequences,[1] (2) the *migrants themselves* (settlers, sojourners, refugees, and exiles) and their incorporation in a new social formation, with a focus on the establishment of diasporic communities, transnational spaces, and bipolar identities, and which also addresses the issue of the lack of fit between state and transnation, the expansion of dual citizenship rights, and the remittances that diasporans send to the homeland,[2] and (3) *backward motion*, with a focus on the returnee population and their reincorporation in the sending country.[3] However, little emphasis has been placed on the pluridimensionality of the dediasporization phenomenon. Such an emphasis could serve as a counterweight to broad literature on structural and cultural assimilation.[4]

Of course, assimilation has been used as a frame of analysis more in the study of integration of migrants than in the reincorporation of returnees because researchers tend to assume that the latter is a passing problem unlikely to endure because these individuals are now in their homeland. Although it is important to study the diasporization process to understand the unfolding of immigration, it is as important to understand the dediasporization process, because it too shapes both homeland and hostland policies and because it is an aspect of the globalization process. Because dediasporization can occur in both the sending and the receiving countries, it deserves some attention: it can clarify both homeland and hostland identities, the parameters of diasporic identity, and the making, unmaking, and remaking of returnee identities.

Dediasporization has been defined "as the regrouping or in-gathering of dispersed people . . . when a community returned to its place of origin."[5] This definition emphasizes only one aspect of the process and equates it with physical relocation to the homeland. In this chapter, by contrast, dediasporization is defined as the process by which a diasporic subject either reacquires homeland citizenship by returning to the sending country, effects generational assimilation in the host state, or reinscribes himself or herself in the transnational circuit of the transnation-state. This definition identifies three distinct locales where dediasporization can be effected: the homeland, the hostland, and the translocal arena of the transnation-state. For those who were not born in the homeland, as Nicholas Van Hear states, "return is somewhat of a misnomer."[6] It is not return per se to one's former place of residence, but rather to an ancestral territory.

As we will see, dediasporization for individuals who never gave up their citizenship or acquired a new citizenship usually is a smooth process that requires only one's return to one's homeland as if one has never left it. For those who once held another citizenship, however, states have established formal procedures for dediasporization, which entail a residence period and the recovery of some citizenship rights.

Dediasporization activates a process that entails the participation of three sets of actors to ensure a successful outcome and cannot be assumed to be the work of the diasporan alone. This is so because the individual, the state, and society have distinct roles to play in the deployment of the process, and none of them can assume or ignore the contributions of the others, in the various phases of dediasporization.

The individual must be willing to initiate the process (although as we will also see, there are exceptions to this requirement), and there are multiple reasons for doing so: desire to return to the homeland, generational factors, or the subjective redefinition of oneself through assimilation in the hostland. However, in practice and objectively speaking, a diasporan cannot dediasporize himself or herself without going through formal state procedures to reacquire one's nationality and citizenship. This is why the role of the state is so important in the process.

The state intervenes in the process to assure itself of the eligibility of such a person to reacquire state citizenship, with all of its privileges and obligations. Such mechanisms are often inserted in the constitution or special laws, which provide a frame of reference for this type of legal intervention. States that consider their diasporas still to be citizens have less elaborate procedures to validate one's citizenship after one's return to the homeland. In contrast, states that do not endorse the concept that "once a subject, always a subject" have established more complicated procedures to regain citizenship. Here again, considerations for regaining citizenship vary greatly in relation to residency, the abdication of one's citizenship, and one's legal status upon return (whether it was a personal decision or a prisoner extradition).

The level of citizenship that the state is willing to confer on an individual also varies: full citizenship (Israel), limited citizenship but barred from seeking the office of the presidency (Haiti), the acquisition of nationality but not citizenship (the dual nationality laws of Mexico). The individual may have different reasons for regaining his or her citizenship, but the state follows procedures fixed in law to make a decision on each case. One may assume that not all cases meet the state's test and that not all of the requests are granted or are granted with longer delay in comparison with other cases. This further underlines state importance in the dediasporization process.

The integration of citizens in society also depends on the state's bestowal of legal legitimacy. The consequent recognition of the diasporan by society through social practices glues the system together, and this is perhaps the most difficult test for the diasporan to pass. Chinese have been living in the Caribbean for more than a century, but they are still considered by the locals as foreigners. In many societies, returnees face the same dilemma. Their past experiences abroad as citizens of another country place them in a different category. They are seen as having a different social standing because of their transnational relations and sometimes because of their wealth.

In Haiti, the populace refers to returnees as diasporas, a distinct status that separates them from the rest of society. Likewise, Russian German returnees from Kazakhstan and Uzbekistan have confronted a similar dilemma after they have regained or acquired German citizenship and begun living in Germany. Regina Romhild notes that "in contrast to their official acknowledgement as German citizens with full rights from the day of their arrival onwards they are primarily perceived as Russians in everyday interactions with German and non-German residents."[7] Social recognition may not be crucial once the legal procedure is achieved, but it still marks a distinction between the group and the rest of society. Either because of this unresolved issue or because of the unwillingness of returnees to integrate, dediasporized citizens tend to form their own group, keep in contact with each other, speak a foreign language when they meet, maintain manners they acquired abroad, and sometimes participate in a transnational circuit of parents and friends who live abroad. In Israel, for example, some returnees have gone so far as to form their own political party, as in the case of Israel Beiteiny, which caters to the interests of Israelis of Russian background, and to establish a separate organization, as in the case of the Association of Canadian and American Jews, which celebrates American holidays and serves as an ambassador of goodwill on behalf of these two countries.

In all this, the role of the state is central. Indeed, the identity of the state can be revealed through a focus on whether it allows or prevents dediasporization. Those states that prevent immigrants from being dediasporized tie their citizenship or naturalization to that issue. Unable to become a citizen, the immigrant is forced to remain a diasporan because the conversion or transformation into a *non-other* is not legally possible. So laws against reattainment of full citizenship are also laws of permanent exclusion and diasporization. Here the state intervenes through its legal system to establish a discriminatory system that actively prevents dediasporization. Such a state is inclusionary only at the internal exclusionary level, but is not exclusionary at the macro-inclusionary level. By such a practice a state eliminates the ambiguity of the diasporic identity, for the status is permanent and not transitory.

A preventive policy by the state leads to the establishment of a diaspora zone, and space for the flourishing of diasporic identity. Not only does such a policy reveal the identity of the state, but it also reveals the identity of the diaspora, because this is the result of negotiation between the two entities. Individuals placed in a distinct legal site are called to create their own consciousness from this space. It also places the diaspora in a structural position where it can entertain its relations with the sending state. In other words, the exclusionary policy of the state limits the domain of expansion of the diaspora and its eventual dediasporization through assimilation.

The capacity for dediasporization is not simply a state affair, but falls also under the domain of the individual who must act to pursue this option. The maintenance of a diaspora status depends on the ability of the individual or community to maintain "two types of autonomy": vis-à-vis the hostland, to prevent full assimilation and a lack of cultural specificity, and vis-à-vis the homeland, in order to be able "to freely select its strategies of integration and its own criteria of identification and socialization."[8] Dediasporization implies that the individual or group has foresworn its ability to maintain its distance vis-à-vis these two entities and has lost its active diaspora status. Assimilation, however, does not ipso facto imply dediasporization, because such a status can be in a dormant phase and can be revived in a situation of persecution. The willingness of the individual to participate in such a scheme is essential for the process to be fully realized.

Elected and Appointed Dediasporized Officials in the Homeland Government

Diasporans who return to the homeland and become public officials bring a new dynamic to the functioning of government and create new issues or problems pertaining to the transnational integration of the national political process[9]. It is important to discuss five of these issues in the Haitian political context because of the way in which they change the forms of the everyday contours of national politics: the government placing itself above constitutional norms to accommodate the diasporans; the multinational composition of the legislature and the cabinet made up of dediasporized politicians, with their diverse democratic agendas; the financial advantage of these politicians at the expense of nondiasporan candidates in matters related to electoral campaigns; the extra burden of complying with requests that comes as strings attached to aid from international donors; and the thorny issue of state loyalty.

An interview I had with the former senator Wesner Emmanuel, a member of the Lavalas caucus in the Haitian parliament (Forty-fifth Legislature, 1991–1997) exemplifies the salience of these issues concerning the role of diasporans in homeland politics.

> There were seventeen diasporans out of the twenty-seven seats in the forty fifth legislature from 1991 to 1997 in the senate. There were a large number of them in the chamber of deputies, as well. The reason for this was that to be a candidate, you must have some money. When the diasporans came, it was not the case that they had a lot of money, but they were reputed to have more money than the rest of us because they were from the diaspora, and that yielded the balance to their advantage, and psychologically speaking, this impacted the other candidates. . . .
>
> Since Jean Claude Duvalier, the constitutional principle that prevents foreigners from exerting certain functions in the Haitian government does not apply. Technocrats, like Flambert, coming from the diaspora, who were not at all Haitian, served in the Jean Claude Duvalier Cabinet. This was invoked and spoken about in the political milieu. Frankly, the Jean Claude Duvalier government was made of technocrats recruited from among well-qualified individuals from Europe and North America that were appointed as cabinet ministers. They did not

accomplish much because, despite their good dispositions, the political will to change the system was not there. The government did not perform well.

And since then, different transitional governments have turned this practice into a routine. Aristide systematically gave preference to the diaspora over the locals to serve in the cabinet. I personally think that he was challenging the opposition. One has the impression that it was his personal choice. He openly selected potential candidates from the diaspora to seek parliamentary seats. Several of those he had selected became senators, deputies, or served in the cabinet. Like G . . . , for example, he was a cabinet minister, but he is not even a Haitian.

I have the proof. He came for a visit in Haiti during the Jean Claude administration. I was a teacher. He came to present his geography manual. He had had political problems. That day, he came to attend a meeting at the Ministry of Education. I was there and offered to give him a ride to the house where he was staying, near the Canado school building. That's where he was.

The Canadian embassy intervened on his behalf after he was arrested. Liberated from the jail where he was in custody, he immediately left for Canada. Then he came back to serve as minister of public works. He even wanted to be prime minister. I am telling you that I personally know that he was not Haitian.

The strangest thing is that in the forty-sixth legislature, there was a senator named S . . . , a diasporan from Boston. I believe this is a unique case in the annals of the National Assembly. He left his wife in Boston. He was originally from the Central Plateau and returned to seek a seat in the parliament. When he was elected to the senate after he had run a very successful campaign, his spouse sent his American passport to the president of the senate. At that time, I was the first secretary of the bureau of the senate, and the scandal exploded in our faces. That was, no doubt, a premeditated blow. While we were in a meeting analyzing his dossier, he was there at the upper house scheduled to speak. He was one of the speakers at the tribune, and I listened to all of them. What may seem paradoxical is that when we voted on the issue, there were diasporans like him who voted for his expulsion from the senate. He briefly said, after the vote was over, that he was surprised and shocked and did not understand why the other supposedly dediasporized senators had voted against him. . . .

Legislator Leonard representing Les Cayes came from Venezuela and speaks fluent Spanish; Duly Brutus and Serge Gilles came from France; Renaud Bernardin came from Canada; other senators came from the U.S., Canada, France, Mexico, Venezuela: the senate has become a global body. They came with their societal projects.

I must say that in Haiti, the word "diaspora" is a pejorative term used with a bit of jealousy or envy by the populace, implying that you

> have enriched yourself abroad, and now you come back to the country to show off. When they come from the popular class, they tend to distinguish themselves by their golden chains etc., while the more educated ones are able to mesh easily with the population and are less distinguishable from the people of their class or neighborhood.
>
> When I traveled with them as an official delegation from the parliament, I became aware that Senator X and Y were not Haitian. When we arrived at a U.S. or Canadian airport, these individuals instead of staying with us in the lane for foreigners, they used the lane for U.S. or Canadian citizens!

Dediasporized politicians thus confront a set of issues that are peculiar to this group, and in this sense, they are being held to standards higher than the rest of the population and are placed in a specific category.

With regard to the government placing itself above constitutional norms to accommodate the diasporans, we can note that the question of dediasporization or renationalization was at the center of the constitutional debate in 1987. In the end, dual nationality was rejected, and a new procedure for dediasporization was instituted in the constitution. Constitutionally, the only way a diasporan can be elected to serve in some public offices is through the double process of *dediasporization* and *renationalization*. However, this constitutional norm has not been followed, despite the constraints of the constitution. Instead, extra constitutional policies have been followed for a variety of reasons: to meet donor nations' requirements or expectations, to bring technocrats to run the machinery of government, and as a gesture of goodwill toward the "Tenth Department."

During the Lavalas administration, for example, both President Aristide and President Préval appointed nondediasporized diasporans to cabinet posts. It was known by the populace that these individuals were Canadian or American citizens and continued to pay yearly income tax to the U.S. or Canadian government. The presence of diasporans—dediasporized or not—in the running of the ministries gives a little more confidence to the electorate that the affairs of the nation are in good and competent hands.

Because of the presence of diasporans, the cabinet and the parliament have become global bodies with sets of issues similar to those one ordinarily finds in other multinational workplaces. These are individuals who spent a good portion of their adult life abroad and who returned to the homeland with a vision of democracy attuned to their experience in a certain country, with a network of friends abroad, and with perceptible language problems in some cases. Some speak Spanish with a Mexican or Venezuelan accent, some French with a Canadian or Parisian accent, some English with a New York or Puerto Rican accent. These individuals are sometimes connected, because of their past work, to such multinational bodies as the World Bank, the United Nations, Inter American Bank of Development, OAS, or to U.S. French, or Canadian government or civil institutions. Some earned their cabinet posts because of the politicking of one of these institutions on their behalf or were simply on loan to the Haitian government for a limited period of time. These individuals are nodes of international networks, and their actions must be gauged in the context of these transnational linkages.

The relative wealth of diasporans in respect to local middle-class candidates—wealth accumulated during their years abroad—places them in a more advantageous political situation than their counterparts. In addition to their own savings, these individuals have also the possibility of doing fund-raising abroad. In the past, diasporic candidates for elected offices in Haiti have organized fund-raising events in Boston, Miami, Washington, DC, New York, and Chicago or have asked their collaborators to raise funds on their behalf. One major consequence of this state of affairs is that this extra money frees them from certain vicissitudes to engage in full-time campaigning and certainly makes them more competitive or gives them an edge over other candidates.

For Jacques Despinosse, president of the Haitian American Democratic Club in North Miami, for example, who has received several letters asking for contributions, "these candidates here have an unfair edge over their opponents."[10] In addition to the monetary advantage, they also gain from the ability of Miami or New York endorsers to spread the word on Haitian television and radio programs and among their friends and family members in Haiti. This connection is important not only in the campaign context, but also because it enables them to provide services to their constituencies. For example, cabinet ministers who had lived abroad have tapped into the resources of the diaspora for certain projects or used their networks to access key policy makers in Washington, Paris, or Ottawa. These ediasporized politicians have emerged as the brokers who reinvigorate the Haitian political process and who internationalize the governance of the Haitian economy. Leslie Casimir, who had observed candidates for office in Haiti who have been campaigning and doing fund-raising in the United States, explains how this was carried out in Little Haiti in Miami during the 1995 general elections:

> Creole-language talk show hosts are urging listeners to go back home to vote. They are giving radio air time to candidates who fly weekly to Miami to raise money for their campaigns. Leaflets with the candidates' pictures plaster the walls of Little Haiti businesses.
>
> Primarily, however, the candidates are trolling Little Haiti more for campaign donations than votes. And some Haitians are responding. This weekend, Véyé-Yo, a Miami-based Haitian political group, sponsored a fund-raiser at its office on Northeast 54th Street for the 80 or so candidates running under the banner of Lavalas, which is Aristide's party. By 3 P.M. Sunday, the group had raised $3,000.[11]

A peculiarity of dediasporized technocrats in the homeland government is caused by requests from international donors and lending agencies that include the expectation that their requests will be fulfilled as a requirement for providing aid. These international bodies want to ensure that competent individuals will be in charge and, as we have noted, are sometimes ready to loan individuals to the government. The government in turn wants to project itself as staffed by professionals capable of administering the affairs of the state, while for their part the diasporans join the government to serve the public good.

A major issue here is that such dediasporized technocrats spend an inordinate amount of time doing the paperwork necessary to meet donors' requirements. Managing these ministerial portfolios can itself be a full-time job, since it requires the assessment of progress, the preparation of progress reports, negotiations of new loans and renegotiations of old loans, juggling schedules of repayment, calculation of the payment of interest, and the actual implementation of projects. In the long term, this has the potential to destabilize the government because the management of loans takes precedence over government priorities. Ministers in this environment find themselves navigating between government priorities and international donors' priorities. It is not that these priorities take different directions, but rather, they emphasize different areas: *transparency to insure that the money is appropriated to a specific project and prevent corruption versus performance and results that insure the popularity of the regime.*

Finally, the loyalty question for dediasporized individuals—whether this arises formally or informally—remains a moot point. They remain socially connected to both countries because of the contacts they maintain with friends and associates abroad and because of invitations they may receive from the local embassy to attend holiday events or because of business relations they maintain with the embassy for the purpose of enhancing their entrepreneurial activities. The loyalty question comes to the fore during periods of political turmoil, when such dediasporized individuals seek the protection of the embassy or even return to their former country of residence to wait until things calm down or simply to resume their diasporic life.

At the collapse of the first Aristide administration, for example, most of the dediasporized ministers and government operatives returned to their former country of residence. The same thing was witnessed again when his government was overthrown a second time in 2004. They were back in New York, Miami, Boston, and Montreal, where I was able to interview some of them. Dediasporized individuals not only have an edge over the locals during the electoral campaigns because of their fund-raising abroad and their international contacts, but they also have an edge over the locals in moments of political crisis because they can easily get out of the country on time and thereby protect their life and assets. Therefore, engaging in political activities is more dangerous for the locals than for the dediasporized. The same observation applies to political operatives in civil society who function within nonprofit organizations. They sustain the democratic process at the grassroots level precisely because they are aware of the extra protection provided to them by their external contacts or even the possibility to return to diasporic life if things turn really sour.

By focusing on elected officials in the homeland, one has a better understanding of the set of issues they confront and how these politicians who pretended to dediasporize themselves end up being tentacles of the diaspora. The legal process of dediasporization is not capable of disentangling itself from the transnational social linkage with overseas contacts to produce totally dediasporized citizens. Dediasporization remains legal and partial, since such individuals activate the means of communication and of mobility by which they maintain their connections with the diaspora.

The Materiality of Logistics

The question of dediasporization cannot be understood outside the materiality of the logistic that strains the process itself. This variety of materiality explains the different forms that dediasporization takes in relation to the effect it has on politics. Not all of the dediasporized individuals maintain the same relations with the hostland. Some return, but leave their wife and children behind and continue to commute back and forth from the homeland to the hostland. A few return with their family. Some return with their wife but leave the children behind. Some maintain their primary residence in the hostland and commute to the homeland. Some return, but continue to own a house abroad. Most of those who return have to confront a housing issue in terms of finding an appropriate home for the family, or building a new house, or managing two households at home and abroad and the additional cost involved.

Former Senator Wesner Emmanuel compares the logistics problems of returnees to those of legislators from the countryside who must travel and reside in Port-au-Prince when the Haitian Parliament is in session. According to him,

> The logistics problems that diasporan politicians confront when they are elected or appointed to a public post are similar to those confronted by rural politicians when they are elected to the parliament or selected to serve in the central government. Housing is a problem for both. Long-standing political networks developed over the years in the home district cannot be transplanted to Port-au-Prince. Networks of friends and advisors cannot be transplanted to another locale. However, there is always a parent or relative with whom one can stay. It's simply for the reason of comfort that one may take residence in a hotel. The way in which the government functions, one can easily meet a dignitary from a foreign country in a hotel, in an upper-class restaurant in Petionville, or at the ministry itself. There is always in each ministry an official lounge for official visits to welcome and discuss state affairs with foreign dignitaries and important visitors.

This problem of logistics that diasporan politicians must resolve early on was explained to me by Frantz Voltaire, the chief of staff of Prime Minister Malval:

> I was commuting back and forth between the U.S. and Canada, and I was invited and participated in the negotiations at Governors Island. Robert Malval, whom I had known for many years, had invited me to attend among the collaborators he was going to select. Robert completed high school in the U.S., attended the University of Miami, and ended up at the Ecole des Sciences Politiques in Paris.
>
> Robert and I had a long discussion on whether he should accept the post of Prime Minister after this reality check at Governors Island. He was solicited earlier by Aristide to serve as an intermediary between the president, the bourgeoisie, and the army. We had had discussions in which I thought that he was one of the most appropriate people to

bridge the gaps between the opposite forces in Haiti, being at the same time a man of character, a team player, a straight talker, a businessman, and an intellectual, but someone who also had good contacts with various sectors of the Haitian social milieu.

When the Miami conference took place, he brought several businesspersons with him to meet with Aristide, and tried to establish a mechanism of consultation and dialogue. At this meeting, Aristide proposed him as Prime Minister. He doubted if he should accept the offer or not, but his family did not want him to take the position. He hesitated, believing that he was not the man for the hour. He saw himself more as a broker than as a political figure. And finally we had a long conversation and he said to me, "If I accept the position because of all of this pressure, are you ready to collaborate with me?" I told him that I had been living abroad for many years, and I had teaching obligations at the university and as director of a not-for-profit documentation center. It was true that I could have made myself available, but I was not sure if I was the right person for the occasion.

He replied that the fact that I did not hold a position in the first Aristide administration—even though I was a consultant to the Ministry of Foreign Affairs under Sabalat, who himself was a friend of Malval—was a plus. He said that because of the trust that exists between us and the fact that we have been friends for many years, "I want you to join me in the government." After some thoughtful reflections, I decided to collaborate with him despite all the hesitations I had pertaining to the conditions in which I was going to encounter in Port-au-Prince.

Effectively in terms of logistics, I had had the habit, since 1986, of traveling regularly to Haiti. I had an apartment in Port-au-Prince. I could, in principle, use this loft, but Robert had made different arrangements for my accommodations. He told me that, given the fact that the government would be there only for a few months, the intensity of the work to be done, and the security problem, he had prepared an apartment for me in his house, since we were called on to work for nineteen hours per day and both my wife and children are abroad. This arrangement freed me from certain household constraints and protected me from some local pressure.

We agreed ahead of time that we would not live in and use the National Palace because symbolically, we did not want to be under the control of the military guards. Instead, staying and working in his house—which became the official office of the Prime Minister and his staff—gave us more autonomy of action and made us less dependent on the armed forces.

I had new networks of contacts in place, since I had a double role to fulfill: I was the director of the cabinet of the Prime Minister in the absence of the president-in-exile and the intermediary between the ministers, and I was the spokesperson for the government. I was the spokesperson who gave press conferences and who publicly intervened to manage disagreements between various factions of the fragile coalition.

Among the diasporans who held cabinet posts during the Malval administration was Ti-Loulou Déjoie, who came from Puerto Rico. His wife and children were living abroad. Effectively, politicians in this situation maintain a different rapport with the country—that is, these are individuals who did not have to worry about the locals pressuring their wives and who have no household economies to manage on a daily basis. Berry was in the same predicament: his wife lived in Canada.

Claudette Werleigh and her husband had returned to live in Haiti in the 1970s. Herve Dennis had been living in Paris, Belgium, and Denmark. Since Denmark, he had been living in Haiti since the late 1970s. Malary had studied in the U.S. and had previously returned to practice law in Haiti.

On the dediasporization question, it is a legal problem in Haiti, since certain functions require Haitian nationality. I did not have such a problem, since the position I occupied does not require one to hold Haitian nationality. This is why I did not change my citizenship status.

In my case, since I needed to move around in my capacity as an intermediary, I maintained contacts with Montreal, with the people at the documentation center, and with those who were attentive to what was going on in Haiti. I maintained contacts with the Haitian Canadian diaspora in a permanent fashion. When I traveled to Québec, I met with various people and groups to give them a briefing of the political situation. I gave them my interpretation of things. I must add that whenever the crisis reached a peak, I was interviewed, and the mainstream Canadian press published reports on my activities. I think they were more than thirty journal articles on me. They presented Frantz Voltaire, who had left Canada to help manage the affairs of Haiti. In fact, I benefited from a kind of implicit solidarity with the mainstream Canadian media. Everything that I said in these interviews that was published in the mainstream Canadian press benefited the government that I served.

On several occasions, during periods of acute crisis, the Canadian embassy had offered me hospitality at the home of the first secretary of the embassy. Here again, I must say that financial aid from the Canadian embassy had allowed the prime minister's office—when we had little resources—to continue to pay our staff and to function as the central office of the government. It was neither the French nor the Americans who came to rescue us, but the Canadians, who financed a number of logistic solutions so that our secretarial staff could function without interruption.

The dual citizenship issue that would allow a diasporan who does not want to forgo his Canadian or American citizenship to become eligible for certain posts is a controversial proposition. People simultaneously have strong opinions on both sides. Given the instability of the political system, giving up one's citizenship requires a good deal of soul searching, a move most people are not ready to make because of the risks involved. Resigning one's position abroad in order to fill a transitional position in Haiti is another risky move. Here is how a female diasporan who returned to Haiti to serve as a Haitian government employee in the National Palace, but now lives in Washington, DC, puts it:

> Some of the diasporans do resign their positions before serving as an official of the Haitian government. I resigned my position. But it depends on what kind of position they held in the U.S. before they went. I did it, but I did not have to. I did it because I had another commitment. Given the history of what has happened, I would not advise anyone to do this, because after my last experience, I will never work for the Haitian government, even if I were friendly with anyone. I learned my lesson, although Malval and Smark Michel are people of the word. If you are contracted by the OAS, UNDP, for example, anyone can sabotage you and make you lose your job overnight. When it comes time to renew the contract, they can decrease the amount you are paid without you knowing about it, without any respect for the terms of the contract. They simply lower your wages so that they can get more people in there. So you see, they don't respect any norms.

Diasporic participation at the cabinet level thus brings its own set of issues. It provides an international team of individuals who have diverse democratic experiences, but who are sometimes not attuned to local realities and whose different efforts to position themselves make them difficult to manage because of the competition among ministries. The diasporic presence at the ministerial level substantively changes the traditional rules of the game. Traditionally, cabinet ministers in Haiti used to be friends who became ministerial colleagues. Now—since some come from abroad—they are ministerial colleagues who may or may not become friends.

The Haitian Case in Comparative Perspective

Haiti has established a formal procedure for the dediasporization of returnees and the naturalization of aliens, as we have previously noted. The procedure to regain one's prior status as a citizen of Haiti is a matter of law and is inscribed in the constitution of 1987. The three pertinent clauses read as follows:

> Art. 12–1: After five years of continuous residence in the territory of the Republic, any foreigner may obtain Haitian nationality by naturalization.
>
> Art. 12–2: Haitians by naturalization shall be allowed to exercise the right to vote, but must wait five years after the date of their naturalization to be eligible to hold public office other than those reserved by the constitution and by law for native-born Haitians.
>
> Art. 15: Dual Haitian and foreign nationality is in no case permitted.

Returnees who hold an American or any other type of citizenship are considered aliens by the Haitian government until they satisfy the conditions set out above. These clauses were discussed and inserted in the constitution at a time when Haitian Americans were returning to the homeland in large numbers after the fall of the Duvalier dynasty to seek elective political office and were barred as aliens from doing so.

Dediasporization in this case is a slow process that entails a waiting time of about ten years before an individual can be totally integrated into the polity. Here again, dediasporization is not total but partial. A returnee who has acquired another citizenship can under no circumstances be elected or selected to serve as president of the republic or prime minister, even after he or she has regained Haitian nationality.

Legal dediasporization is a formal process, but it does not necessarily affect one's attachment to the former host country. In fact, returnees establish separate communities, speak English among themselves, celebrate American holidays, serve as ambassadors of goodwill explaining American practices and customs to others, and maintain contact with friends and family in the United States through the telephone, e-mail, or periodic visits.

The identity of the state is also revealed as it develops or fails to develop policies pertaining to the dediasporization of returnees. When migrants return to their homeland, they cannot dediasporize themselves by their own will. State intervention is necessary to spell out how this can be done and the conditions under which *total dediasporization* is possible or not allowed. In doing so, the state determines how malleable its citizenship boundaries are. Some states permit only *partial dediasporization* by allowing individuals to own property, but they are not allowed to seek some political offices, such as the presidency, for example, or to vote in legislative and presidential elections.

Countries have advanced various reasons why a diasporan may not be permitted to achieve complete dediasporization, often because of the presumed double allegiance of such persons and for national security reasons.[12] Some allow them to vote at the legislative, but not at the national level. Other countries such as France go to the other extreme by indicating after which generation the descendant of an immigrant is no longer a citizen. In the first scenario, the state establishes the rules for dediasporization or prevents it from happening completely. In the other scenarios, the state never recognizes the loss of citizenship and reentry is considered purely a matter of procedure. If diasporans are still citizens of the homeland, their right to vote from abroad is upheld.

Dediasporization presents itself in various ways, depending upon whether the initiative comes from the diasporic community, the sending state, or the receiving state. Each type has its own logic and each affects the diaspora differently. For example, the diaspora develops an internal policy to dediasporize itself as it seeks to cut its ties from the homeland or to return there. Diverse routes are followed to accomplish this goal, and the reasons for so doing may vary from one individual to another, from one contingent to another, or from one period to another. What we want to stress here is that the initiative is developed by the diasporic community.

The receiving state intervenes in the dediasporization process either by implementing its assimilation policy so as to integrate the group into society by preventing it from entering or resettling definitively in its country of adoption or, if they are already in the country, by inviting them to leave voluntarily through the enactment of a repatriation act or by expelling them from the country, as in the case of Indians in Uganda during the İdi Amin regime or in the case of Jews in Nazi Germany. These are external acts by which the receiving state attempts to dediasporize the group either by way of complete integration or by expulsion.

The sending state may develop a repatriation policy to encourage or even to facilitate the return of diasporans to the homeland. This often happens after a diaspora is harassed or persecuted by the receiving state, especially if it refuses to allow the diaspora permanent status or legal entry into the country. Under pressure from the international community and as a result of public embarrassment at home, the government of the sending state may end the crisis by welcoming the refugees back home. Such repatriation schemes involve the return of the population to the homeland, but here, dediasporization is more of a politics of relocation than of renaturalization if repatriated individuals are denied the legal right to seek the office of the presidency or other high offices because they have given up that right by accepting citizenship in another state.

The most recent form of dediasporization is a much more radical project than previous forms. It concerns individuals who have placed themselves between the diaspora, to which they no longer want to belong, and the mainstream, which does not provide them with full membership. It is neither assimilation nor relocation. It does not entail relocation to the homeland, and neither those who seek this form of dediasporization condition nor those in the mainstream consider it as full assimilation. This form of dediasporization is essentially a subjective condition, rather than an objective one. It is a deliberate and rational choice of an identity made by diasporans in order to hide or eliminate their foreignness or their diasporan identity. Members of this group want to cut its ties with the homeland, seeing this strategy as a springboard for success in the hostland. This is achieved by marrying out, speaking an unaccented English, and cutting ties with the homeland or even with groups that continue to celebrate their ties to the homeland.

To this subjective type of dediasporization, one must oppose the two prevalent types of objective dediasporization: the renaturalized diaspora, in which diasporans regain complete state citizenship, and the dediasporized diaspora, in which the diasporans achieve transnational citizenship. The first entails the return to the homeland, but the other does not. However, both involve regaining full citizenship rights in the homeland and the ability to participate fully in its public life: representation in parliament and access to public offices in the legislative, judicial, and executive branches. While the renaturalized diaspora is waging a local battle for inclusion, the dediasporized diaspora is engaged in a transnational battle because working to be able to exert their homeland rights of citizenship while they are living abroad and as citizens of another country. It dislocates citizenship rights from within the nation-state and relocates it inside the transnation-state. However, the ability to exert rights outside the legal boundaries of the state creates problems of jurisdiction and taxation. In this scheme, there would be representation without taxation, because the state may not be in a position to enforce its laws on those who live outside its legal boundaries.

Because of different state policies vis-à-vis their diaspora, these objective types of dediasporization take various forms. One must distinguish the states that allow dual citizenship from those that do not and also from those that allow the second and third generations to maintain homeland citizenship even if they were born abroad. In the dual citizenship regime, dediasporization is linked to or a factor of location. Returning to the homeland effects it, since one never loses one's citizenship. The result is the coexistence of two citizenships, each linked to a location. The state that does not allow the loss of one's citizenship because of migration dediasporizes its returnees as a matter of procedure. In both cases, dediasporization is theoretically total and complete, partly because citizenship was never forfeited. The more complicated process occurs in the states that do not allow more than one citizenship and that exclude from membership those who acquire citizenship in another state.

Dual Nationality versus Dual Citizenship

The dediasporization process thus involves different mechanisms in polities that recognize dual citizenship and/or dual nationality. For many years, dual citizenship was anathema for most countries because of the dual loyalty it implies, even though the sphere of state's influence over such individuals was territorialized. However, the resentment was felt equally by the sending state that provided services without being able to collect taxes from such individuals and by the receiving states that were fearful of fifth columns in their midst. Since the collapse of the Soviet Bloc, several countries have revisited their dual citizenship and nationality laws and have moved to amend them. Israel did so two years after its inception as a state.

The Israeli Law of Return of 1950, with consecutive amendments in 1954 and 1970, is perhaps the most generous and liberal dediasporization mechanism because it automatically grants citizenship to the Jewish returnee. However, such a privilege is not extended to those who are engaged in activities "against the Jewish people," those who are "likely to endanger public health or the security of the state," or those "with a criminal past." Article 1 of the Law of Return says, "Every Jew has the right to come to this country as an *oleh* immigrant." The amendments of 1970 grant this right to members of the extended family. Article 4A(a) of this amendment reads, "The rights of the Jew under this Law and the rights of an *oleh* under the Nationality Law, 5712–1952, as well as the rights of an *oleh* under any other enactment, are also vested in a child and a grandchild of a Jew, the spouse of a Jew, the spouse of a child of a Jew and the spouse of a grandchild of a Jew, except for a person who has been a Jew and has voluntarily changed his religion."

The major stumbling bloc in the application of such a dediasporization scheme came about with the controversy over the definition of Jewish identity: "Who is a Jew?" The matter was supposedly settled with Article 4B of the 1970 amendment, which reads "For the purpose of the Law, 'Jew' means a person who was born of a Jewish mother or has become converted to Judaism and who is not a member of another religion." Jews from the Left and the Right have found cause to challenge this definition, which they find either too liberal or too restrictive.

Dediasporization in the case of the reunification of two territories is not a uniform process because there are diverse ways this is undertaken. The reunification of East and West Germany provides one model, while the reunification of Hong Kong with China on July 1, 1997, provides another. In the German case, there was complete integration under a unitary state, while in the Hong Kong case, there were special provisions made under the principle "One country, two systems" to allow those who wanted to hold Chinese citizenship and those who preferred British special status to make their choice before the handover of Hong Kong by the British:

> All persons who on 30 June 1997 are, by virtue of a connection with Hong Kong, British Dependent Territories Citizens (BDTCs) under the law in force in the United Kingdom will cease to be BDTCs with effect from 1 July 1997, but will be eligible to retain an appropriate status which, without conferring the right of abode in the United Kingdom, will entitle them to continue to use passports issued by the Government of the United Kingdom. This status will be acquired by such persons only if they hold or are included in such a British passport issued before 1 July 1997, except that eligible persons born on or after 1 January 1997 but before 1 July 1997 may obtain or be included in such a passport up to 31 December 1997.[13]

The act of dediasporization through reunification in both cases is also an act of diasporization. It diasporizes some and dediasporizes others who have or may request a British passport or Chinese citizenship, in the case of foreigners. While the Sino-British Joint Declaration on the Question of Hong Kong establishes the legal framework and parameters for the reunification, the Basic Law of the Hong Kong Special Administrative Regime of the People's Republic of China addresses the question of the boundaries of citizenship for Hong Kong residents. Article 24 of the Basic Law stipulates the following:

> The permanent residents of the Hong Kong Special Administrative Region shall be:
> 1) Chinese Citizens born in Hong Kong before or after the establishment of the Hong Kong Special Administrative region;
> 2) Chinese citizens who have ordinarily resided in Hong Kong for a continuous period of not less than seven years before or after the establishment of the Hong Kong Special Administrative Region;
> 3) Persons of Chinese nationality born outside Hong Kong of those residents listed in categories 1 and 2;
> 4) Persons not of Chinese nationality who have entered Hong Kong with valid travel documents, have ordinarily resided in Hong Kong for a continuous period of not less than seven years and have taken Hong Kong as their place of permanent residence before or after the establishment of the Hong Kong Special Administrative Region;
> 5) Persons under 21 years of age born in Hong Kong of those residents listed in category 4 before or after the establishment of the Hong Kong Special Administrative Region;
> 6) Persons other than those residents listed in categories 1 to 5, who, before the establishment of the Hong Kong Special Administrative region, had the right of abode in Hong Kong only.
>
> In its Article 26, it further stipulates that "Permanent residents of the Hong Kong Special Administrative Region shall have the right to vote and the right to stand for election in accordance with law."

The acquisition of Chinese citizenship through the reunification scheme also prevents one from upholding dual nationality status. Under Article 3 of the Nationality Law of the People's Republic of China of 1980, one reads, "The people's Republic of China does not recognize dual nationality for any Chinese national."

Dediasporization in the German case was immediate and total because the two countries were able to negotiate their unification directly, without using a third party that was also negotiating its exit. In contrast, in the Hong Kong case, the British government negotiated both the unification of Hong Kong with China and its own exit from Hong Kong.

The Mexican model is still different from the other two cases. It provides to its diaspora dual nationality but not dual citizenship.[14] Although Mexican dual nationals may buy and sell land, inherit property, and invest in Mexico with the same privileges extended to Mexican citizens, they are prohibited from holding political office and from voting in general presidential elections.[15] In other words, as S. Mara

Perez Godoy puts it, "while nationality has officially transcended geo-political national boundaries, citizenship has not yet been legally expanded."[16] This is a very delimited type of dediasporization.

Dual nationality is one area in which the process of dediasporization becomes more complex, especially in the case of children born with two nationalities. Peter J. Spiro explains the four routes that may lead to this outcome:

> [H]istorically the largest number has resulted from the interplay of different birthright nationality laws under which citizenship at birth can be ascribed both by location (the rule of *jus soli*) and by parentage (*jus sanguinis*), so that the child born in one nation to a parent holding citizenship in another nation will hold both nationalities at birth. . . . Second, dual nationality has more recently also resulted from the marriage of persons with different nationality. . . . The children of these unions will often be entitled . . . to the nationalities of both parents. . . . Third, a native-born American citizen will become a dual national if he or she naturalizes in another country. . . . Finally, dual nationality in the U.S. context also arises where a foreign national naturalizes here but retains his or her original nationality.[17]

The physical return to one's ancestral homeland may not be sufficient to dediasporize a person because it may not be the place where one was born.

These cases highlight the ways in which dediasporization has its own set of politics, is handled differently depending on the country and the circumstances, and depends on a variable set of factors.

Typology of Dediasporization Practices

Dediasporization practices have taken various forms, and it is important to analyze some of them in order to understand the backward process of transnational migration and the limits of diasporization. An unusual form of dediasporization is proposed in the ideology of Zionism, which repositions the diasporic Jew inside a religious framework different from the categories of the nation-state. Zionism provided to the diasporic Jew a new meaning, a new sense of direction, and a new experience. As Aron Rodrigue puts it, "Zionism, a strategy of exit as well as a mimesis of the western model, emerged as a powerful response to the Jewish diasporic predicament in the age of the nation-state. Zionism attempted to 'naturalize' the Jew by negating and abolishing the Diaspora."[18] This strategy of exit by which a subjective form of dediasporization is effected while one is still in a physical and tangible condition of diaspora would give way to an ultimate form of dediasporization with the creation of the state of Israel. As Daphna Golan puts it, "the ideology of the new state was based on the negation of exile."[19] With Zionism, the Jew negates the status imposed on the community and forges a transnational and global community status. In other words, Zionism unites the disparate diasporas and transforms them into a global nation located across the boundaries of nation-states.

The reclaiming of the homeland and its institutionalization into a nation-state is an extreme form of dediasporization, and it is also an act of self-affirmation. It redefines one's identity and sets the conditions under which that identity can express itself. We may identify this as the *self-dediasporization model* and contrast it with the *reincorporationist dediasporization model.* In the latter model, the diasporan returns home and must confront the state, which may or may not allow them complete dediasporization. He or she applies for membership to regain citizenship rights, which cannot be regained by will and strength, but only by following a set of legal procedures. In other words, the diasporan reenters a social formation that already has in place its dediasporization rules. This entails some negotiation, the promulgation of new laws, or the reinterpretation of old laws.

Because the diasporan is dediasporized by an external body, according to a set of laws, reincorporationist dediasporization may be severely circumscribed. Individuals sent to the homeland by the receiving country after they have been convicted for their criminal practices or records do not willingly want to go back home because, as criminals or ex-cons, they are not welcome, and the country is unwilling to reincorporate them with full citizenship rights. They are often placed in jail or under surveillance upon their arrival and are relinquished to the population when they are deemed to be worthy to do so only as second-class citizens unable to seek higher political office. Dediasporization in such cases may be said to be aborted because it is achieved by relocation, but does not result in regaining the full legal rights of citizenship.

In the self-dediasporization model, however, the diasporan does not confront the state, but participates in it. Diasporans return to the ancestral territory, establish a new state, and create the laws and conditions that dediasporize them. Thus, the returnees of the Jewish Diaspora dediasporized themselves with the formation of the state of Israel. They went further by placing all Jews wherever they may live in a state of latent dediasporization with the Israeli Law of Return. For Golan, "the Israeli Law of Return embodies the notion that Israel is not only a Jewish state, but also the state of all Jews the world over."[20] One may speak then of dediasporization in terms of reversibility. In that vein, Kenneth Surin speaks of "the dispersal of the Jewish people and that dispersal's 'reversal' in the creation of the state of Israel."[21]

The most common type of dediasporization is voluntary return undertaken by individuals for personal reasons (unemployment, marital considerations, the education of children, business ventures, or retirement). Dediasporization is also undertaken by the receiving country, often with little regard for the welfare of individuals (such a repatriation scheme creates a crisis-management problem for the sending country, negatively affects its reputation, and engenders public humiliation for the forced returnees). It also may be undertaken by the sending country in need of expertise, which may solicit diasporans and facilitate their return. Such repatriation may be done by steps or abruptly as people well in advance prepare their eventual return.

Until the mid-twentieth century, the *assimilationist dediasporization* model was the main strategy used to achieve dediasporization. State-centered and individual-centered approaches are two distinct trajectories of assimilation that must be distinguished from each other. In the state-centered approach, assimilation is pursued to prevent the fragmentation of the state, avoid social conflict, and solve problems related to the diasporans' lack of integration into the host society. More often, it is done to prevent the rise of a state within a state. The principal concern here is the issue of integration.

In the individual-centered approach, the initiative is taken by the diasporans to forsake their identity for the benefit of acquiring a new identity, to erase cultural difference, and to acquire a new group consciousness, that of the state of adoption. Robin Cohen notes that "many members of a particular ethnic group may intend to and be able to merge into the crowd, lose their prior identity and achieve individualized forms of social mobility. (The changing of ethnically identifiable names by new immigrants signals this intention.)" For him, without a "strong tie to the past or a block to assimilation," dediasporization is likely to occur.[22]

Generational dediasporization evokes the passing of time and is an older form that occurs after a group has lived for many years in a foreign territory. With time and after some generations have succeeded each other, they end up cutting their emotional ties with their family's original homeland and adopt the new territory as their homeland precisely because they were born and live there. This formal choice is sometimes made after a change of status of the homeland from colony to independence or commonwealth status, when people are given an opportunity either to reincorporate with the ancestral homeland or to continue business as usual. It may take several generations before such a dediasporization will occur, and it can be an individual or group phenomenon. Alain Touraine explains such a choice in terms of socialization, identifying it with the third generation as Gordon did earlier in the development of his theory of assimilation.[23]

One must distinguish the legal aspects of both assimilationist and generational dediasporization from the emotional aspects. The emotional aspect—family, history, and so on—may remain for sentimental reasons long after one has cut legally one's ties to the homeland. A diasporan may assimilate, but may still have family left behind and therefore is not emotionally detached from the motherland. Likewise the third-generation emigrant from France who was born and lives in his native country for his entire life has little to do emotionally with the country of his grandfather, yet he is legally a French citizen. In the eyes of French law, he has remained a French citizen without perhaps being aware of it.

Annexationist dediasporization by the state occurs when it annexes territories where its diasporans live. By annexing surrounding territories, the Soviet Union dediasporized Russian diasporic communities. However, with the collapse of the Soviet Union, these communities became once again diasporas.[24] In commenting on the situation of Russians in Estonia and Latvia, Graham Smith argues that "the ethnic patron attempts to 'diasporize' the Russians and the West seeks to secure individual liberties through homeland-citizenship and 'dediasporization,' while the nationalizing regimes envisage a homeland-nation in which there is no space for diasporic identities."[25]

Reunificationist dediasporization occurs when the homeland and the diasporic site become once again part of the same country at the end of the contractual arrangement that leased such a territory and legal control over it to a third party or when a secessionist territory is reattached to the homeland.[26] The return of Hong Kong by the British to the People's Republic of China in 1997 is an exemplary form of the former, while the return of Taiwan to China, if it happens, or perhaps as it will eventually happen, will constitute another form of reunificationist dediasporization.

Transnational dediasporization occurs when the homeland redefines itself as a transnation and sees the diaspora as a constitutive element of its makeup. With the transnational identity of the nation-state, the diaspora becomes a dediasporized diaspora because it is no longer a diaspora vis-à-vis a homeland, since it is reconstructed as part of the homeland. We have seen that in the case of Russians in the Baltic states who became part of the Soviet Union and thereby a dediasporized diaspora. But with the collapse of the Soviet Union, they have regained their diaspora status. It is thus important to factor in time because of the changing political conditions of the state. Time also plays a role in the subjective makeup of the dediasporized identity because some may identify with the homeland when they agree with the government policies and withdraw their identification when they are in disagreement with the government or the general orientation of the country.

Contractual dediasporization is the phenomenon by which temporary or guest workers under state agreement with a foreign country are welcome as guests for a specified period and to undertake specific tasks. It is understood by both sides that at the end of the specified period they will voluntarily return home and thereby dediasporize themselves as part of a routine course of action. As Despina Sakka et al. put it, "the notion of return had been included in the initial migration plan."[27] In this scheme, diasporization and dediasporization are conceived as part of the same process of a state-induced migration project.

Hybrid dediasporization refers to a condition whereby dediasporization is partial or exists side by side with diasporization. One may think of the way the state of Israel defines itself as a Jewish state, thereby encompassing Jewish people wherever they live, or of the way Germany that assigns citizenship rights through blood or descent and not in terms of territorial residence, thereby making German citizenship accessible to anyone with German blood, wherever they may live.[28]

Regaining Lost Status

Dediasporization forces us to think about how identity is shaped by residence: new identities result from migration and diasporization and dediasporization. If rights can be decoupled from identities as Yasemin Soysal suggests, one may ask can they then be recoupled by return migration?[29] Status and identity refer to different conceptual domains.

Status change means that one cannot regain it once the border has been crossed. A single person once married acquires a different legal status in society, and that person cannot fully regain the same social status he or she once had. Divorce returns that person to a different status. In instances, however, the regaining of the former status is possible. For example, a young man who joins the military changes his status from civilian to military, but after retirement, he regains his full civilian social status with all the rights and privileges. In some cases, the social status is even enhanced. Where does dediasporization fit in this scheme of things?

The two examples above involve two actors: the individual and the state. The question of status is thus resolved within the confines of the nation-state. In contrast, in the case of dediasporization, three actors are interpellated: the individual citizen, the hostland, and the homeland. Each constructs status change and status reversal from a different perspective, and each makes claims that may undermine claims made by the other actors.

Helmuth Berking has recently suggested that diasporic identity is constructed from above by the hostland, which projects a policy vision vis-à-vis these others, who remain such after many generations in the country.[30] The mainstream develops its own narrative as to who the natives and outsiders are. The regime of dediasporization that they deploy is supposed to benefit the state and serve the common good of the nation. Diasporic identity is constructed internally to respond to diaspora needs to adapt to their new conditions, to the homeland and the hostland. The regime deployed here is supposed to benefit the diasporic community and serve the common good of the hostland and the homeland. Diasporic identity is transnationally constructed by the homeland to make claims on the diaspora for the benefit of the homeland and the diaspora.

What distinguishes the dediasporization process from the other types of status reversal is that in the previous examples, regaining the lost status or identity means a motion inside the nation-state, while here it means a motion from the transnational to the national and therefore brings another country and a displaced population into the process.

The dediasporization process may be complete according to the norms of one sector/actor and not the others. Regaining a previous status may not be possible—especially in the case of the state that does not allow a returnee to seek higher political offices. Once the status is lost, not all privileges can be regained. Dediasporization still places the citizen in a different category—a citizenship that has most of the characteristics of the regular citizen, but also some aspects of diaspora status and identity. Dediasporization resembles more the divorcee case than the military case, that is, it implies a third status.

Typology of Rediasporization Practices

Dediasporization may not be the permanent state of a diasporic individual. It may be succeeded by rediasporization. Rediasporization refers to two different processes: the relocation of the group to another diasporic site, or the new diasporization of a dediasporized group. With regard to the first, Van Hear speaks of rediasporization as "when a migrant community was . . . further dispersed."[31] Rediasporization, in its other meaning, implies prior dediasporization. One cannot be rediasporized unless one was dediasporized at one time. Rediasporization may be voluntary or involuntary, self-initiated or imposed by an external entity. It is self-initiated when an individual decides to emigrate once more from his or her homeland. It is imposed when an individual is forced to leave his or her country and to enter once more the diasporic condition.

Those who return home and reclaim their homeland citizenship may eventually emigrate from the homeland for political, economic, or personal reasons. Sometimes they find that although they thought that they could reintegrate with the homeland society, they would be better off in the diaspora. Sometimes political circumstances such as a revolution force them to seek asylum elsewhere. Other times, unable to find employment or because of pressure from their diasporic children, they end up reemigrating to their former diasporic sites. All of these examples illustrate the diaspora-dediaspora-rediaspora scheme as it is experienced in everyday life.

Rediasporization may also occur without an intervening relocation to the homeland. Often individuals choose to rediasporize themselves inside another diasporic group. This is carried out to hide from harassment and to escape what one perceives to be the negative characteristics of one's own group. For example, to prevent deportation to the Dominican Republic, sometimes Dominican immigrants in New York identify themselves as Puerto Ricans. Also, a wife may convert her identity into that of her husband's group if that is perceived to be more beneficial for her pursuits. This is clearly a deliberate choice, no matter what the reason is or the consequences might be. For others, this rediasporized identity is imposed by the state. This can be seen, for example, in the census when individuals are assigned to a specific group identity irrespective of the birth place or the objective identity of the individual. For example, in the United States, Jamaicans are placed in the Afro-American category even though some of them do not identify themselves as such. So the voluntary rediasporization follows a logic different from the involuntary type.

A singular feature of rediasporization occurs in the case of assimilationist and generational dediasporization and does not require relocation or may not even come from homeland initiatives or events. For example, emigrants from the homeland may revive the diasporic consciousness of individuals who have long been assimilated into the culture of the host country. Arab immigrants have in the past revived traditional practices of Islam in Dearborn, Michigan among those who were assimilated.[32] Michel Wieviorka has reported how Jewish immigrants from Poland, Romania, Lithuania, and Russia have revived diasporic Jewish consciousness among those long established in France.[33] Events in the hostland may also lead to the revitalization of diasporic consciousness, as happened with the persecution of Jews in France during the Vichy regime.

Rediasporization is always a possibility. For some, dediasporization is a slow process that begins with spatial dediasporization: individuals who return home, but are not willing to reacquire homeland citizenship because they want to reassure themselves that this is the right choice for them. They may decide it is not. Spatial dediasporization thus may lead to a return to diasporic status, especially if the conditions for homeland living do not meet an individual's criteria.

Assimilation, Integration, and Transnational Rediasporization

Stanley J. Tambiah establishes that diasporas interact not just with the host community and the country of origin, but also with other diasporic sites. He argues that they follow three processes of incorporation: "assimilation, exclusion, and integration," adding a fourth, "multiculturalism," which he considers to be a subset of integration because it implies the right to difference.[34] In fact, assimilation or integration, full or partial, with homeland or hostland, entails more than just the incorporation of the diaspora within a given state.

I mention these processes again here in the context of rediasporization because I want to emphasize that often incorporation—or rather, reincorporation—occurs not only within the confines of a nation-state, but also inside transnational diasporic circuits, a process that is difficult for the nation-state to thwart. Former diasporans can be reincorporated into the transnational diaspora. Dediasporized individuals thus can simultaneously be rediasporized individuals. While the relations with the homeland tend to be between center and periphery, that asymmetry is lost in the transnational relations between present and former diasporans. These are relations among equals.

Conclusion

If transnationality unsettles the notion of a nation-state as a bounded entity, it also unsettles the notion of a diaspora, because diaspora is a diaspora of a nation-state or a bounded unit. Therefore, in the new regime of transnationality, dediasporization has to be reproblematized as well.

Physical dediasporization implies return to the homeland, but not disengagement or disentanglement from the transnational circuit. Returnees continue to be part of that circuit because of social relations established while abroad. This explains why the returnees are in a distinct category, socially speaking, but also explains why the locals continue to see them as the others.

Complete dediasporization requires two different kinds of exit: exit from the hostland and exit from the diasporic circuit. The first is physical and is achieved when one regains one's place of birth or the homeland. The other, however, is social and requires the abandonment of the diasporic circuit for the construction of a different type of locally dominated set of social relations.

Transnationality complicates the dediasporization process because it makes it more difficult to achieve. Although physical return to the homeland is possible, disentanglement from social relations is not always possible because it entails the willingness of actors in one's web of relationships to do so and therefore is not under the exclusive control of the returnees.

What this analysis of the micropolitics of dediasporization tells us is that international migration implies not only diasporization, but also the possibility for dediasporization and that dediasporization is the other side of the migratory process. We refer to this as "micropolitics" to suggest that regaining this status is not automatic, but rather proceeds from negotiation and interaction with the state. States develop elaborate mechanisms to deal with individuals who want to reintegrate and regain a lost status or who must do so because of annexation or reunification. Dediasporization is not simply an individual decision because, as we have emphasized, state intervention is crucial for this transformation to occur.

Conclusion: Diasporic Politics and Transnational Political Space

The study of diasporic politics compels us not only to deessentialize and reconceptualize the concept of the nation because of the mobility that diasporic politics adds to the seemingly circumscribed character of the politics of the nation-state, but also to do away with any monolithic notion of diaspora. A diasporic protopolitical system may take various forms pertaining to time and space: periods of internal crisis, political turmoil, electoral campaigns, invasion or wars, and the national context of such a system's incorporation.

Even after generations, diasporas do not become uninterested in politics related to the homeland. Such is the case in the Anglo-American community. The pro-Britain and pro-Europe American foreign policy orientation (code named "special relations") attests unequivocally to this fact of life. In this case, the transnationality of Euro-American diasporic politics has become routinized and part of the orientation of the mainstream political system. This practice has become naturalized and transformed into a habitus, part of the ethos of everyday life, while diasporic politics undertaken by any other immigrant group—including Jewish American political practices vis-à-vis Israel—has not.

As we began by noting, there are three frames of reference that have been used to analyze diasporic politics, and each has its own strengths and weaknesses. The *assimilation, integration, and incorporation scheme*, with its orientation on participation and assimilation is the dominant discourse in the mainstream political science literature. It sees the successful participation by ethnics in American politics in terms of voting behaviors and electoral politics as the best ticket for their integration and success in American society. So a good deal of effort is put in evaluating their level of participation in American politics. In contrast, the *transnational politics approach* emphasizes more the attachment and connections of diasporans to their homeland than their loyalty to the hostland. According to this approach, even when they participate in hostland politics, they do so by using the homeland political frame of reference. Referring to political practices of first generation Greek immigrants Roudometof and Karpathakis note, "while this new generation brings with it a new sensitivity to American politics and affairs, its frame of reference remains Greek national politics."[1] The *diasporic politics approach* used here emphasizes three things: the transnational practices and interests of diasporic actors in both homeland and hostland politics, the use of ethnic politics to influence homeland and hostland politics, and the temporal structure that influences the ethnic and transnational orientation of diasporic politics. One aspect or the other may be emphasized at times by diasporan political actors and communities. So one must distinguish a routine transnational orientation from an incidental one, although both practices belong to the same diasporic political continuum.

The diasporic political model proposes that the larger arena of the relations between the diaspora and the homeland, among diasporic sites, and between the diaspora and hostland political institutions is the natural context that gives meaning to diaspora engagement in the political field. This model generates three important propositions. First, the priority of transnational political relations reflects the peculiar conditions in which the diaspora finds itself and symbolizes one moment of its existence, for example, the moment in which recent arrivals, refugees, opponents of the homeland regime, and so on determine the nature of diasporic politics. These conditions often explain the strong external profile of the diaspora in the early years of its resettlement abroad. Second, the shift from an emphasis on transnational relations to an emphasis on political integration within the host country is a normal course of adaptation of this unit in the transnational circuit. Third, engagement in both hostland and homeland affairs is in some cases sustained by the electorate, irrespective of the desires of elected politicians, or it may be sporadically fed by events in the homeland. These various manifestations of diasporic politics show that the process is not monolithic, but polyvalent, with multiple shapes. This larger context also explains why a problem in any part of the network may elicit reactions from other sites and how one site may at times help maintain or reactivate the transnational posture of a dormant site.

To understand the various facets of diasporic politics, one must move beyond the forms that transnational relations take to encompass their meanings. Transnationality may occur without direct physical relations or interactions with the homeland. In this context, transnationality manifests itself, for example, when diasporic politics takes the responsibility of making claims for the recognition of diasporans' status. Usually, communities that seek political asylum for their members use this route. As Manuchehr Sanadjian notes, diasporans enter into politics by "wearing the mask of the politically persecuted . . . in their efforts to represent their transnational migration as a flight from political persecution."[2] Transnationality is invoked here for the purpose of eliciting acknowledgment of the status of a political refugee.

Furthermore, participation in domestic politics may be undertaken for the purpose of assisting the homeland, as one votes for a presidential candidate whose foreign policy is pro-homeland government. One can hardly think of an anti-Castro Cuban American in Miami voting for a presidential candidate who is pro-Castro, the same way that one would not expect a presidential candidate to win the general election if his or her political platform is openly anti-Britain, because such a campaigner is unlikely to get a large number of votes from the Anglo-American constituency. Also, a homeland crisis may lead to participation in hostland politics to help diffuse the crisis. This must be contrasted with the engagement of some in politics for purely domestic ends.

Likewise, diasporic participation in homeland politics may also be for the benefit of the hostland. Some Haitian American activists who took part in anti-Lavalas protests in Boston and New York in 2001 sought to undermine the Aristide administration in an effort to replace it by a government more in line with American foreign policy objectives and interests in the Caribbean region.

Some sending states have established a formal structure for the management of transnational relations. For example, the Croatian state has a special ministry—the Ministry of Return and Exiles—to deal with immigrants. We are told that "in the elections of 1995 twelve seats were reserved for diaspora representatives in the Croatian parliament."[3] Haiti has also established a Ministry of Diasporic Affairs. So formal channels and institutions are being developed to account for diasporic transnational practices.

Transnational Political Space

Diasporic politics is choreographed inside a transnational political space because of connections to the homeland and other diasporic sites and because of the influence of any unit in the network on its shape and behavior. The various turbulences in the relationships that maintain the transnational network comprise the nodes of this cross-border political space.

Political activities that occur within the transnational space make sense most forcefully through the logic of diasporic politics. Three levels of effect can be identified: on the host country, on the homeland, and on the transnational circuit, including the diaspora and its shifting identity.

The transnational diasporic space provides a public sphere that can be mobilized for action. This sphere encompasses diasporans in diverse nations and the homeland, and one site can draw on the resources of others. For example, if one site decides to mount a protest, it can request help from the network and get the protest going in every site where the diaspora has its strengths.

The transnational diasporic sphere has used the discourse of human rights as its major form of legitimacy instead of race, revolutionary rhetoric, or even hemispheric solidarity. This sphere has nurtured this lingua franca that gives much substance and unity of practices to its transnational actions and in a sense distinguishes it from any other political sphere.

The Shift in Haitian American Diasporic Politics

As we have seen, since the mid-1990s, a new political consciousness caused by both the Immigration Act of 1996 and the political stalemate in Haiti has moved the Haitian diaspora to reposition itself politically. This was facilitated by the forward movement of a younger generation of politicians better prepared and more interested in American politics than in Haitian politics. A number of activities contributed to that new posture. Radio conversations in Florida and New York advocated this change without much retaliation from the old guards. When Haitian Americans ventured to make such a statement earlier, they were always reprimanded or humiliated for being unpatriotic, insensitive, or outright conservative in their thinking. Now the public sphere is more receptive to this kind of political discourse and orientation. Political organizations in the diaspora in Miami and New York whose goal is to help foster the success of Haitians for public office have seen the light of the day. Formal meetings to discuss and assess the political needs of the diaspora have been held in Miami, New York, and Boston in an effort to identify consensus points and to develop strategies to push the agenda of the community and also to help candidates for elective office win.

What these changes seem to indicate is that Haitian Americans no longer want to be exclusively in the position of serving as lobbyists on behalf of the Haitian government. While the diaspora is taking care of Haiti, they have begun to ask, who is taking care of the diaspora? They no longer want to invest all their political capital in a full-time effort to help Haiti. On the contrary, they are developing their political organizations to become major players in U.S. politics and to use that leverage to deal with both American society and Haitian society. The recent spate of attempts in the diasporic community to seek elective political office (at the state, county, and city levels) with a group of good candidates vying for seats in state legislatures, for judgeships, for mayorships, and for city council memberships is an expression or a translation into reality of this new vision of the role of the Haitian diaspora in American society. The shift here is from attempting to meet the needs of Haiti to attempting to meet the needs of the diaspora or, to put it differently, to moving the focus on the diaspora from the periphery to the center in diasporic politics and the focus on the homeland of yesteryear from the center to the periphery.

Three projects advance this new vision. Increasing political representation by electing Haitian Americans to state legislatures, municipal governments, and eventually to Congress seems to be the most practical way of integrating diasporic politics and American politics. The development of a political action committee in Miami and other similar organizations in Boston and New York that give prominence to ethnic politics over homeland politics is another project in this new vision. The empowerment of the community as a result of the strength of its participation in American politics becomes the sought-after dividend. And finally, as a consequence of the above, activists are being relegated to a backup position to serve the community first and foremost and Haiti is only secondary. In this third project, the leadership of the community is being placed in the hands of elected officials and not in the hands of those with no formal political mandate.

This greater emphasis on engagement in ethnic politics in the United States while downgrading the Haiti orientation was formally recognized during two important national strategic meetings, one organized by the National Coalition for Haitian Rights, held in Miami in the spring of 2002, and the other organized by Representative Marie St. Fleur in Boston in the fall of the same year. Unlike previous Haitian American national meetings, the focus was almost exclusively on the needs of the diaspora, the need to build institutions, and the need to elect Haitian American leaders and to participate actively in mainstream American politics at the local, state, and federal levels.

This shift from a focus on Haiti to a focus on the United States marks a sharp turn of the diasporic community as questions of survival have begun to take precedence over the everyday management of homeland affairs. This turn is also the result of a clash of generations as younger professional Haitians see their future almost exclusively in terms of American parameters, because moving back to Haiti is not an option that most realistically envision.

This new vision entailing new strategies of action and participation in diasporic politics while emphasizing the ethnic and downgrading the transnational is the new agenda of the community. The recent victories at the polls in Florida and Massachusetts put a little pressure on New York, with its sizable Haitian community, to move forward in that direction.

The shift in orientation also means that relations of the diaspora with Haiti need to be reconceptualized. Their form and intensity will depend on whether Haiti continues to be an embarrassment or a point of light for the diaspora. Diasporic politics, with its projected massive involvement in American politics and its low or high levels of transnational interaction, depending on what is at stake, is the new path that the diaspora has set for itself for the success of its integration into American society.

Notes

Introduction: Mapping the Global Arena of Diasporic Politics

1. See, e.g., Olivier Kramsch, Toward a Mediterranean Scale of Governance. In Cross-Border Governance in the European Union, ed. Olivier Kramsch and Barbara Hooper. London: Routledge, 2004, pp. 190–208.
2. Michael B. Preston, Bruce E. Cain, and Sandra Bass, eds., *Racial and Ethnic Politics in California*, Berkeley: Institute of Governmental Studies, 1998; John Mollenkopf, David Olson, and Timothy Ross, Immigrant Political Participation in New York and Los Angeles. In *Governing Urban America: Immigrants, Natives, and Urban Politics*, ed. Michael Jones Correa, New York: Russell Sage Foundation, 2001; Louis DeSipio, *Counting on the Latino Vote: Latinos as a New Electorate*, Charlottesville: University of Virginia Press, 1996; Jan E. Leighley, *Strength in Numbers? The Political Mobilization of Racial and Ethnic Minorities*, Princeton: Princeton University Press, 2001; Pei-Te Lien, Ethnicity and Political Participation: A Comparison between Asian and Mexican Americans. *Political Behavior* 16, no. 2 (1994): 237–264; Carole Jean Uhlaner, Bruce E. Cain, and D. Roderick Kiewiet, Political Participation of Ethnic Minorities in the 1980s. *Political Behavior* 11, no. 3 (1989): 195–231; Jack Citrin et al., *How Race, Ethnicity and Immigration Are Changing the California Electorate*, San Francisco: Public Policy Institute of California, 2002; Wendy K. Tam Cho, Naturalization, Socialization, Participation: Immigrants and (Non-) Voting. *Journal of Politics* 61, no. 4 (1999): 1140–1155; Harry Pachon and Louis DeSipio, *New Americans by Choice: Political Perspectives of Latino Immigrants*, Boulder, CO: Westview, 1994; Katherine Tate, *From Protest to Politics: The New Black Voters in American Elections*, Cambridge, MA: Harvard University Press, 1993.
3. Notable exceptions are the studies that analyze the impact of ethnic groups on American foreign policy or that use a multicultural perspective, see, e.g., Tony Smith, *Foreign Attachments: The Power of Ethnic Groups in the Making of American Foreign Policy*, Cambridge, MA: Harvard University Press, 2000; Samuel P. Huntington, The Erosion of American National Interests. *Foreign Affairs* 76, no. 5 (1997); and Yossi Shain, *Marketing the American Creed Abroad: Diasporas in the US and their Homelands*, Cambridge: Cambridge

University Press, 1999; M. Hechter and D. Okamoto, Political Consequences of Minority Group Formation. *Annual Reviews of Political Science* 4 (2001): 189–215; D. Carment, The International Dimensions of Ethnic Conflict: Concepts, Indicators and Theory. *Journal of Peace Research* 30 (1993): 137–150; M. J. Esman, Two Dimensions of Ethnic Politics: Defense of Homelands, Immigrant Rights. *Ethnic and Racial Studies* 8 (1985): 438–440; Jose Carpizo and Diego Valades, *El Voto de los Mexicanos En El Extranjero*, Mexico City: Universidad Nacional Autonóma de Mexico, 1998; Jesus Martinez-Saldana, At the Periphery of Democracy: The Binational Politics of Mexican Immigrants in Silicon Valley. PhD dissertation, University of California, Berkeley, 1993; Jesus Martinez-Saldana and Raul Ross Pineda, Suffrage for Mexicans Residing Abroad. In *Cross-Border Dialogues: US-Mexico Social Movement Networking*, ed. Davids Brooks and Jonathan Fox, La Jolla, CA: UCSD Center for U.S. Mexican Studies, 2002, pp. 275–293.

4. David A. Smith, Dorothy J. Solinger, and Steven C. Topik, eds., *States and Sovereignty in the Global Economy*, London: Routledge, 1999.
5. Gabriel Sheffer, *Diaspora Politics: At Home Abroad*, Cambridge: Cambridge University Press, 2003; Marian Fitzgerald, Different Roads? The Development of Afro-Caribbean and Asian Political Organization in London. *New Community* 14 (1988): 385–396; Miriam Feldblum, Paradoxes of Ethnic Politics: The Case of Franco-Maghrebis in France. *Ethnic and Racial Studies* 16 (1993): 52–74; Pnina Werbner and Muhammad Anwar, eds., *Black and Ethnic Leadership in Britain*, London: Routledge, 1991; Gary Gerstle and John Mollenkopf, *Immigrants, Civic Culture, and Modes of Political Incorporation*, New York: Russell Sage Foundation, 2001; Sidney Verba et al., *Participation and Political Equality*, Cambridge: Cambridge University Press, 1978; Sidney Verba et al., *Voice and Equality: Civic Voluntarism in American Politics*, Cambridge, MA: Harvard University Press, 1995.
6. See also B. Anderson, Exodus. *Critical Enquiry* 20, no. 2 (1994): 314–327; Nina Glick Schiller and Georges E. Fouron, *Long-Distance Nationalism and the Search for Home*, Durham: Duke University Press, 2001; Z. Skrbis, *Long-Distance Nationalism. Diasporas, Homelands and Identities*, Aldershot, Hants: Ashgate, 1999.
7. Anver Saloojee and Myer Siemiatychi, Formal and Non-Formal Political Participation by Immigrants and Newcomers: Understanding the Linkages and Posing the Questions. *Canadian Issues Themes Canadiens*, April 2003, pp. 42–46.
8. Gabriel Sheffer, Ethno-National Diasporas and Security. *Survival* 36, no. 1 (1994): 60–79; Aline Angoustures et Valérie Pascal, Diasporas et Financement des Conflits. In *Economie des Guerres Civiles*, ed. François J. Rufin and Jean-Christophe Rufin, Paris: Hachette, 1996, pp. 495–498; and Kevin Hill and John Hughes, *Cyberpolitics: Citizen Activism in the Age of the Internet*, New York: Rowman and Littlefield, 1998; Michael Dahan and Gabriel Sheffer, Ethnic Groups and Distance Shrinking Communication Technologies *Nationalism and Politics* 7 (2001): 85–107; Peggy Levitt, *The Transnational Villagers*, Berkeley: University of California Press, 2001; David H. Goldberg, *Foreign Policy and Ethnic Interest Groups: American and Canadian Jews Lobby for Israel*,

New York: Greenwood, 1990; Edward Tivnan, *The Lobby: Jewish Political Power and American Foreign Policy*, New York: Simon and Schuster, 1987; Robert H. Trice, *Interest Groups and the Foreign Policy Process: US Policy in the Middle East*, Beverly Hills: Sage, 1976; Dimitri C. Contas and Athanassios G. Platias, eds., *Diasporas in World Politics: The Greeks in Comparative Perspective*, London: Macmillan, 1993.

9. Milton Gordon, *Assimilation in American Life*, New York: Oxford University Press, 1964.
10. Jose Itzigsohn, Immigration and the Boundaries of Citizenship: The Institutions of Immigrants' Political Transnationalism. *International Migration Review* 34, no. 4 (2000): 1126–1154; Michel S. Laguerre, State, Diaspora and Transnational Politics. *Millennium: Journal of International Studies* 28, no. 3 (1999): 633–651.
11. On the transnational diasporic field as a category of analysis, see Nina Glick Schiller et al., *Towards a Transnational Perspective on Migration*, New York: New York Academy of Sciences, 1992.
12. Shain, *Marketing the American Creed Abroad*; Tony Smith, *Foreign Attachments*; Gabriel Sheffer, *Diaspora Politics: At Home Abroad*, Cambridge: Cambridge University Press, 2003.

1 The Practice of Diasporic Politics

1. Michael Preston, Bruce E. Cain, and Sandra Bass, eds., *Racial and Ethnic Politics in California*, Berkeley: Institute of Governmental Studies, 1998; Leland Saito, *Race and Politics: Asian Americans, Latinos, and Whites in a Los Angeles Suburb*, Urbana: University of Illinois Press, 1998; Andrew L. Aoki and Don T. Nakanishi, Asian Pacific Americans and the New Minority Politics. *Political Science and Politics* 34, no. 3 (2001): 605–610; James S. Lai et al., Asian Pacific American Campaigns, Elections, and Elected Officials. *Political Science and Politics* 34, no. 3 (2001): 611–618.
2. Rodolfo de la Garza, Martha Menchaca, and Louis DeSipio, *Barrio Ballots: Latino Politics in the 1990 Elections*, Boulder: Westview, 1994; Pei-te Lien, *The Political Participation of Asian Americans: Voting Behavior in Southern California*, New York: Garland, 1997; Carole J. Uhlaner, Bruce Cain, and D. Roderick Kiewiet, Political Participation of Ethnic Minorities in the 1980s. *Political Behavior* 17 (1989): 195–231; Kin Geron et al., Asian Pacific Americans Social Movements and Interest Groups. *Political Science and Politics* 34, no. 3 (2001): 619–624; Pei-Te Lien et al., Asian Pacific American Public Opinion and Political Participation. *Political Science and Politics* 34, no. 3 (2001): 625–631; Claire Jean Kim et al., Interracial Politics: Asian Americans and Other Communities of Color. *Political Science and Politics* 34, no. 3 (2001): 631–644.
3. Bruce E. Cain, Asian Americans' Electoral Power: Imminent or Illusory. *Election Politics* nos. 28–29 (Spring 1988); Jan Leighley, *Strength in Numbers? The Political Mobilization of Racial and Ethnic Minorities*, Princeton: Princeton University Press, 2001; Sidney Verba, Kay Lehman

Schlozman, and Henry Brady, *Voice and Equality: Civic Voluntarism in American Politics*, Cambridge, MA: Harvard University Press, 1995.

4. Y. M. Alex-Assensoh and L. Hanks, eds., *Black and Multiracial Politics in America*, New York: New York University Press, 2000; Michael Jones-Correa, *Between Two Nations: The Political Predicament of Latinos in New York City*, Ithaca: Cornell University Press, 1998; Tony Affigne, Latino Politics in the United States: An Introduction. *Political Science and Politics* 34, no. 3 (2000): 523–528; Rodney Hero et al., Latino Participation, Partisanship, and Office Holding. *Political Science and Politics* 34, no. 3 (2000): 529–535; Christine Marie Sierra, Latino Immigration and Citizenship. *Political Science and Politics* 34, no. 3 (2000): 535–540; Benjamin Marquez et al., Representation by Other Means: Mexican American and Puerto Rican Social Movement Organizations. *Political Science and Politics* 34, no. 3 (2000): 541–546; Valerie Martinez-Ebers et al., Latino Interests in Education, Health and Criminial Justice Policy. *Political Science and Politics* 34, no. 3 (2000): 547–554; Lisa J. Montoya et al., Latina Politics: Gender, Participation, and Leadership. *Political Science and Politics* 34, no. 3 (2000): 555–562; Ronald J. Schmidt, Sr. et al., Latino Identities: Social Diversity and US Politics. *Political Science and Politics* 34, no. 3 (2000): 563–568.
5. Lawrence Bobo and Frank D. Gilliam, Jr., Race, Sociopolitical Participation, and Black Empowerment. *American Political Science Review* 84 (1990): 377–393; Steven J. Rosenstone and John M. Hansen, *Mobilization, Participation, and Democracy in America*, New York: Macmillan, 1993.
6. Gabriel Sheffer, *Diaspora Politics: At Home Abroad*, Cambridge: Cambridge University Press, 2003; Yossi Shain, *Marketing the American Creed Abroad: Diasporas in the US and their Homelands*, New York: Cambridge University Press, 1999; Tony Smith, *Foreign Attachments: The Power of Ethnic Groups in the Making of American Foreign Policy*, Cambridge, MA: Harvard University Press, 2000; Randall Hansen and Patrick Weil, *Dual Nationality, Social Rights and Federal Citizenship in the US and Europe*, New York: Berghahn, 2002; Bruce Cain and Brendan J. Doherty, *The Impact of Dual Citizenship on Political Participation*. The Nation of Immigrants Conference, Institute of Governmental Studies, University of California at Berkeley, May 2–3, 2003.
7. Nakanishi stresses the need to broaden the scope of analysis by including "both nondomestic and nonelectoral political activities." He further remarks that "homeland issues continue to dominate their ethnic political leadership agendas and the front pages of their vernacular media, and compete with, if not at times overwhelm, efforts to steer the evergrowing numbers of naturalized citizens towards greater involvement in the American electoral process" (Don T. Nakanishi, When Numbers do not Add Up: Asian Pacific Americans and California Politics. In *Racial and Ethnic Politics in California*, ed. Michael B. Preston, Bruce Cain, and Sandra Bass, Berkeley: Institute of Governmental Studies, 1998, pp. 11 and 31. See also Michel S. Laguerre, State, Diaspora and Transnational Politics. *Millennium: Journal of International Studies* 28, no. 3 (1999): 633–651; Paul Y. Watanabe, Global Forces, Foreign Policy, and Asian Pacific Americans. *Political Science and Politics* 34, no. 3 (2001): 639–644.

8. See, e.g., A. A. Parham, *The Diasporic Public Sphere: Internet-Mediated Community and Civic Life in Transnational Haiti*. PhD dissertation, Department of Sociology, University of Wisconsin at Madison, 2003.
9. Samuel Denny Smith, *The Negro in Congress 1870–1901*, Chapel Hill: University of North Carolina Press, 1940; William Clay, *Just Permanent Interests: Black Americans in Congress, 1870–1991*, New York: Amistad, 1992; Rodolphe Lucien Desdunes, *Our People and Our History*, Baton Rouge: Louisiana State University Press, 1973; Michel S. Laguerre, *Diasporic Citizenship: Haitian Americans in Transnational America*, New York and Basingstoke: Macmillan, 1998; Jose Itzigsohn, Immigration and the Boundaries of Citizenship: The Institutions of Immigrants' Political Transnationalism. *International Migration Review* 34, no. 4 (2000): 1126–1154; Nina Glick-Schiller, The Implications of Haitian Transnationalism for US-Haiti Relations: Contradictions of the Deterritorialized Nation-State. *Journal of Haitian Studies* 1, no. 1 (1995): 111–123. Also useful are P. Evans, Fighting Marginalization with Transnational Networks: Counter-Hegemonic Globalization. *Contemporary Sociology* 29, no. 1 (2000): 230–241; W. I. Robinson, Beyond Nation-State Paradigms: Globalization, Sociology and the Challenges of Transnational Studies. *Sociological Forum* 13, no. 4 (1998): 561–594.
10. Desdunes, *Our People and Our History*.
11. Eric Green, Haitian American Elected Mayor, City Councilman in South Florida. *Washington File*, May 22, 2001, U.S. Department of State International Information Programs.
12. Marjorie Valbrun, Striking a Minor Chord. *Boston Magazine*, January 2002.
13. Joseph P. Kahn, Brothers Ink Two Childhood Friends Work to Give a Voice to Greater Boston's Haitian American Community. *The Boston Globe*, February 7, 2001, p. F1.
14. Carlos Monje, Jr., St. Fleur a Big Winner in the 5th District. *The Boston Globe*, July 7, 1999.
15. For House District 108. *The Miami Herald*, October 16, 2002.
16. Jacqueline Charles, Carolyn Salazar, and Draeger Martinez, Dade Vote is Historic for Two New Legislators. *The Miami Herald*, November 6, 2002.
17. See, e.g., Haitian-American Democrats To Honor Politicians at Banquet. *The Miami Herald*, December 30, 1999; Michael Vasquez, Haitian Americans Review Achievements. *The Miami Herald*, January 17, 2002; Sonji Jacobs, Haitian American Group Celebrates Anniversary, Commitment to GOP. *The Miami Herald*, July 8, 2002.
18. Cited in Marjorie Valbrun, Caribbean Immigrants' Political Moves Stir Tensions. *The Wall Street Journal*, June 30, 1998.
19. Cited in Marjorie Valbrun, Coming out Party: Haitian American Women Step Out from Behind Scenes and Into US Politics. *APF Reporter* vol. 20 #4 Index, 2003.
20. Suzan Clarke, Haitians Work for the American Dream. *The Journal News*, Westchester County, NY, July 16, 2004.
21. According to the Associated Press, Councilman Jacques Despinosse (North Miami) said in an interview that "by concentrating on local crime, traffic problems and flood insurance policy, Haitians here can pragmatically carry

weight back home, just as Jewish-Americans help shape Middle East policy and Cubans in Miami helped dictate the U.S.'s stance on Cuba." Website: <http://www.caribvoice.org/Features/celestin.html>.

22. According to the article in the *Miami Herald* in 1996 alone, 24,556 Haitians were naturalized in Florida. *The Miami Herald*, December 20, 1999.
23. See, e.g., E. A. Torriero, Haitian-Americans Say Past Rule Was Better. *The Orlando Sentinel*, February 20, 2004; Mark Hayward, NH Haitian-Americans Fear for Nation's Democracy. *The Union Leader*, Manchester, NH, February 27, 2004; C. Kalimah Redd, Fearing for Homeland and Kin: Haitian Americans Are Worried About Political Violence On The Island. *The Boston Globe*, February 26, 2004.
24. Cited in Ken Thomas, South Florida Haitians Achieve Political Clout. *The Associated Press State and Local Wire*, May 29, 2001.
25. Kathy Glasgow, A New Political Complexion. *Miami New Times*, May 3, 2001.
26. Marie St. Fleur, Haitian Americans at a Crossroad in Our Journey. *Boston Haitian Reporter*, vol. 1, issue 1, May 2001.
27. Gary Pierre-Pierre, For Haitians, Leadership Split Is a Generation Gap. *The New York Times*, September 24, 1997, sec. B, p. 4, col. 1.
28. Gabriel Sheffer, ed., *Modern Diasporas in International Politics*, London: Croom Helm, 1986; Y. Shain, ed., *The Frontiers of Loyalty: Political Exiles in the Age of the Nation-State*, Middletown, CT: Wesleyan University Press, 1989; and A. Iwanska, *Exiled Governments: Spanish and Polish*, Cambridge: Schenkman, 1981.

2 State, Diaspora, and Transnational Politics

1. Pamela M. Graham, Reimagining the Nation and Defining the District: Dominican Migration and Transnational Politics. In *Caribbean Circuits: New Directions in the Study of Caribbean Migration*, ed. Patricia R. Pessar, Staten Island: Center for Migration Studies, 1997, pp. 91–125; Gregory M. Maney, Transnational Mobilization and Civil Rights in Northern Ireland. *Social Problems* 47, no. 2 (2000): 153–179; Silvia Maria Perez Godoy, Social Movements and International Migration: The Mexican Diaspora Seeks Inclusion in Mexico's Political Affairs, 1968–1998. PhD dissertation, University of Chicago, 1999; Graham Smith, Transnational Politics and the Politics of the Russian Diaspora. *Ethnic and Racial Studies* 22, no. 3 (1999): 500–523; Louis DeSipio et al., *Immigrant Politics at Home and Abroad: How Latino Immigrants Engage the Politics of their Home Communities and the United States*, Claremont, CA: Tomas Rivera Policy Institute, 2003; Michael Jones-Correa, *Between Two Nations: The Political Predicament of Latinos in New York City*, Ithaca: Cornell University Press, 1998.
2. Nina G. Schiller et al., The Implications of Haitian Transnationalism for US-Haiti Relations: Contradictions of the Deterritorialized Nation-State. *Journal of Haitian Studies* 1, no. 1 (1995): 111–123.

3. During the nineteenth century, there were two independent states in the Caribbean, namely Haiti and the Dominican Republic. On their policies vis-à-vis their respective diasporas, see Frank Moya Pons, *The Dominican Republic: A National History*, New Rochelle, NY: Hispaniola Books, 1995, pp. 245–263 and Michel S. Laguerre, *The Complete Haitiana, 1900–1980*, Millwood, NY: Kraus International, 1982, pp. 609–624.
4. Kimberly Hamilton and Kate Holder, International Migration and Foreign Policy: A Survey of the Literature. *The Washington Quarterly* 14, no. 2 (1991): 195–211.
5. Michel S. Laguerre, *Diasporic Citizenship: Haitian Americans in Transnational America*, London: Macmillan, 1998; Walker Conner, The Impact of Homelands Upon Diasporas. In *Modern Diasporas in International Politics*, ed. Gabriel Sheffer, London: Croom Helm, 1986, pp. 16–46.
6. Zlatko Skrbis, Homeland-Diaspora Relations: From Passive to Active Interactions. *Asian and Pacific Migration Journal* 6, nos. 3–4 (1997): 439–455.
7. For recent literature on nation and national identity, see Maxim Silverman, *Deconstructing the Nation: Immigration, Racism and Citizenship in France*, London: Routledge, 1992; Etienne Balibar and Immanuel Wallerstein, eds., *Race, Nation, Class: Ambiguous Identities*, London: Verso, 1991; B. A. Roberson, ed., *International Society and the Development of International Relations Theory*, London: Pinter, 1998; and Jean-Marie Guehenno, *The End of the Nation-State*, Minneapolis: University of Minnesota Press, 1995.
8. The state is seen here as a constructed reality and its meanings or what it is supposed to perform in the international arena is also socially constructed. On the notion of constructivism as applied to the state, see Stefano Guzzini, A Reconstruction of Constructivism in International Relations. *European Journal of International Relations* 6, no. 2 (2000): 147–182; Ted Hopf, The Promise of Constructivism in International Relations Theory. *International Security* 23, no. 1 (1998): 171–200; Jeffrey T. Checkel, The Constructivist Turn in International Relations Theory. *World Politics* 50, no. 2 (1998): 324–348; Thomas J. Biersteker; and Cynthia Weber, *State Sovereignty as Social Construct*, Cambridge: Cambridge University Press, 1996.
9. William F. Stinner, Klaus de Albuquerque, and Roy S. Bryce-Laporte, eds., *Return Migration and Remittances: Developing a Caribbean Perspective*, Washington, DC: Research Institute on Immigration and Ethnic Studies, Smithsonian Institution, 1982. According to Associated Press journalist Mark Stevenson, "there are an estimated 30,000 foreigners in Haiti, including about 20,000 Americans. Many also have Haitian passports, but it is not known how many" (Americans Flee Violence of the Haitian Uprising. *San Jose Mercury News*, February 21, 2004).
10. James Clifford, Diasporas. *Cultural Anthropology* 9, no. 3 (1994): 302–338; Robin Cohen, Diasporas and the Nation-State. *International Affairs* 72, no. 3 (1996): 507–520; William Safran, Diasporas in Modern Societies. *Diaspora* 1, no. 1(1991): 83–99; Kachig Tololyan, Rethinking Diaspora(s): Stateless Power in the Transnational Moment. *Diaspora* 1, no. 1 (1991): 3–36; Daniel Boyarin and Jonathan Boyarin, Diaspora: Generation and the Ground of

Jewish Identity. *Critical Inquiry* 19 (1993): 693–725; Elliott P. Skinner, The Dialectic Between Diasporas and Homelands. In *Global Dimension of the African Diaspora*, ed. Joseph Harris, Washington, DC: Howard University Press, 1982, pp. 11–40; Floya Anthias, Evaluating Diaspora: Beyond Ethnicity. *Sociology: The Journal of British Sociological Association* 32, no. 3 (1998): 557–580; Carlton Wilson, Conceptualizing the African Diaspora. *Comparative Studies of South Asia, Africa and the Middle East* 17, no. 2 (1997): 118–122; Magdalene Ang-Lygate, Charting the Spaces of (Un)Location: On Theorizing Diaspora. In *Black British Feminism: A Reader*, ed. Heidi Safia Mirza, London: Routledge, 1997, pp. 168–186; Phil Cohen, Rethinking the Diasporama. *Patterns of Prejudice* 33, no. 1 (1999): 3–22; April Gordon, The New Diaspora-African Immigration to the United States. *Journal of Third World Studies* 15, no. 1 (1998): 79–103.

11. Carlos B. Gil, Cuauthemoc Cardenas and the Rise of Transborder Politics. In *Hopes and Frustrations: Interviews with Leaders of Mexico's Political Opposition*, ed. Carlos B. Gil, Wilmington, DE: Scholarly Resources, 1992, pp. 287–303; Carlos Gonzales Gutierrez, The Mexican Diaspora in California: Limits and Possibilities for the Mexican Government. In *The California-Mexican Connection*, ed. Abraham F. Lowenthal and Katrina Burgess, Stanford, CA: Stanford University Press, 1993, pp. 221–235.
12. Razmik Panossian, Between Ambivalence and Intrusion: Politics and Identity in Armenia-Diaspora Relations. *Diaspora* 7, no. 2 (1998): 149–196; Ivan Cizmic, Political Activities of Croatian Immigrants in the USA and the Creation of an Independent Croatia. *Drustvena Istrazivanja* 7, nos. 33–34 (1998): 5–25.
13. These models of state-diaspora relations are not specific to Haiti; they can be used to explain various moments of Mexican migration to the United States, Turkish migration to Germany, South Asian migration to Canada and Korean migration to Japan (Thomas Faist, Developing Transnational Social Spaces: The Turkish-German Example. In *Migration and Transnational Social Spaces*, ed. Ludger Pries, Aldershot: Ashgate, 1999, pp. 36–72).
14. Rodolphe L. Desdunes, *Our People and Our History*, Baton Rouge: Louisiana State University Press, 1973.
15. Susan. H. Buchanan, Scattered Seeds: The Meaning of Migration for Haitians in New York City. PhD dissertation, Department of Anthropology, New York University, 1980.
16. Michel S. Laguerre, *The Global Ethnopolis: Chinatown, Japantown and Manilatown in American Society*, London: Macmillan and New York: St. Martin's, 1999.
17. See, e.g., Yossi Shain, *Marketing the American Creed Abroad: Diasporas in the US and their Homelands*, Cambridge: Cambridge University Press, 1999, 175–176.
18. Yossi Shain, ed., *Governments-in-Exile in Contemporary World Politics*, New York: Routledge, 1991; Alicja Iwanska, *Exiled Governments: Spanish and Polish*, Cambridge, MA: Schenkman, 1981; Lewis J. Edinger, *German Exile Politics: The Social Democratic Executive Committee in the Nazi Era*, Berkeley: University of California Press, 1956.

19. Jean Jean-Pierre, The Tenth Department. In *The Haiti Files: Decoding the Crisis*, ed. James Ridgeway, Washington, DC: Essential Books, 1994, pp. 56–59.
20. Maria Cristina Garcia, *Havana USA: Cuban Exiles and Cuban Americans in South Florida, 1959–1994*, Berkeley: University of California Press, 1996, pp. 120–168.
21. Linda Basch et al., *Nations Unbound Transnational Projects: Postcolonial Predicaments and Deterritorialized Nation-States*, Amsterdam: Gordon and Breach, 1994.
22. In a speech before a group of diasporic artists at the National Palace on May 7, 1999, President René Préval states that "la reconnaisance des Haitiens d'origine vivant à l'étranger comme CITOYENS à part entière, et cela qu'ils aient acquis ou non une autre nationalite, a été et est encore pour moi un objectif fondamental." To implement this vision, he proposes the following:

    1. L'établissement d'un lien plus organique entre divers groupements régionaux constitués à l'etranger et les instances locales visées, pour faciliter le développement régional et renforcer le processus de décentralisation qui est à la fois une exigence constitutionnelle et un instrument du développement durable.
    2. L'insertion des actions des ONG haitiennes de l'exterieur dans l'orientation générale définie par l'Executif quel que soit le secteur d'intervention, pour que ces dernières deviennent ainsi des partenaires de l'Etat.
    3. La mobilisation des "ressources humaines haitiennes" à travers les diverses associations socioprofessionnelles établies à l'extérieur et leur utilisation dans differents projets que l'Etat pourrait mettre de l'avant.
    4. La participation au scrutin lors d'elections au pays aux divers niveaux prévus par la Constitution, pour ceux qui ont conservé leur nationalité d'origine.
    5. "L'identification dans les lois traitant des étrangers de certaines dispositions irritantes pour les Haitiens d'origine ayant acquis une autre nationalité, afin de proposer les modifications nécessaires qui leur donneraient un statut particulier en attendant tout amendement constitutionnel visant à leur redonner la nationalité haitienne." (Discours du Président de la République, son Excellence M. René Préval, Lors de la Réception en l'Honneur des Peintres Haitiens Vivant à l'Etranger, le 7 Mai 1999, au Palais National, Port-au-Prince: Ministère des Haitiens Vivant à L'Etranger, 1999).

23. See also Carlos Gonzales Gutierrez, Decentralized Diplomacy: The Role of Consular Offices in Mexico's Relations with its Diaspora. In *Bridging the Border: Transforming Mexico-US Relations*, ed. Rodolfo O. de la Garza and Jesus Velasco, Lanham, MD: Rowman and Littlefield, 1997, pp. 49–67.
24. Zlatko Skrbis, The Distant Observers? Towards the Politics of Diasporic Identification. *Nationalities Papers* 25, no. 3 (1997): 601–610.
25. Paul Arthur, Diasporan Intervention in International Affairs: Irish America as a Case Study. *Diaspora* 1, no. 2 (1991): 143–162; Shain, *Marketing the American Creed Abroad.*
26. Panossian, Between Ambivalence and Intrusion, pp. 149–196.

27. James Goodman, National Multiculturalism and Transnational Migrant Politics: Australian and East Timorese. *Asian Pacific Migration Journal* 6, nos. 3–4 (1997): 457–480.
28. Ivo D. Duchacek, Multicommunal and Bicommunal Polities and their International Relations. In *Perforated Sovereignties and International Relations: Trans-Sovereign Contacts of Subnational Governments*, ed. Ivo D. Duchacek, Daniel Latouche, and Garth Stevenson, New York: Greenwood, 1988, pp. 3–28.
29. Ibid., p. 5.
30. Michel S. Laguerre, Business and Corruption: Framing the Haitian Military Question. *California Management Review* 36, no. 3 (1994): 89–106 and *The Military and Society in Haiti*, Knoxville: University of Tennessee Press, 1993.
31. See also Michael Clough, Grass-Roots Policy Making: Say Good-Bye to the "Wise Men." *Foreign Affairs* 73, no. 1 (1994): 2–7.
32. Michel S. Laguerre, The Role of the Diaspora in Haitian Politics. In *Haiti Renewed*, ed. Robert I. Rotberg Washington, DC: Brookings Institution Press, 1997, pp. 170–182. On the participation of immigrants in homeland affairs, see also Anna Karpathakis, Home Society Politics and Immigrant Political Incorporation: The Case of Greek Immigrants in New York City. *International Migration Review* 33, no. 1 (1999): 55–78; and Purnima Mankekar, Reflections on Diasporic Identities: A Prolegomenon to an Analysis of Political Bifocality. *Diaspora* 3, no. 3 (1994): 463–485; Shain, *Marketing the American Creed Abroad*; and Maria de los Angeles Torres, Transnational Political and Cultural Identities: Crossing Theoretical Borders. In *Borderless Borders: U.S. Latinos, Latin Americans, and the Paradox of Interdependence*, ed. Frank Bonilla, Edwin Melendez, Rebecca Morales, and Maria de los Angeles Torres, Philadelphia: Temple University Press, 1998, pp. 169–182.
33. Robert W. Cox, Civil Society at the Turn of the Millennium: Prospects for an Alternative World Order. *Review of International Studies* 25, no. 1 (1999): 3–28.
34. Gabriel Sheffer, ed., *Modern Diasporas in International Politics*, London: Croom Helm, 1986.
35. Georg Sorensen, IR Theory after the Cold War. *Review of International Studies* 24, no. 5 (1998): 83–100.
36. John. F. Stack, Jr., Ethnic Groups as Emerging Transnational Actors. In *Ethnic Identities in a Transnational World*, ed. John. F. Stack, Jr., Westport: Greenwood, 1981, pp. 17–45; Lawrence H. Fuchs, Minority Groups and Foreign Policy. *Political Science Quarterly* 74. no. 2 (1959): 165–175.
37. David Held and Anthony McGrew, The End of the Old Order? Globalization and the Prospects for World Order. *Review of International Studies* 24, no. 5 (1998): 219–243; E. H. Carr, *The Twenty Years' Crisis 1919–1939*, London: Macmillan, 1962; William I. Robinson, Beyond Nation-State Paradigms: Globalization, Sociology, and the Challenge of Transnational Studies. *Sociological Forum* 13, no. 4 (1998): 561–594.
38. James Petras, Imperialism and NGOs in Latin America. *Monthly Review* 49, no. 7 (1997): 10–27.

39. Charles Chatfield, Introduction. In *Transnational Social Movements and Global Politics*, ed. Jackie Smith et al., Syracuse: Syracuse University Press, 1997; see also Margaret E. Keck and Kathryn Sikkink, *Activists Beyond Borders*, Ithaca, NY: Cornell University Press, 1998.
40. On the role played by ethnicity and identity in influencing the shape of IR, see Friedrich Kratochwil and Yosef Lapid, eds., *The Return of Culture and Identity in IR Theory*, Boulder: Lynne Rienner, 1996; Chris Brown, Cultural Diversity and International Political Theory. *Review of International Studies* 26, no. 2 (2000): 199–214; Mark Laffey, Locating Identity: Performativity, Foreign Policy and State Action. *Review of International Studies* 26, no. 3 (2000): 429–444; Harold Troper, The Canadian Jewish Polity and the Limits of Political Action: The Campaigns on Behalf of Soviet and Syrian Jews. In *Ethnicity, Politics, and Public Policy*, ed. Harold Troper and Morton Weinfeld, Canada: University of Toronto Press, 1999, pp. 224–252; Yossi Shain, Multicultural Foreign Policy. In *New Tribalisms: The Resurgence of Race and Ethnicity*, ed. Michael W. Hughey, New York: New York University Press, 1998, pp. 299–316; David A. Dickson, American Society and the African American Foreign Policy Lobby: Constraints and Opportunities. *Journal of Black Studies* 27, no. 2 (1996): 139–151; Paul Arthur, Diasporan Intervention in International Affairs: Irish America as a Case Study. *Diaspora* 1, no. 2 (1991): 143–162.
41. J. H. Leurdijk, From International to Transnational Politics: A Change of Paradigm. *International Social Science Journal* 26, no. 1 (1974). R. B. J. Walker, ed., *Contending Sovereignties: Redefining Political Community*, Boulder: Lynne Rienner Publishers, 1990.
42. Gabriel Sheffer, ed., *Modern Diasporas in International Politics*, London: Croom Helm, 1986.
43. Yossi Shain, The Foreign Policy Role of US Diasporas and Its Domestic Consequences. In *Representing and Imagining America*, ed. Philip John Davies, Keele: Keele University Press, 1996, pp. 101–114.
44. I am grateful to an economist assigned to the Caribbean desk at the World Bank for this information.
45. David Schoenbaum, *The United States and the State of Israel*, New York: Oxford University Press, 1993; Yossi Shain and Mark Thompson, The Role of Political Exiles in Democratic Transitions: The Case of the Philippines. *Journal of Developing Societies* 6, no. 1 (1990): 71–86.
46. Charles McC. Mathias, Jr., Ethnic Groups and Foreign Policy. *Foreign Affairs* 59, no. 5 (1981): 975–998.
47. Michael J. Shapiro and Hayward R. Alker, eds., *Challenging Boundaries: Global Flows, Territorial Identities*, Minneapolis: University of Minnesota Press, 1996.
48. Guehenno, *The End of the Nation-State*.
49. Y. N. Soysal, *Limits of Citizenship: Migrants and Postnational Membership in Europe*, Chicago: University of Chicago Press, 1994.
50. Jonathan Ree, Cosmopolitanism and the Experience of Nationality. In *Cosmopolitics: Thinking and Feeling Beyond the Nation*, ed. Pheng Cheah

and Bruce Robbins, Minneapolis: University of Minnesota Press, 1998, pp. 77–90.

51. Michael Banks and Martin Shaw, eds., *State and Society in International Relations*, London: Harvester and Wheatsheaf, 1991.
52. E. Fuat Keyman, *Globalization, State, Identity/Difference: Toward a Critical Social Theory of International Relations*, Atlantic Highlands, NJ: Humanities Press, 1997.
53. Christopher K. Ansell and Steven Weber, Organizing International Politics: Sovereignty and Open Systems. *International Political Science Review* 20, no. 1 (1999): 73–93.
54. Ibid., 75. State-globalization relations should be seen not in oppositional, binary terms, but rather as part of the same continuum, that is the implosion of the global in the local and the implosion of the local in the global. These are formal and informal relations between units in the same interactional and networked universe. One may thus speak not of loss or gain when the state or the global has the upper hand, but rather of "inter-state socialization" or "transitional adjustment." In other words, the state is not "here" and globalization "there." The local state is part of the global process. Of course, when international norms prevail over local practices, the state is sometimes forced to adjust its ways, but that is not always the case. It is so because globalization does not necessarily entail homegeneity. In fact, globalization because it does not undermine the existence of localities (globalized localities), is a central mechanism in the production of heterogeneity. On this issue, see, e.g., David Armstrong, Globalization and the Social State. *Review of International Studies* 24, no. 4 (1998): 461–478 and Roland Robertson, *Globalization, Social Theory and Global Culture*, London: Sage, 1992.
55. Ansell and Weber, Organising International Politics, p. 75.
56. Ibid., p. 77.

3 Diasporic Lobbying in American Politics

1. Sajal Lahiri and Pascalis Raimondos-Moller, in Lobbying by Ethnic Groups and AID Allocation, 2000, argue that ethnic lobbies are a universal phenomenon and not specific to any country. Reviewing the lobby scene in western Europe and the United States, they refer to the prominence of the "Jewish lobby in the United States, the Arab and African lobbies in France, the Indian lobby in the United Kingdom, the Turkish lobby in Germany" and find that "the relationship between the pattern of aid and ethnic composition is striking." They further correlate foreign aid with the strength of the ethnic lobbies to unveil a common pattern, that is "about 25% of United States bilateral [aid] goes to Israel, 12% of British [aid] goes to India, 5% of German [aid] goes to Turkey, and 5% of French [aid] goes to Cameroon"(p. C65).

   The success of ethnic lobbies cannot be easily evaluated because of the other factors that influence the outcomes of policy decisions in which they are involved. However, for Charles B. Kelly, "ethnic lobbies' strength is based on their organization, the imperatives of the electoral system, and the merits of their cases." He sees electoral politics as providing an avenue through which ethnic lobbyists can access and influence elected officials. He notes that "the ability to deliver votes, as well as money and other campaign resources, provides access to office holders and office seekers. Elections and the congressional committee structure are tailor-made for influencing the American political system." He traces the activist role of Congress in foreign policy to the period after the Second World War and attributes it to pressure from ethnic lobbies. He attributes the nexus of the relations between both to "the attention that lobbies give Congress contributes to its activism in foreign affairs, which, in turn, provides an entry wedge for lobbies."

2. Jeffrey M. Berry, *Lobbying for the Poor: The Political Behavior of Public Interest Groups*, Princeton: Princeton University Press, 1977, p. 5.
3. Charles B. Keely, The Effects of International Migration on U.S. Foreign Policy. In *Threatened Peoples, Threatened Borders: World Migration and US Policy*, ed. Michael S. Teitelbaum and Myron Weiner, New York: W. W. Norton, 1995, pp. 215–243.
4. Kevin W. Hula, *Lobbying Together: Interest Group Coalitions in Legislative Politics*, Washington, DC: Georgetown University Press, 1999.
5. Alexis de Tocqueville, *Democracy in America*, Chicago: University of Chicago Press, 2000.
6. Hula, *Lobbying Together*, pp. 23, 39.
7. Ibid., p. 40.
8. Vered Talai, Mobilization and Diffuse Ethnic Organizations: The London Armenian Community. *Urban Anthropology* 13, nos. 2–3 (1984): 197–217.
9. Marcel Mauss, *The Gift*, Glencoe: Free Press, 1954.
10. Sajal Lahiri and Pascalis Raimondos-Moller, Lobbying by Ethnic Groups and AID Allocation. *The Economic Journal* 110, no. 462 (2000): C63.
11. Bruce C. Wolpe and Bertram J. Levine, *Lobbying Congress: How the System Works*, Washington, DC: Congressional Quarterly, 1996, p. 89.
12. Lawrence H. Fuchs, Minority Groups and Foreign Policy, *Political Science Quarterly* 74, no. 2 (1959): 161.
13. Michael S. Teitelbaum and Myron Weiner, Introduction. In *Threatened Peoples, Threatened Borders: World Migration and US Policy*, ed. Michael S. Teitelbaum and Myron Weiner, New York: W. W. Norton, 1995, p. 26.
14. Ibid., p. 27.
15. Sharon Stanton Russell, Migration Patterns of US Foreign Policy Interest. In *Threatened Peoples, Threatened Borders: World Migration and US Policy*, ed. Michael S. Teitelbaum and Myron Weiner, New York: W. W. Norton, 1995, p. 70.
16. Aristide R. Zolberg, From Invitation to Interdiction: US Foreign Policy and Immigration Since 1945. In *Threatened Peoples, Threatened Borders: World Migration and US Policy*, ed. Michael S. Teitelbaum and Myron Weiner, New York: W. W. Norton, 1995, p. 136.
17. Russell, Migration Patterns of US Foreign Policy Interest, p. 71.

18. Yossi Shain, Multicultural Foreign Policy. In *New Tribalisms: The Resurgence of Race and Ethnicity*, ed. Michael W. Hughey, New York: New York University Press, 1998, pp. 299–316.
19. John P. Paul, The Greek Lobby and American Foreign Policy: A Transnational Perspective. In *Ethnic Identities in a Transnational World*, ed. John F. Stack, Jr., Westport, CT: Greenwood, p. 68.
20. Andrew Stark, Political Discourse Analysis and the Debate over Canada's Lobbying Legislation. *Canadian Journal of Political Science* 25, no. 3 (1992): 523.
21. Alicia Iwanska, *Exiled Governments: Spanish and Polish*, Cambridge: Schenkman, 1981, pp. 43–44.
22. Yossi Shain, Ethnic Diasporas and US Foreign Policy. *Political Science Quarterly* 109, no. 5 (1995): 811–841.
23. Ibid., p. 816.
24. Stark, Political Discourse Analysis and the Debate Over Canada's Lobbying Legislation, p. 523.
25. Paolo Dell'Aquila, Tribus et Associations Virtuelles. *Sociétés* 2, no. 68 (2000): 63–68; Tiger Li, Computer-Mediated Communications and the Chinese Students in the US. *The Information Society* 7, no. 2 (1990): 125–137.
26. Lisa Drouillard, Miami's Little Havana: A Nation in Exile *Alternate Routes* 14 (1997): 3–20.
27. Jackie Smith, Organizing Global Action. *Peace Review* 6, no. 4 (1994): 419–425.
28. Edwin Harwood, American Public Opinion and U.S. Immigration Policy. *The Annals of the American Academy of Political Science and Social Science* 487(1986): 201–212.
29. Harold Troper, The Canadian Jewish Polity and the Limits of Political Action: The Campaigns on Behalf of Soviet and Syrian Jews. In *Ethnicity, Politics, and Public Policy: Case Studies in Canadian Diversity*, ed. Harold Troper and Morton Weinfeld, Canada: University of Toronto, 1999, pp. 224–252.
30. Shain, Ethnic Diasporas and US Foreign Policy, p. 812.
31. Ibid., p. 813.
32. Myron Weiner, Asian Politics and U.S. Foreign Policy. In *Immigration and U.S. Foreign Policy*, ed. Robert W. Tucker et al., Boulder, CO: Westview, 1990, p. 207.
33. Ibid.
34. Fuchs, Minority Groups and Foreign Policy, pp. 161, 167.
35. Yossi Shain, The Foreign Policy Role of US Diasporas and Its Domestic Consequences. In *Representing and Imagining America*, ed. Philip John Davies, Keele: Keele University Press, 1996, p. 109.
36. Paul Arthur, Diasporan Intervention in International Affairs: Irish America as a Case Study. *Diaspora* 1, no. 2 (1991): 152.
37. David Sadd and G. Neal Lendenmann, Arab American Grievances. *Foreign Policy* 60 (1985): 18.
38. Paul, The Greek Lobby and American Foreign Policy, p. 54.

39. Patricia Ellis and Zafar Khan, Diasporic Mobilization and the Kashmir Issue in British Politics. *Journal of Ethnic and Migration Studies* 24, no. 3 (1998): 471–488.
40. Shain, The Foreign Policy Role of US Diasporas and its Domestic Consequences, p. 101.
41. Jack Wertheimer, Jewish Organizational Life in the United States since 1945. *American Jewish Yearbook* 95 (1995): 3–98.
42. The Montreal declaration would not have occurred if it were not in connivance with the Port-au-Prince academic group.

    Pétition d'intellectuels haïtiens à la veille des élections présidentielles du 26 novembre 2000.

    > Les soussignés, alarmés par les déroutements successifs du processus démocratique, par les menaces que font peser sur le pays les coups de force, les attentats aux droits des citoyens, les violences orchestrées, se déclarent solidaires des 193 pétitionnaires de la protestation citoyenne.
    > Ils se joignent à tous ceux qui défendent les principes démocratiques et travaillent à l'instauration de l'État de droit pour condamner l'impunité et la confiscation des pouvoirs. Ils s'élèvent contre les procédés d'intimidation qui entretiennent un climat de peur et d'insécurité, démobilisent les individus et les collectifs, poussent à l'exil, conduisent à l'isolement du pays et risquent d'enfermer le peuple haïtien dans l'impasse politique et la régression économique.
    > Alertés par la gravité de la situation du pays après plus de dix ans de tribulations, d'échecs, de destructions, d'accumulation de cadavres, conscients de l'ampleur d'une crise pluridimensionnelle qui remue notre société dans ses profondeurs, les soussignés en appellent à tous les compatriotes, à tous les démocrates, aux partis politiques, aux organisations de la société civile pour qu'ils opposent un refus sans appel à la manipulation et au détournement des procédures démocratiques, et qu'ils oeuvrent sans relâche à la promotion de la libre délibération publique et de la négociation, la seule qui soit compatible avec un projet de société authentiquement démocratique.

43. Charles McC Mathias, Ethnic Groups and Foreign Policy. *Foreign Affairs* 59 (1981): 975–998. Joseph S. Roucek et al., *America's Ethnic Politics*, Westport: Greenwood, 1982.
44. Keely, The Effects of International Migration on US Foreign Policy, p. 242.
45. Yossi Shain, Multicultural Foreign Policy. In *New Tribalisms: The Resurgence of Race and Ethnicity*, ed. Michael W. Hughey, Washington Square, NY: New York University, 1998, pp. 299–316.

4 Virtual Diasporic Public Sphere

1. Michel S. Laguerre, *The Military and Society in Haiti*, Knoxville: University of Tennessee Press, 1993.
2. For discussions of "public sphere" as a category of analysis, see J. Habermas, *The Structural Transformation of the Public Sphere*, Cambridge: MIT, 1989 and C. Calhoun, ed., *Habermas and the Public Sphere*, Cambridge: MIT, 1992.
3. For a recent attempt at assessing the use of the Internet in the Haitian American diaspora, see A. A. Parham, The Diasporic Public Sphere: Internet-Mediated Community and Civic Life in Transnational Haiti. PhD dissertation, Department of Sociology, University of Wisconsin at Madison, 2003. See also Michel S. Laguerre, *The Digital City: The American Metropolis and Information Technology*, New York and Basingstoke: Palgrave Macmillan, 2005.
4. Poll of Haitian-Americans on Haiti's Crisis, U.S. Haiti Policy, and Haitian President Jean Bertrand Aristide. *New California Media/Pacific News Service*, Executive Summary, February 19, 2004, online version.
5. Guy-Robert Saint-Cyr, Lettre de Port-au-Prince: Les Deux Fronts Distincts d'Opposition au Président Haitien. *Le Devoir*, Tuesday February 17, 2004.
6. Steve Miller, Haitians in U.S. Lash Out at Hill Black Caucus Ties. *The Washington Times*, March 8, 2004.
7. Paul A. Barthole, Reclaim Haitian American Loyalty. *The Miami Herald*, Wednesday March 24, 2004.
8. Jacqueline Charles and Dan Devise, Aristide Critic: Television Host Named Haitian Prime Minister. *Knight Ridder/Tribune News Service*, March 9, 2004, p. k. 6987.
9. Patrick Eliancy, Mobilisation à Miami en Solidarité avec la Presse Haitienne. *AlterPresse*, October 18, 2002.
10. Alva James-Johnson, Haitian Protesters Call For the Ouster of President Aristide in Fort Lauderdale. *Moun*, January 24, 2004. Web site: <www.moun.com/Articles/jan2004/1-25.3.htm>
11. Vario Serant, Haiti/Crise: Ils Préfèrent Ecouter des Chimères à Washington. *Alter Presse*, July 10, 2003.
12. Lydia Polgreen, Haiti's New Leader Sees a Long Transition. *The New York Times*, March 12, 2004, p. A6 (L), col. 01.
13. According to Gilles Sassine, "the need for communication and information has lead the way for the significant growth in cybercafés in the Port-au-Prince Metropolitan Area. Community access/cyber café is offered by more than a dozen companies (examples: Labonet in Port-au-Prince, Computerworld in Petionville). Each company has a park of a dozen computers placed for public access, charges members and other users between 50 and 75 gourdes per hour [$1 to $1:50], or between 300 and 650 gourdes [$10 to $15] per month for 20 hours of use in some cases and unlimited access in others. These enterprises ask between 3 and 5 gourdes per page printed." See Gilles Sassine, IT Usage [in Haiti]." Website: <http://www.american.edu/carmel/gs9261a/Telecom_infra.htm>, 2003.

14. National Organization for the Advancement of Haitians, An Open Letter to the Leaders of Haiti. Website: <http://www.noahhaiti.org>, December 29, 2003.
15. Guy S. Antoine, An Open Letter to Members of NOAH. Website: <http://www.intermedia haiti.com>, December 30, 2003.
16. Jean Bertrand Aristide, Commentary. *Pacific News Service*, March 5, 2004.
17. Lyn Duff and Dennis Bernstein, Haitians Under the Gun Getting the Word Out on Cell Phone. *Pacific News Service*, March 19, 2004.

5 Dediasporization: Homeland and Hostland

1. Roy Bryce-Laporte, ed., *Sourcebook on the New Immigration: Implications for the United States and the International Community*, New Brunswick: Transaction, 1980.
2. Charles Hirschman et al., *The Handbook of International Migration: The American Experience*, New York: Russell Sage Foundation, 1999.
3. William F. Stinner et al., *Return Migration and Remittances: Developing a Caribbean Perspective*, Washington, DC: Smithsonian Institution, 1982.
4. Nathan Glazer, Is Assimilation Dead? In *Multiculturalism and American Democracy*, ed. Arthur M. Melzer et al., Lawrence: University Press of Kansas, 1998, pp. 15–36.
5. Nicholas Van Hear, *New Diasporas: The Mass Exodus, Dispersal and Regrouping of Migrant Communities*, Seattle: University of Washington Press, 1998, pp. 48–49.
6. Ibid., p. 48.
7. Regina Romhild, Home-Made Clivages: Ethnonational Discourse, Diasporization, and the Politics of Germanness. *Anthropological Journal of European Cultures* 8, no. 1 (1999): 99–120, p. 114.
8. C. Saint-Blancat, Une Diaspora Musulmane en Europe. *Archives de Sciences Sociales des Religions* 92 (October–December 1995): 9–24, p. 10.
9. See, e.g., Joseph J. Levy, *Entretiens avec Georges Anglade: L'Espace d'Une Génération*, Montréal: Liber, 2004.
10. Leslie Long Casimir, Campaign Trail Leads to Little Haiti. *The Miami Herald*, June 19, 1995.
11. Ibid.
12. David A. Martin, New Rules on Dual Nationality for a Democratizing Globe: Between Rejection and Embrace. *Georgetown Immigration Law Journal* 14, no. 1 (1999): 1–34.
13. Government of the People's Republic of China and Government of the United Kingdom of Britain and Northern Ireland, *Sino-British Joint Declaration on the Question of Hong Kong*, Beijing: Foreign Languages Press, 1984, p. 61.
14. Martin, New Rules on Dual Nationality, pp. 1–34; Jorge A. Vargas, Dual Nationality for Mexicans. 18 *Chicano-Latino Law Review* 1 (1996).
15. Paula Gutierrez, Comment, Mexico's Dual Nationality Amendment: They Do Not Undermine Citizens' Allegiance and Loyalty or US Political Sovereignty. 19 *Loyola L.A. International and Comparative Law Journal* 999 (1997);

Pablo Lizzaraga Chavez, Note. Creating a United States-Mexico Political Double Helix: The Mexican Government's Proposed Dual Nationality Amendment. *Stanford Journal of International Law* 33 (1997): 119–168.

16. Silvia Mara Perez Godoy, Social Movements and International Migration: The Mexican Diaspora Seeks Inclusion in Mexico's Political Affairs, 1968–1998. PhD dissertation, Department of Sociology, University of Chicago, 1998.
17. Peter J. Spiro, Embracing Dual Nationality. Occasional Paper no. 1, Carnegie Endowment for International Peace, 1998.
18. Daphna Golan, V. Y. Mudimbe, Aron Rodrigue, and Steven J. Zipperstein, The Jewish Diaspora, Israel and Jewish Identities: A Dialogue. *The South Atlantic Quarterly* 98 (1/2): 104.
19. Ibid., p. 109.
20. Ibid., p. 111.
21. Kenneth Surin, Afterthoughts on Diaspora. *The South Atlantic Quarterly* 98 (1/2): 275.
22. Robin Cohen, *Global Diasporas*, Seattle: University of Washington Press, 1997, p. 24.
23. Alain Touraine, Vrais et Faux Problèmes. In *Une Société Fragmentée? Le Multiculturalisme en Débat*, ed. Michel Wieviorka et al., Paris: Editions La Découverte, 1996; Milton Gordon, *Assimilation in American Life*, New York: Oxford University Press, 1964.
24. Pal Kolsto, Territorialising Diasporas: The Case of Russians in the Former Soviet Republics. *Millennium: Journal of International Studies* 28, no. 3 (1999): 607–632.
25. Graham Smith, Transnational Politics and the Politics of the Russian Diaspora. *Ethnic and Racial Studies* 22, no. 3 (1999): 500–523.
26. Petra Bauer-Kaase, Germany in Transition: The Challenge of Coping with Unification. In *German Unification: Processes and Outcomes*, ed. M. Donald Hancock and Helga A. Welsch, Boulder: Westview, 1994, pp. 285–311.
27. Despina Sakka et al., Return Migration: Changing Roles of Men and Women. *International Migration* 37, no. 4 (1999): 740–764, p. 742.
28. Yossi Shain, *Marketing the American Creed Abroad: Diasporas in the US and their Homelands*, Cambridge: Cambridge University Press, 1999, p. 168.
29. Yasemin Nuhoglu Soysal, *The Limits of Citizenship*, Chicago: University of Chicago Press, 1994.
30. Helmuth Berking, Homes Away from Home: On Tensions Between Diaspora and Nation-State. *Berliner Journal für Soziologie* 10, no. 1 (2000): 49–60.
31. Van Hear, *New Diasporas*, 195.
32. Sameer Y. Abraham et al., The Southend: An Arab Muslim Working Class Community. In *Arabs in the New World*, ed. Sameer Y. Abraham and Nabeel Abraham, Detroit: Wayne State University, 1983.
33. Michel Wievorka, Culture, Société et Démocratie. In *Une Société Fragmentée? Le Multiculturalisme en Débat*, ed. Michel Wievorka et al., Paris: Editions La Découverte, 1996, pp. 11–60.
34. Stanley J. Tambiah, Transnational Movements, Diaspora, and Multiple Modernities. *Daedalus* 129, no. 1 (2000): 163–194.

Conclusion: Diasporic Politics and Transnational Political Space

1. Victor Roudometof and Anna Karpathakis, Greek Americans and Transnationalism; Religion, Class and Community. In *Communities Across Borders: Immigrants and Transnational Cultures*, ed. Paul Kennedy and Victor Roudometof, London: Routledge, 2002, p. 42.
2. Manuchehr Sanadjian, Transnational Expansion of "Class Struggle" and the Mediation of Sport in Diaspora: The World Cup and Iranian Exiles. In *Communities Across Borders: New Immigrants and Transnational Cultures*, ed. Paul Kennedy and Victor Roudometof, London: Routledge, 2002, p. 93.
3. Maja Povrzanovic Frykman, Homeland Lost and Gained: Croatian Diaspora and Refugees in Sweden. In *New Approaches to Migration? Transnational Communities and the Transformation of Home*, ed. Nadje Al-Ali and Khalid Koser, London: Routledge, 2002, p. 120.

Bibliography

Abou-El-Haj, Barbara. 1997. Languages and Models for Cultural Exchange. In *Culture, Globalization and the World System*, edited by Anthony D. King. Minneapolis: University of Minnesota Press.

Abraham, Sameer Y. et al. 1983. The Southend: An Arab Muslim Working Class Community. In *Arabs in the New World*, edited by Sameer Y. Abraham and Nabeel Abraham. Detroit: Wayne State University Press.

Abu-Lughod, Janet. 1997. Going Beyond Global Babble. In *Culture, Globalization and the World System*, edited by Anthony D. King. Minneapolis: University of Minnesota Press.

Affigne, Tony. 2000. Latino Politics in the United States: An Introduction. *Political Science and Politics* 34 (3): 523–528.

Agnew, J., and J. Duncan, eds. 1989. *The Power of Place: Bringing Together the Geographical and Sociological Imagination*. Boston: Unwin Hyman.

Alex-Assensoh, Y. M., and L. Hanks, eds. 2000 *Black and Multiracial Politics in America*. New York: New York University Press.

Anderson, B. 1994. Exodus. *Critical Enquiry* 20 (2): 314–327.

Anderson, Grace. 1974. *Networks of Contacts*. Waterloo: Wilfred Laurier University Publications.

Ang-Lygate, Magdalene. 1997. Charting the Spaces of (Un)Location: On Theorizing Diaspora. In *Black British Feminism: A Reader*, edited by Heidi Safia Mirza. London: Routledge.

Angoustures, Aline, and Valérie Pascal. 1996. Diasporas et Financement des Conflits. In *Economie des Guerres Civiles*, ed. François J. Ruffin and Jean-Christophe Ruffin. Paris: Hachette, pp. 495–498.

Ansell, Christopher K., and Steven Weber. 1999. Organizing International Politics: Sovereignty and Open Systems. *International Political Science Review* 20 (1): 73–93.

Anthias, Floya. 1998. Evaluating Diaspora Beyond Ethnicity. *Sociology: The Journal of the British Sociological Association* 32 (3): 557–580.

Antoine, Guy S. An Open Letter to Members of NOAH. Website: <http://www.intermediahaiti.com>, December 20, 2003.

Aoki, Andrew L., and Don T. Nakanishi. 2001. Asian Pacific Americans and the New Minority Politics. *Political Science and Politics* 34 (3): 605–610.

Aristide, Jean Bertrand. Commentary, *Pacific News Service*. March 5, 2004.

Armstrong, David. 1998. Globalization and the Social State. *Review of International Studies* 24 (4): 461–478.

Arthur, Paul. 1991. Diasporan Intervention in International Affairs: Irish America as a Case Study. *Diaspora* 1 (2): 143–162.

Ashton, T. S. 1980. *The Industrial Revolution, 1760–1830.* London: Oxford University Press.

Bahbha, H., ed. 1990. *Nation and Narration.* London: Routledge.

Balibar, Etienne, and Immanuel Wallerstein, eds. 1991. *Race, Nation, Class: Ambiguous Identities.* London: Verso.

Bamyeh, Mohammed A. 1993. Transnationalism. *Current Sociology* 41 (3): 1–95.

Banks, Michael, and Martin Shaw, eds. 1991. *State and Society in International Relations.* London: Harvester and Wheatsheaf.

Banton, M. 1983. *Racial and Ethnic Competition.* New York: Cambridge University Press.

Barnard, C. I. 1958. *The Functions of the Executive.* Cambridge: Harvard University Press.

Barrera, M. 1979. *Race and Class in the Southwest.* South Bend: University of Notre Dame Press.

Barth, F., ed. 1969. *Ethnic Groups and Boundaries.* Boston: Little, Brown.

Barthole, Paul A. Reclaim Haitian American Loyalty. *The Miami Herald.* March 24, 2004.

Basch, Linda et al. 1994. *Nations Unbound: Transnational Projects, Postcolonial Predicaments and Deterritorialized Nation-States.* Amsterdam: Gordon and Breach.

Bastide, Roger 1970. *Le Prochain et le Lointain.* Paris: Editions Cujas.

Bauer-Kaase, Petra. 1994. Germany in Transition: The Challenge of Coping with Unification. In *German Unification: Processes and Outcomes*, edited by M. Donald Hancock and Helga A. Welsch. Boulder: Westview.

Belanger, Jacques et al., eds. 1999. *Being Local Worldwide.* Ithaca: ILR Press.

Berking, Helmuth. 2000. Homes Away from Home: On Tensions Between Diaspora and Nation-State. *Berliner Journal fur Soziologie* 10 (1): 49–60.

Berry, Jeffrey M. 1977. *Lobbying for the Poor: The Political Behavior of Public Interest Groups.* Princeton: Princeton University Press.

Biersteker, Thomas J., and Cynthia Weber. 1996. *State Sovereignty as Social Construct.* Cambridge: Cambridge University Press.

Blauner, R. 1972. *Racial Oppression in America.* New York: Harper and Row.

Bobo, Lawrence, and Frank D. Gilliam, Jr. 1990. Race, Sociopolitical Participation, and Black Empowerment. *American Political Science Review* 84: 377–393.

Borja, Jordi, and Manuel Castells. 1997. *Local and Global: Management of Cities in the Information Age.* London: Earthscan Publications.

Boyarin, Daniel, and Jonathan Boyarin. 1993. Diaspora: Generation and the Ground of Jewish Identity. *Critical Inquiry* 19: 693–725.

Brown, Chris. 2000. Cultural Diversity and International Political Theory. *Review of International Studies* 26 (2): 199–214.

———. 2000. Cosmopolitan, World Citizenship and Global Civil Society. *Critical Review of International, Social and Political Philosophy* 3 (1): 7–26.

Bryce-Laporte, Roy, ed. 1980. *Sourcebook on the New Immigration: Implications for the United States and the International Community*. New Brunswick: Transaction.

Buchanan, Susan H. 1980. Scattered Seeds: The Meaning of Migration for Haitians in New York City. PhD dissertation, Department of Anthropology, New York University.

Cain, Bruce E. 1988. Asian Americans' Electoral Power: Imminent or Illusory. *Election Politics*. Spring: 28–29.

Cain, Bruce E., and Brendan J. Doherty. *The Impact of Dual Citizenship on Political Participation*. The Nation of Immigrants Conference, Institute of Governmental Studies, University of California at Berkeley, May 2–3, 2003.

Calhoun, C., ed. 1992. *Habermas and the Public Sphere*. Cambridge: MIT.

Carment, D. 1993. The International Dimensions of Ethnic Conflict: Concepts, Indicators and Theory. *Journal of Peace Research* 30: 137–150.

Carpizo, Jose, and Diego Valados. 1998. *El Voto de los Mexicanos en el Extranjero*. Mexico City: Universidad Nacional Autonoma de Mexico.

Carr, E. H. 1962. *The Twenty Years' Crisis 1919–1939*. London: Macmillan.

Casimir, Leslie Long. Campaign Trail Leads to Little Haiti. *The Miami Herald*. June 19, 1995.

Castells, Manuel. 1991. *The Informational City*. Oxford: Basil Blackwell.

———. 1996. *The Rise of the Network Society*. Cambridge: Blackwell.

Castells, Manuel, and Peter Hall. 1994. *The Technopoles of the World: The Making of the Twenty-First Century Industrial Complexes*. London: Routledge.

Chaliand, Gerard, ed. 1989. *Minority Peoples in the Age of Nation-States*. London: Pluto Press.

Charles, Jacqueline, and Dan Devise Aristide Critic, Television Host Named Haitian Prime Minister. *Knight Rider/Tribune News Service*, March 9, 2004, p. k. 6987.

Charles, Jacqueline, Carolyn Salazar, and Draeger Martinez Dade. Vote Is Historic for Two New Legislators. *The Miami Herald*. November 6, 2002.

Chatfield, Charles. 1997. Introduction. In *Transnational Social Movements and Global Politics*, edited by Jackie Smith et al. Syracuse: Syracuse University Press.

Chavez, Pablo Lizzaraga. 1997. Creating a United States-Mexico Political Double Helix: The Mexican Government's Proposed Dual Nationality Amendment. *Stanford Journal of International Law* 33, no. 1: 119–151.

Checkel, Jeffrey T. 1998. The Constructivist Turn in International Relations Theory. *World Politics* 50 (2): 324–348.

Chisholm, D. 1989. *Coordination Without Hierarchy: Informal Structures in Multiorganizational Systems*. Berkeley: University of California Press.

Cho, Wendy K. Tam. 1999. Naturalization, Socialization, Participation: Immigrants and (Non-) Voting. *Journal of Politics* 61 (4): 1140–1155.

Citrin, Jack et al. 2002. *How Race, Ethnicity, and Immigration are Changing the California Electorate*. San Francisco: Public Policy Institute of California.

Cizmic, Ivan. 1998. Political Activities of Croatian Immigrants in the USA and the Creation of an Independent Croatia. *Drustvena Istrazivanja* 7 (33–34): 5–25.

Clarke, Suzan. 2004. Haitians Work for the American Dream. *The Journal News*, Westchester County, NY, July 16, 2004.

Clay, William. 1992. *Just Permanent Interests: Black Americans in Congress, 1870–1991*. New York: Amistad.

Clifford, James. 1994. Diasporas. *Cultural Anthropology* 9 (3): 302–338.

Clough, Michael. 1994. Grass-Roots Policy Making: Say Good-Bye to the "Wise Men." *Foreign Affairs* 73 (1): 2–7.

Cohen, Abner. 1971. Cultural Strategies in the Organization of Trading Diasporas. In *The Development of Indigenous Trade and Markets in West Africa*, edited by Claude Meillassoux. Oxford: Oxford University Press.

Cohen, Robin. 1996. Diasporas and the Nation-State. *International Affairs* 72 (3): 507–520.

———. 1997. *Global Diasporas*. Seattle: University of Washington Press.

Comeau, Y. 1987. Resurgence de la Vie Quotidienne et de ses Sociologies. *Sociologie et Société* 19 (2): 115–123.

Connell, John, and Richard P. C. Brown. 1995. Migration and Remittances in the South Pacific: Towards New Perspectives. *Asian and Pacific Migration Journal* 4 (1): 1–33.

Conner, Walker. 1986. The Impact of Homelands Upon Diasporas. In *Modern Diasporas in International Politics*, edited by Gabriel Sheffer. London: Croom Helm.

Contas, Dimitri C., and Athanassios G. Platias, eds. 1993. *Diasporas in World Politics: The Greeks in Comparative Perspective*. London: Macmillan.

Cox, Kevin R. 1997. Globalization and Its Politics in Question. In *Spaces of Globalization*, edited by Kevin R. Cox. New York: Guilford Press.

Cox, Robert W. 1999. Civil Society at the Turn of the Millenium: Prospects for an Alternative World Order. *Review of International Studies* 25 (1): 3–28.

Curtin, Philip D. 1990. The Environment Beyond Europe and the European Theory of the Empire. *Journal of World History* 1 (2): 131–150.

Dahan, Michael, and Gabriel Sheffer. 2001. Ethnic Groups and Distance Shrinking Communication Technologies. *Nationalism and Politics* 7 (1): 85–107.

Davis, K. 1953. Management and Communication and the Grapevine. *Harvard Business Review* 31: 43–49.

De la Garza, Rodolfo, Martha Menchacha, and Louis DeSipio. 1994. Barrio Ballots: Latino Politics in the 1990 Elections. Boulder: Westview.

DeSipio, Louis. Building a New Foreign Policy Among Friends: National Efforts to Construct Long-Term Relationships with Latin American Emigres in the United States. Paper read at the Conference on "States and Diasporas," Columbia University, May 8, 1998.

———. 1996. *Counting on the Latino Vote: Latinos as a New Electorate*. Charlottesville: University of Virginia Press.

De Tocqueville, Alexis. 2000. *Democracy in America*. Chicago: University of Chicago Press.

Dell'Aquila, Paolo. 2000. Tribus et Associations Virtuelles. *Sociétés* 2 (68): 63–68.

Desdunes, Rodolphe L. 1973. *Our People and Our History*. Baton Rouge: Louisiana State University Press.

Dickson, David A. 1996. American Society and the African American Foreign Policy Lobby: Constraints and Opportunities. *Journal of Black Studies* 27 (2): 139–151.

Dirlik, Arif. 1996. The Global in the Local. In *Global/Local: Cultural Production and the Transnational Imaginary*, edited by Rob Wilson and Wimal Dissanayake. Durham: Duke University Press.

Dominguez, Virginia. 1994. *White By Definition: Social Classification in Creole Louisiana*. New Brunswick: Rutgers University Press.

Drouillard, Lisa. 1997. Miami's Little Havana: A Nation in Exile. *Alternate Routes* 14: 3–20.

Duchacek, Ivo D. 1988. Multicommunal and Bicommunal Polities and their International Relations. In *Perforated Sovereignties and International Relations: Trans-Sovereign Contacts of Subnational Governments*, edited by Ivo D. Duchacek, Daniel Latouche, and Garth Stevenson. New York: Greenwood.

Duff, Lynn, and Dennis Bernstein. Haitians Under the Gun Getting the Word Out on Cell Phone. *Pacific News Service*, March 19, 2004.

Eade, John, ed. 1997. *Living the Global: Globalization as Local Process*. New York: Routledge.

Edinger, Lewis J. 1956. *German Exile Politics: The Social Democratic Executive Committee in the Nazi Era*. Berkeley: University of California Press.

Eliancy, Patrick. Mobilisation à Miami en Solidarité avec la Presse Haitienne. *AlterPresse*. October 18, 2002.

Ellis, Patricia, and Zafar Khan. 1998. Diasporic Mobilization and the Kashmir Issue in British Politics. *Journal of Ethnic and Migration Studies* 24 (3): 471–488.

Esman, M. J. 1985. Two Dimensions of Ethnic Politics: Defense of Homelands, Immigrant Rights. *Ethnic and Racial Studies* 8: 438–440.

Fabian, Johannes. 1983. *Time and the Other*. New York: Columbia University Press.

Faist, Thomas. 1999. Developing Transnational Social Spaces: The Turkish-German Example. In *Migration and Transnational Social Spaces*, edited by Ludger Pries. Aldershot: Ashgate.

Featherstone, Mike, ed. 1990. *Global Culture, Nationalism and Modernity*. London: Sage.

———. 1993. Global and Local Cultures. In *Mapping the Futures*, edited by Jon Bird et al. New York: Routledge.

———. 1996. Localism, Globalism, and Cultural Identity. In *Global/Local: Cultural Production and the Transnational Imaginary*, edited by Rob Wilson and Wimal Dissanayake. Durham: Duke University Press.

Feldblum, Miriam. 1993. Paradoxes of Ethnic Politics: The Case of Franc-Maghrebis in France. *Ethnic and Racial Studies* 16: 52–74.

Fitzgerald, Marian. 1988. Different Roads? The Development of Afro-Caribbean and Asian Political Organization in London. *New Community* 14: 385–396.

Fitzpatrick, P. 1988. The Rise and Rise of Informalism. In *Informal Justice*, edited by R. Matthews. London: Sage, pp.178–198.

Friedman, J. 1990. Being in the World: Globalization and Localization. In *Global Culture*, edited by Mike Featherstone. London: Sage.

Fuchs, Lawrence H. 1959. Minority Groups and Foreign Policy. *Political Science Quarterly* 74 (2): 161–167.

Gans, Herbert J. 1979. Symbolic Ethnicity: The Future of Ethnic Groups and Cultures in America. *Ethnic and Racial Studies* 2 (1): 1–20.

Garcia, Maria Cristina. 1996. *Havana USA: Cuban Exiles and Cuban Americans in South Florida, 1959–1994*. Berkeley: University of California Press.

Gerstle, Gary, and John Mollenkopf. 2001. *Immigrants, Civic Culture, and Modes of Political Incorporation*. New York: Russell Sage Foundation.

Gerth, H. H., and C. Wright Mills, eds. 1977. *From Max Weber*. London: Routledge.

Gil, Carlos B. 1992. Cuauthemoc Cardenas and the Rise of Transborder Politics. In *Hopes and Frustrations: Interviews with Leaders of Mexico's Political Opposition*, edited by Carlos B. Gil. Wilmington, DE: Scholarly Resources.

Glasgow, Kathy A. New Political Complexion. *Miami New Times*. May 3, 2001.

Glazer, Nathan. 1998. Is Assimilation Dead? In *Multiculturalism and American Democracy*, edited by Arthur M. Melzer et al. Lawrence: University Press of Kansas.

Godoy, Silvia Maria Perez. 1999. Social Movements and International Migration: The Mexican Diaspora Seeks Inclusion in Mexico's Political Affairs, 1968–1998. PhD dissertation, University of Chicago.

Golan, Daphna, V. Y. Mudimbe, Aron Rodrigue, and Steven J. Zipperstein. 1999. The Jewish Diaspora, Israel and Jewish Identities: A Dialogue. *The South Atlantic Quarterly* 98: 95–116.

Goldberg, David H. 1990. *Foreign Policy and Ethnic Interest Groups: American and Canadian Jews Lobby for Israel*. New York: Greenwood.

Goodman, James. 1997. National Multiculturalism and Transnational Migrant Politics: Australian and East Timorese. *Asian Pacific Migration Journal* 6 (3–4): 457–480.

Gordon, April. 1998. The New Diaspora-African Immigration to the United States. *Journal of Third World Studies* 15 (1): 79–103.

Gordon, Milton. 1964. *Assimilation in American Life*. New York: Oxford University Press.

Government of the People's Republic of China and Government of the United Kingdom of Britain and Northern Ireland. 1984. *Sino-British Joint Declaration on the Question of Hong Kong*. Beijing: Foreign Languages Press.

Graham, Pamela M. 1997. Reimagining the Nation and Defining the District: Dominican Migration and Transnational Politics. In *Caribbean Circuits: New Directions in the Study of Caribbean Migration*, edited by Patricia R. Pessar. Staten Island: Center for Migration Studies.

Green, Eric Haitian American Elected Mayor, City Councilman in South Florida. *Washington File*. May 22, 2001, U.S. Department of State International Information Programs.

Guehenno, Jean-Marie. 1995. *The End of the Nation-State*. Minneapolis: University of Minnesota Press.

Gutierrez, Carlos Gonzales. 1997. Decentralized Diplomacy: The Role of Consular Offices in Mexico's Relations with its Diaspora. In *Bridging the Border:*

Transforming Mexico-U.S. Relations, edited by Rodolfo O. de la Garza and Jesus Velasco. Lanham, MD: Rowman and Littlefield.

———. 1993. The Mexican Diaspora in California: Limits and Possibilities for the Mexican Government. In *The California-Mexican Connection*, edited by Abraham F. Lowenthal and Katrina Burgess. Stanford, CA: Stanford University Press.

Gutierrez, Paula. 1997. Comment, Mexico's Dual Nationality Amendment: They Do Not Undermine Citizens' Allegiance and Loyalty or US Political Sovereignty. 19 *Loyola L.A. International and Comparative Law Journal* 999–1026.

Guzzini, Stefano. 2000. A Reconstruction of Constructivism in International Relations. *European Journal of International Relations* 6 (2): 147–182.

Habermas, J. 1989. *The Structural Transformation of the Public Sphere*. Cambridge: MIT.

Hadot, Jean. 1972. Community, Utopia and Primitive Christianity. *Archives Internationales de Sociologie de la Coopération et du Développement* 31: 7–22.

Hall, Stuart. 1997. The Local and the Global: Globalization and Ethnicity. In *Culture, Globalization and the World System*, edited by Anthony B. King. Minneapolis: University of Minnesota Press.

Hamilton, Kimberly, and Kate Holder. 1991. International Migration and Foreign Policy: A Survey of the Literature. *The Washington Quarterly* 14 (2): 195–211.

Handlin, Oscar. 1951. *The Uprooted*. Boston: Little, Brown.

Hannerz, Ulf. 1990. Cosmopolitans and Locals in World Culture. In *Global Culture*, edited by Mike Featherstone. London: Sage.

Hansen, Randall, and Patrick Weil. 2002. *Dual Nationality, Social Rights and Federal Citizenship in the US and Europe*. New York: Berghahn.

Harding, P., and R. Jenkins. 1989. *The Myth of the Hidden Economy*. Philadelphia: Open University Press.

Harvey, David. 1993. From Space to Place and Back Again: Reflections on the Condition of Postmodernity. In *Mapping the Futures: Local Cultures, Global Change*, edited by Jon Bird et al. New York: Routledge.

Harwood, Edwin. 1986. American Public Opinion and U.S. Immigration Policy. *The Annals of the American Academy of Political Science and Social Science* 487: 201–212.

Hayward, Mark NH Haitian-American Fear for Nation's Democracy. *The Union Leader* (Manchester, NH), February 27, 2004.

Hechter, M., and D. Okamoto. 2001. Consequences of Minority Group Formation. *Annual Reviews of Political Science* 4: 189–215.

Held, David, and Anthony McGrew. 1998. The End of the Old Order? Globalization and the Prospects for World Order. *Review of International Studies* 24 (5): 219–243.

Held, David et al. 1999. *Global Transformations: Politics, Economics and Culture*. Stanford: Stanford University Press.

Hero, Rodney et al. 2000. Latino Participation, Partisanship, and Office Holding. *Political Science and Politics* 34 (3): 529–535.

Hill, Kevin, and John Hughes. 1998. *Cyberpolitics: Citizen Activism in the Age of the Internet*. New York: Rowman and Littlefield.

Hirschman, Charles et al. 1999. *The Handbook of International Migration: The American Experience*. New York: Russell Sage Foundation.

Hopf, Ted. 1998. The Promise of Constructivism in International Relations Theory. *International Security* 23 (1): 171–200.

Hula, Kevin W. 1999. *Lobbying Together: Interest Group Coalitions in Legislative Politics*. Washington, DC: Georgetown University Press.

Huntington, Samuel P. 1997. The Erosion of American National Interests. *Foreign Affairs* 76 (5): 28–49.

Itzigsohn, Jose. 2000. Immigration and the Boundaries of Citizenship: The Institutions of Immigrants' Political Transnationalism. *International Migration Review* 34 (4): 1126–1154.

Iwanska, Alicia. 1981. *Exiled Governments: Spanish and Polish*. Cambridge: Schenkman.

Jacobs, Sonji. Haitian American Group Celebrates Anniversary, Commitment to GOP. *The Miami Herald*. July 8, 2002.

Jameson, Frederic et al., eds. 1998. *The Cultures of Globalization*. Durham: Duke University Press.

James-Johnson, Alva. Haitian Protestors Call for the Ouster of President Aristide in Fort Lauderdale. *Moun*. January 24, 2004.

Jean-Pierre, Jean. 1994. The Tenth Department. In *The Haiti Files: Decoding the Crisis*, edited by James Ridgeway. Washington, DC: Essential.

Jenkins, Rhys Owen. 1984. *Transnational Corporations and Industrial Transformation in Latin America*. New York: St. Martin's.

Jones-Correa, Michael. 1998. *Between Two Nations: The Political Predicament of Latinos in New York City*. Ithaca: Cornell University Press.

Karpathakis, Anna. 1999. Home Society Politics and Immigrant Political Incorporation: The Case of Greek Immigrants in New York City. *International Migration Review* 33 (1): 55–78.

Kearney, Michael. 1995. The Local and the Global: The Anthropology of Globalization and Transnationalism. *Annual Review of Anthropology* 24: 547–565.

Keck, Margaret E., and Kathryn Sikkink. 1998. *Activists Beyond Borders*. Ithaca, NY: Cornell University Press.

Keely, Charles B. 1995. The Effects of International Migration on U.S. Foreign Policy. In *Threatened Peoples, Threatened Borders: World Migration and U.S. Policy*, edited by Michael S. Teitelbaum and Myron Wiener. New York: W. W. Norton, pp. 215–243.

Keith, Michael, and Steve Pile, eds. 1993. *Place and the Politics of Identity*. New York: Routledge.

Keyman, E. Fuat. 1997. *Globalization, State, Identity/Difference: Toward a Critical Social Theory of International Relations*. Atlantic Highlands, NJ: Humanities Press.

Kibria, Nazli. 1998. Multicultural America and the New Immigration. *Society* 35 (6): 84–88.

Kim, Claire Jean et al. 2001. Interracial Politics; Asian Americans and Other Communities of Color. *Political Science and Politics* 34 (3): 631–644.

King, Anthony D. 1997. Preface to the Revised Edition. In *Culture, Globalization and their World System*, edited by Anthony B. King. Minneapolis: University of Minnesota Press.

Knight, Franklin W. et al. 1989. The African Diaspora. In *UNESCO General History of Africa*, edited by J. F. Ade Ajayi. Vol. 4. Berkeley: University of California Press.

Kolsto, Pal. 1999. Territoriliasing Diasporas: The Case of Russians in the Former Soviet Republics. *Millenium: Journal of International Studies* 28 (3): 607–632.

Kratochwil, Friedrich, and Yosef Lapid, eds. 1996. *The Return of Culture and Identity in IR Theory*. Boulder: Lynne Rienner.

Laffey, Mark. 2000. Locating Identity: Performativity, Foreign Policy and State Action. *Review of International Studies* 26 (3): 429–444.

Laguerre, Michel S. 1984. *American Odyssey: Haitians in New York City*. Ithaca: Cornell University Press.

———. 1994. Business and Corruption: Framing the Haitian Military Question. *California Management Review* 36 (3): 89–106.

———. 1982. *The Complete Haitiana, 1900–1980*. Millwood, NY: Kraus International.

———. 1998. *Diasporic Citizenship: Haitian Americans in Transnational America*. London: Macmillan.

———. 2005. *The Digital City: The American Metropolis and Information Technology*. New York and Basingstoke: Palgrave Macmillan.

———. 2000. *The Global Ethnopolis: Chinatown, Japantown, and Manilatown in American Society*. London: Macmillan.

———. 1994. Headquarters and Subsidiaries: Haitian Immigrant Family Households in New York City. In *Minority Families in the United States: A Multicultural Perspective*, edited by Ronald L. Taylor. Englewood Cliffs, NJ: Prentice-Hall, pp. 47–61.

———. 1994. *The Informal City*. New York and Basingstoke: Macmillan.

———. 1993. *The Military and Society in Haiti*. Knoxville: University of Tennessee Press.

———. 1999. *Minoritized Space: An Inquiry into the Spatial Order of Things*. Berkeley: University of California-Institute of Governmental Studies Press (now Berkeley Public Policy Press).

———. 1997. The Role of the Diaspora in Haitian Politics. In *Haiti Renewed*, edited by Robert I. Rotberg. Washington, DC: Brookings Institution Press.

———. 1999. State, Diaspora and Transnational Politics. *Millennium: Journal of International Studies* 28 (3): 633–652.

———. 1995. *Transnational Citizenship*. Keynote address delivered at the annual meetings of the Sociology of Education Association, Asilomar Conference Center, Pacific Grove, California, February 3–5.

———. 2004. *Urban Multiculturalism and Globalization in New York City*. New York and Basingstoke: Palgrave Macmillan.

Lahiri, Sajal, and Pascals Raimondos-Moller. 2000. Lobbying by Ethnic Groups and AID Allocation. *The Economic Journal* 110 (462): C63–C65.

Lai, James S. et al. 2001. Asian Pacific American Campaigns, Elections, and Elected Officials. *Political Science and Politics* 34 (3): 611–618.

Laidi, Zaki, ed. 1997. *Le Temps Mondial*. Paris: Editions Complexe.

Leighley, Jan E. 2001. *Strength in Numbers? The Political Mobilization of Racial and Ethnic Minorities*. Princeton: Princeton University Press.

Lien, Pei-Te. 2001. Asian Pacifc Americans' Social Movements and Interest Groups. *Political Science and Politics* 34 (3): 619–624.

———. 1994. Ethnicity and Political Participation: A Comparison Between Asian and Mexican Americans. *Political Behavior* 16 (2): 237–264.

———. 1997. *The Political Participation of Asian Americans: Voting Behavior in Southern California*. New York: Garland Publishing

Lien, Pei-Te et al. 2001. Asian Pacific American Public Opinion and Political Participation. *Political Science and Politics* 34 (3): 625–631.

Leurdijk, J. H. 1974. From International to Transnational Politics: A Change of Paradigm. *International Social Science Journal* 26 (1): 53–69.

Levitt, Peggy. 1996. Transnationalizing Civil and Political Change: The Case of Transnational Organization Ties between Boston and the Dominican Republic. PhD dissertation, Department of Sociology, MIT.

———. 2001. *The Transnational Villagers*. Berkeley: University of California Press.

Levy, Joseph J. 2004. *Entretiens avec Georges Anglade: L' Espace d'Une Génération*. Montreal: Liber

Li, Tiger. 1990. Computer-Mediated Communications and the Chinese Students in the U.S. *The Information Society* 7 (2): 125–137.

Light, Ivan. 1999. Immigrant Incorporation in the Garment Industry of Los Angeles. *International Migration Review* 23 (1): 5–25.

Light, Ivan, and Edna Bonacich. 1988. *Immigrant Entrepreneurs: Koreans in Los Angeles 1965–1982*. Berkeley: University of California Press.

Lozano, B. 1989. *The Invisible Work Force*. New York: Free Press.

Mair, A. 1994. Honda's Global Flexifactory Network. *International Journal of Operations and Production Management* 14 (3): 6–23.

———. 1994. *Honda's Global Local Corporation*. London: Macmillan.

———. 1997. *Strategic Location: The Myth of the Postnational Enterprise*. New York: Guilford Press.

Mandaville, Peter G. 1999. Territory and Translocality: Discrepant Idioms of Political Identity. *Millennium: Journal of International Studies* 28 (3): 653–675.

Maney, Gregory M. 2000. Transnational Mobilization and Civil Rights in Northern Ireland. *Social Problems* 47 (2): 153–179.

Mankekar, Purnima. 1994. Reflections on Diasporic Identities: A Prolegomenon to an Analysis of Political Bifocality. *Diaspora* 3 (3): 463–485.

Marquez, Benjamin et al. 2000. Representation by Other Means: Mexican American and Puerto Rican Social Movement Organizations. *Political Science and Politics* 34 (3): 541–546.

Martin, David A. 1999. New Rules on Dual Nationality for a Democratizing Globe: Between Rejection and Embrace. *Georgetown Immigration and Law Journal* 14 (1): 1–34.

Martinez-Ebers, Valerie et al. 2000. Latino Interests in Education, Health and Criminal Justice Policy. *Political Science and Politics* 34 (3): 547–554.

Martinez-Saldana, Jesus. 1993. At the Periphery of Democracy: The Binational Politics of Mexican Immigrants in Silicon Valley. PhD dissertation, University of California, Berkeley.

Martinez-Saldana, Jesus, and Raul Ross Pineda. 2002. Suffrage for Mexicans Residing Abroad. In *Cross-Border Dialogues: U.S.-Mexico Social Movement Networking*, edited by David Brooks and Jonathan Fox. La Jolla, CA: UCSD Center for U.S. Mexican Studies, 275–292.

Massey, Douglas S. et al. 1998. *Worlds in Motion: Understanding International Migration at the End of the Millennium*. Oxford: Clarendon Press.

Mathias, Charles McC, Jr. 1981. Ethnic Groups and Foreign Policy. *Foreign Affairs* 59 (5): 975–998.

Mauss, Marcel 1954. *The Gift*. Glencoe: Free Press.

Mercure, D. 1979. L'Etude des Temporalités Sociales. *Cahiers Internationaux de Sociologie* LXVII: 263–276.

Miller, Steve. Haitians in U.S. Lash Out at Hill Black Caucus Ties. *The Washington Times*. March 8, 2004.

Mittar, V. 1988. *Growth of the Urban Informal Sector in a Developing Economy*. New Delhi: Deep and Deep Publications.

Mollenkopf, John, David Olson, and Timothy Ross. 2001. Immigrant Political Participation in New York and Los Angeles. In *Governing Urban America: Immigrants, Natives, and Urban Politics*, edited by Michael Jones Correa. New York: Russell Sage Foundation.

Monje Jr., Carlos. St. Fleur a Big Winner in the 5th District. *The Boston Globe*. July 7, 1999.

Montoya, Lisa J. et al. 2000. Latina Politics: Gender, Participation, and Leadership. *Political Science and Politics* 34 (3): 555–562.

Nakanishi, Don T. 1998. When Numbers Do Not Add Up: Asian Pacific Americans and California Politics. In *Racial and Ethnic Politics in California*, edited by Michael B. Preston, Bruce Cain, and Sandra Bass. Berkeley: Institute of Governmental Studies Press.

O'Meara, Patrick et al. 2000. *Globalization and the Challenges of a New Century*. Bloomington: Indiana University Press.

Pachon, Harry, and Louis DeSipio. 1994. *New Americans by Choice: Political Perspectives of Latino Immigrants*. Boulder: Westview.

Panossian, Razmik. 1998. Between Ambivalence and Intrusion: Politics and Identity in Armenia-Diaspora Relations. *Diaspora* 7 (2): 149–196.

Parham, A. A. 2003. The Diasporic Public Sphere: Internet-Mediated Community and Civic Life in Transnational Haiti. PhD dissertation, Department of Sociology, University of Wisconsin at Madison.

Paul, John P. 1981. The Greek Lobby and American Foreign Policy: A Transnational Perspective. In *Ethnic Identities in a Transnational World*, edited by John F. Stack, Jr. Westport, CT: Greenwood.

Petras, James. 1997. Imperialism and NGOs in Latin America. *Monthly Review* 49 (7): 10–27.

Pierre-Louis, *François*. 2006. *Haitians in New York City: Transnationalism and Hometown Associations*. Gainesville, FL: University Press of Florida.

Pierre-Pierre, Gary. For Haitians, Leadership Split is a Generation Gap. *The New York Times*. September 24, 1997, sec. B, p. 4, col. 1.

Polgreen, Lydia. Haiti's New Leader Sees a Long Transition. *The New York Times*. March 12, 2004, p. A (L), col. 01.

Pons, Frank Moya. 1995. *The Dominican Republic: A National History*. New Rochelle, NY: Hispaniola.

Portes, A. et al. 1989. *The Informal Economy*. Baltimore: Johns Hopkins University Press.

———. 1999. Transnational Communities. *Ethnic and Racial Studies* Special Issue 22 (2): 217–477.

Preston, Michael B., Bruce E. Cain, and Sandra Bass, eds. 1998. *Racial and Ethnic Politics in California*. Berkeley: Institute of Governmental Studies.

Prával, René. 1999. Discours du Président de la République, son Excellence M. Rene Preval, Lors de la Réception en l'Honneur des Peintres Haitiens Vivant a l'Etranger, le 7 Mai 1999, au Palais national. Port-au-Prince: Ministere des Haitiens Vivant à l'Etranger.

Rakowitz, Robert Nissim. 1997. Exodus from the Babylonian Captivity: The Jews of Modern Iraq. *International Journal of Group Tensions* 27 (3): 177–191.

Redd, Kalimah. Fearing for Homeland and Kin: Haitian Americans Are Worried About Political Violence On the Island. *The Boston Globe*. February 26, 2004.

Ree, Jonathan. 1998. Cosmopolitanism and the Experience of Nationality. In *Cosmopolitics: Thinking and Feeling Beyond the Nation*, edited by Pheng Cheah and Bruce Robbins. Minneapolis: University of Minnesota Press.

Richards, E. G. 1998. *Mapping Time: The Calendar and its History*. New York: Oxford University Press.

Roberson, B. A., ed. 1998. *International Society and the Development of International Relations Theory*. London: Pinter.

Robertson, Roland. 1992. *Globalization: Social Theory and Global Culture*. London: Sage.

———. 1995. Globalization: Time-Space and Homogeneity-Heterogeneity. In *Global Modernities*, edited by Mike Featherstone et al. London: Sage.

Robinson, William I. 1998. Beyond Nation-State Paradigms: Globalization, Sociology, and the Challenge of Transnational Studies. *Sociological Forum* 13 (4): 561–594.

Roucek, Joseph S. et al. 1982. *America's Ethnic Politics*. Westport: Greenwood.

Rodrik, Dani. 2000. Sense and Nonsense in the Globalization Debate. In *Globalization and the Challenges of a New Century*, edited by Patrick O'Meara et al. Bloomington: Indiana University Press.

Roethlisberger, F. J., and W. J. Dickson. 1947. *Management and the Worker*. Cambridge, MA: Harvard University Press.

Romhild, Regina. 1999. Home-Made Cleavages: Ethnonational Discourse, Diasporization, and the Politics of Germanness. *Anthropological Journal of European Cultures* 8 (1): 99–120.

Rosenstone, Steven J., and John M. Hansen. 1993. *Mobilization, Participation, and Democracy in America*. New York: Macmillan.

Roudometof, Victor, and Anna Karpathakis. 2002. Greek Americans and Transnationalism; Religion, Class, and Community. In *Communities Across Borders: Immigrants and Transnational Cultures*, edited by Paul Kennedy and Victor Roudometof. London: Routledge.

Rouse, Roger. 1991. Mexican Migration and the Social Space of Postmodernism. *Diaspora* 1: 8–23.

Russell, Sharon Stanton. 1995. Migration Patterns of U.S. Foreign Policy Interest. In *Threatened Peoples, Threatened Borders: World Migration and U.S. Policy*, edited by Michael S. Teitelbaum and Myron Weiner. New York: W. W. Norton.

Sachs, Jeffrey. 2000. International Economics: Unlocking the Mysteries of Globalization. In *Globalization and the Challenges of a New Century*, edited by Patrick O'Meara et al. Bloomington: Indiana University Press.

Sadd, David, and G. Neal Lendenmann. 1985. Arab American Grievances. *Foreign Policy* 60: 17–30.

Safran, William. 1991. Diasporas in Modern Societies: Myths of Homeland and Return. *Diaspora* 1 (1): 83–99.

Saint-Blancat, C. 1995. Une Diaspora Musulmane en Europe. *Archives de Sciences Sociales des Religions* 92 (October–December): 9–24.

Saint-Cyr, Guy-Robert. 2004. Lettre de Port-au-Prince: Les Deux Fronts Distintcs d'Opposition au Président Haitien. *Le Devoir*. Tuesday, February 17.

Sakka, Despina et al. 1999. Return Migration: Changing Roles of Men and Women. *International Migration* 37 (4): 740–764.

Saito, Leland. 1998. *Race and Politics: Asian Americans, Latinos, and Whites in a Los Angeles Suburb*. Urbana: University of Illinois Press.

Saloojee, Anver, and Myer Siemiatychi. Formal and Non-Formal Political Participation by Immigrants and Newcomers: Understanding the Linkages and Posing the Questions. *Canadian Issues /Themes Canadiens*. April 2003, pp. 42–46.

Sanadjian, Manuchehr. 2002. Transnational Expansion of "Class Struggle" and the Mediation of Sport in Diaspora: The World Cup and Iranian Exiles. In *Communities Across Borders: New Immigrants and Transnational Cultures*, edited by Paul Kennedy and Victor Roudometof. London: Routledge.

Sassen, Saskia. 1991. *The Global City: New York, London, Tokyo*. Princeton: Princeton University Press.

Sauvy, A. 1984. *Le Travail Noir et L'Economie de Demain*. Paris: Calmann-Levy.

Saxenian, Annalee. 2000. Networks of Immigrant Entrepeneurs. In *Silicon Valley Edge: A Habitat for Innovation and Entrepeneurship*, edited by Chong-Moon Lee et al. Stanford: Stanford University Press.

Sayles L. R. 1966. *Human Behavior Organizations*. Englewood Cliffs: Prentice-Hall.

Schiller, H. I. 1985. Electronic Information Flows: New Basis for Global Domination. In *Television in Transition*, edited by P. Drummond and R. Patterson. London: British Film Institute.

Schiller, Nina G. et al. 1995. The Implications of Haitian Transnationalism for the U.S.-Haiti Relations: Contradictions of the Deterritorialized Nation-State. *Journal of Haitian Studies* 1 (1): 111–123.

———. 1992. *Towards a Transnational Perspective on Migration*. New York: New York Academy of Sciences.

Schiller, Nina G., and Georges E. Fouron. 2001. *Long-Distance Nationalism and the Search for Home*. Durham: Duke University Press.

Schmidt Sr., Ronald J. et al. 2000. Latino Identities: Social Diversity and US Politics. *Political Science and Politics* 34 (3): 563–568.

Schoenbaum, David. 1993. *The United States and the State of Israel*. New York: Oxford University Press.

Scott, Allen J. 1993. *Technopolis: High Technology Industry and Regional Development in Southern California*. Berkeley: University of California Press.

Serant, Vario. Haiti/Crise, Ils Préfèrent Ecouter des Chimères à Washington. *AlterPresse*. July 10, 2003.

Shain, Yossi. 1995. Ethnic Diasporas and U.S. Foreign Policy. *Political Science Quarterly* 109 (5): 811–841.

———. 1996. The Foreign Policy Role of U.S. Diasporas and Its Domestic Consequences. In *Representing and Imagining America*, edited by Philip John Davies. Keele: Keele University Press.

———, ed. 1989. *The Frontiers of Loyalty: Political Exiles in the Age of the Nation-State*. Middletown, CT: Wesleyan University Press.

———, ed. 1991. *Governments-in-Exile in Contemporary World Politics*. New York: Routledge.

———. 1999. *Marketing the American Creed Abroad: Diasporas in the US and their Homelands*. Cambridge: Cambridge University Press.

———. 1998. Multicultural Foreign Policy. In *New Tribalisms: The Resurgence of Race and Ethnicity*, edited by Michael W. Hughey. New York: New York University Press.

Shain, Yossi, and Mark Thompson. 1990. The Role of Political Exiles in Democratic Transition: The Case of the Philippines. *Journal of Developing Studies* 6 (1): 71–86.

Shapiro, Michael J. and Hayward R. Alker, eds. 1996. *Challenging Boundaries: Global Flows, Territorial Identities*. Minneapolis: University of Minnesota Press.

Sheffer, Gabriel. 2003. *Diaspora Politics: At Home Abroad*. New York: Cambridge University Press.

———. 1994. Ethno-National Diasporas and Security. *Survival* 36 (1): 60–79.

———, ed. 1986. *Modern Diasporas in International Politics*. London: Croom Helm.

Sierra, Christine Marie. 2000. Latino Immigration and Citizenship. *Political Science and Politics* 34 (3): 535–540.

Silverman, Maxim. 1992. *Deconstructing the Nation: Immigration, Racism and Citizenship in France*. London: Routledge.

Skinner, Elliott P. 1982. The Dialectic Between Diasporas and Homelands. In *Global Dimension of the African Diaspora*, edited by Joseph Harris. Washington, DC: Howard University Press.

Sklair, L. 1991. *Sociology of the Global System*. Hemel Hempstead: Harvester Wheatsheaf.

Skrbis, Zlatko. 1997. The Distant Observers? Towards the Politics of Diasporic Identification. *Nationalities Papers* 25 (3): 601–610.

———. 1997. Homeland-Diaspora Relations: From Passive to Active Interactions. *Asian and Pacific Migration Journal* 6 (3–4): 439–455.

———. 1999. *Long-Distance Nationalism. Diasporas, Homelands and Identities.* Aldershot, Hants: Ashgate.

Smith, David A., Dorothy J. Solinger, and Steven C. Topik, eds. 1999. *States and Sovereignty in the Global Economy.* London: Routledge.

Smith, Graham. 1999. Transnational Politics and the Politics of the Russian Diaspora. *Ethnic and Racial Studies* 22 (3): 500–523.

Smith, Jackie. 1994. Organizing Global Action. *Peace Review* 6 (4): 419–425.

Smith, Jackie et al., eds. 1997. *Transnational Social Movements and Global Politics.* Syracuse: Syracuse University Press.

Smith, Jackie. 1998. Global Civil Society? Transnational Social Movement, Organizations and Social Capital. *American Behavioral Scientist* 42 (1): 93–107.

Smith, M. G. 1984. The Nature and Variety of Plural Units. In *The Prospects of Plural Societies*, edited by D. Maybury-Lewis. Washington, DC: American Ethnological Society.

Smith, Michael P. 1994. Transnational Migration and the Globalization of Grassroots Politics. *Social Text* 39: 15–34.

Smith, Michael P. et al., eds. 1998. *Transnationalism from Below.* New Brunswick: Transaction.

Smith, Neil. 1993. Homeless/Global: Scaling Places. In *Mapping the Futures: Local Culture, Global Change*, edited by Jon Bird et al. New York: Routledge.

Smith, Robert C. 1998. Transnational Localities: Community, Technology and the Politics of Membership Within the Context of Mexico and U.S. Migration. In *Transnationalism From Below*, edited by Michael P. Smith et al.. New Brunswick: Transaction.

Smith, Samuel Denny. 1940. *The Negro in Congress 1870–1901.* Chapel Hill: University of North Carolina Press.

Smith, Tony. 2000. *Foreign Attachments: The Power of Ethnic Groups in the Making of American Foreign Policy.* Cambridge, MA: Harvard University Press.

Soja, Edward, and Barbara Hooper. 1993. The Spaces that Difference Makes. In *Place and the Politics of Identity*, edited by Michael Keith and Steve Pile. London: Routledge.

Sollors, Werner. 1986. *Beyond Ethnicity: Consent and Descent in American Culture.* New York: Oxford University Press.

Sorensen, George. 1998. IR Theory after the Cold War. *Review of International Studies* 24 (5): 83–100.

Soysal, Yasemin Nuhoglu. 1994. *Limits of Citizenship: Migrants and Postnational Membership in Europe.* Chicago: University of Chicago Press.

Spiro, Peter J. 1998. Embracing Dual Nationality. Occasional Paper no. 1, Carnegie Endowment for International Peace.

Stack, Carol. 1975. *All Our Kin.* New York: Harper and Row.

Stack, John F., Jr. 1981. Ethnic Groups as Emerging Transnational Actors. In *Ethnic Identities in a Transnational World*, edited by John F. Stack, Jr. Westport: Greenwood.

Stark, Andrew. 1992. Political Discourse Analysis and the Debate over Canada's Lobbying Legislation. *Canadian Journal of Political Science* 25 (3): 513–534.

St. Fleur, Marie. Haitian Americans at Crossroad in Our Journey. *Boston Haitian Reporter*. Vol. 1, issue 1, May, 2001.

Stinner, William F., Klaus de Albuquerque, and Roy S. Bryce-Laporte, eds. 1982. *Return Migration and Remittances: Developing a Caribbean Perspective*. Washington, DC: Research Institute on Immigration and Ethnic Studies, Smithsonian Institution.

Storper Michael. 1997. Territories, Flows, and Hierarchies in the Global Economy. In *Spaces of Globalization: Reasserting the Power of the Local*, edited by Kevin R. Cox. New York: Guilford Press.

Surin, Kenneth. 1999. Afterthoughts on Diaspora. *The South Atlantic Quarterly* 98: 275–325.

Swyngedouw, Erik. 1997. Neither Global nor Local: Globalization and the Politics of Scale. In *Spaces of Globalization: Reasserting the Power of the Local*, edited by Kevin R. Cox. New York: Guilford Press.

Talai, Vered. 1984. Mobilization and Diffuse Ethnic Organizations: The London Armenian Community. *Urban Anthropology* 13 (2–3): 197–217.

Tambiah, Stanley J. 2000. Transnational Movements, Diaspora, and Multiple Modernities. *Daedalus* 129 (1): 163–194.

Tanzi, V. 1982. *The Underground Economy in the United States and Abroad*. Lexington: D. C. Health.

Tate, Katherine. 1993. *From Protest to Politics: The New Black Voters in American Elections*. Cambridge, MA: Harvard University Press.

Teitelbaum, Michael S., and Myron Weiner, ed. 1995. Introduction. In *Threatened People, Threatened Borders: World Migration and U.S. Policy*. New York: W. W. Norton.

Thomas, Ken. South Florida Haitians Achieve Political Clout. *The Associated Press State and Local Wire*. May 29, 2001.

Tivnan, Edward. 1987. *The Lobby: Jewish Political Power and American Foreign Policy*. New York: Simon and Schuster.

Tololyan, Kachig. 1991. Rethinking Diaspora(s): Stateless Power in the Transnational Moment. *Diaspora* 1 (1): 3–36.

Tomlinson, John. 1999. *Globalization and Culture*. Chicago: University of Chicago Press.

Torres, Maria de los Angeles. 1998. Transnational Political and Cultural Identities: Crossing Theoretical Borders. In *Borderless Borders: U.S. Latinos, Latin Americans, and the Paradox of Interdependence*, edited by Frank Bonilla, Edwin Melendez, Rebecca Morales, and Maria de los Angeles Torres. Philadelphia: Temple of University Press.

Torriero, E. A. Haitian Americans Say Past Rule Was Better. *The Orlando Sentinel*. February 20, 2004.

Touraine, Alain. 1996. Vrais et Faux Problèmes. In *Une Societe Fragmentée? Le Multiculturalisme en Débat*, edited by Michel Wieviorka et al. Paris: Editions La Decouverte.

Trice, Robert H. 1976. *Interest Groups and the Foreign Policy Process: US Policy in the Middle East*. Beverly Hills: Sage.

Troper, Harold. 1999. The Canadian Jewish Polity and the Limits of Political Action: The Campaigns on Behalf of Soviet and Syrian Jews. In *Ethnicity,*

Politics, and Public Policy: Case Studies in Canadian Diversity, edited by Harold Troper and Morton Weinfeld. Canada: University of Toronto Press.

Tuan, Y. F. 1977. *Space and Place: The Perspective of Experience*. Minneapolis: University of Minnesota Press.

Turner, Bryan S., ed. 1993. *Citizenship and Social Theory*. London: Sage.

Turner, Scott. 1998. Global Civil Society, Anarchy and Governance: Assessing an Emerging Paradigm. *Journal of Peace Research* 35 (1): 25–42.

Uhlaner, Carole Jean, Bruce E. Cain, and D. Roderick Kiewlet. 1989. Political Participation of Ethnic Minorities in the 1980s. *Political Behavior* 11 (3): 195–231.

Valbrun, Marjorie. Striking a Minor Chord. *Boston Magazine*. January 2002.

———. Caribbean Immigrants' Political Moves Stir Tensions. *The Wall Street Journal*. June 30, 1998.

———. Coming Out Party: Haitian American Women Step Out from Behind Scenes and Into US Politics. *APF Reporter* vol. 20 #4 Index, 2003.

Van Hear, Nicholas. 1998. *New Diasporas: The Mass Exodus, Dispersal and Regrouping of Migrant Communities*. Seattle: University of Washington Press.

Vasquez, Michael. Haitian Americans Review Achievements. *The Miami Herald*. January 17, 2002.

Verba, Sidney et al. 1978. *Participation and Political Equality*. Cambridge: Cambridge University Press.

———. 1995. *Voice and Equality: Civic Voluntarism in American Politics*. Cambridge, MA: Harvard University Press.

Wah, Tatiana. 2003. *Haiti's Development Through Expatriate Reconnection*. Coconut Creek, FL: Educa Vision.

Walker, R. B. J., ed. 1990. *Contending Sovereignties: Redefining Political Community*. Boulder: Lynne Rienner.

Watanabe, Paul Y. 2001. Global Forces, Foreign Policy, and Asian Pacific Americans. *Political Science and Politics* 34 (3): 639–644.

Weiner, Myron. 1990. Asian Politics and U.S. Foreign Policy. In *Immigration and U.S. Foreign Policy*, edited by Robert W. Tucker et al. Boulder, CO: Westview.

———. 1986. Labor Migrations as Incipient Diasporas. In *Modern Diasporas in International Politics*, edited by Gabriel Sheffer. London: Croom Helm.

Werbner, Pnina. 1996. Stamping the Earth in the name of the Allah: Zikr and the Sacralizing of Space Among British Muslims. *Cultural Anthropology* 11 (3): 309–338.

Werbner, Pnina, and Muhammad Anwar, eds. 1991. *Black and Ethnic Leadership in Britain*. London: Routledge.

Wertheimer, Jack. 1995. Jewish Organizational Life in the United States since 1945. *American Jewish Yearbook* 95: 3–98.

Wieviorka, Michel. 1996. Culture, Société et Démocratie. In *Une Société Fragmentée? Le Multiculturalisme en Débat*, edited by Michel Wieviorka. Paris: Editions La Découverte.

Wilson, Carlton. 1997. Conceptualizing the African Diaspora. *Comparative Studies of South Asia, Africa and the Middle East* 17 (2): 118–122.

Wilson, Rob et al., eds. 1996. *Global/Local: Cultural Production and the Transnational Imaginary*. Durham: Duke University Press.

Wolff, Janet. 1997. The Global and the Specific: Reconciling Conflicting Theories of Culture. In *Culture, Globalization and the World System*, edited by Anthony D. King. Minneapolis: University of Minnesota Press.

Wolpe, Bruce C. and Bertram J. Levine. 1996. *Lobbying Congress: How the System Works*. Washington, DC: Congressional Quarterly.

Young, Oran R., ed. 1997. *Global Governance: Drawing Insights from the Environmental Experience*. Cambridge: Massachusetts Institute of Technology.

Zolberg, Aristide R. 1995. From Invitation to Interdiction: U.S. Foreign Policy and Immigration Since 1945. In *Threatened Peoples, Threatened Borders: World Migration and U.S. Policy*, edited by Michael S. Teitelbaum and Myron Weiner. New York: W. W. Norton.

Index